GOODBYE SARAJEVO

GOODBYE SARAJEVO

A True Story of Courage, Love and Survival

Atka Reid & Hana Schofield

B L O O M S B U R Y

LONDON • BERLIN • NEW YORK • SYDNEY

First published in Great Britain 2011

Copyright © by Hana Schofield and Atka Reid 2011
Map by John Gilkes

Bloomsbury Publishing Plc
36 Soho Square
London W1D 3QY

www.bloomsbury.com

Bloomsbury Publishing, London, New York, Berlin and Sydney

A CIP catalogue record for this book is available from the British Library

ISBN 978 1 4088 1274 7

10 9 8 7 6 5 4 3 2 1

Typeset by Hewer Text UK Ltd, Edinburgh
Printed in Great Britain by Clays ltd, St Ives Plc

This book is dedicated to Andrew and James

In loving memory of Grandma, Mayka, Nako, Zoran,
Azra and Bill,
and all the victims of the war

Map of the former
Yugoslavia

In 1991, Slovenia and Croatia declared their independence from Yugoslavia. After a ten-day conflict, Slovenia broke away successfully. However, the Serbs living in Croatia resisted independence. With the help of the heavily armed Serb-dominated Yugoslav Peoples' Army (JNA), the Serbs overran parts of Croatia, and the term 'ethnic cleansing' entered the modern lexicon. The war in Croatia was still raging when in April 1992, following a national referendum, Bosnia and Herzegovina also declared independence from Yugoslavia. The Bosnian Serbs attacked their Muslim and Croat countrymen, overrunning large swathes of the country with the help of the JNA. Armed with heavy artillery and tanks, the Serbs and the JNA surrounded Sarajevo, Bosnia's capital, enforcing one of the longest and bloodiest sieges in modern history.

The Farewell

Atka

In a parking area, hidden between a building and the branches of some tall trees, a group of men, women and children were squeezing and pushing in front of an old bus. Loud cries, sobs and shouts, mixed with the metallic sound of guns and mortar fire in the distance reminded me of scenes that I had watched in old war movies. It was a May morning in 1992. Since early April, Sarajevo had been under relentless fire from the Serbs who had taken control of the surrounding hills and the city was now almost completely besieged by their tanks and heavy artillery. Under the protection of the United Nations (UN), people were taking the last few buses out of the city in a state of sheer disbelief, panic and confusion. They were fleeing to safety, in the hope that common sense would soon prevail and peace would be restored. We all wanted this madness to pass quickly so that we could go back to our normal lives.

A tiny hand held tightly onto my jersey. I hunched down and looked at my frightened twelve-year-old sister Hana who stared back at me helplessly with her large blue eyes. Tears were streaming down her face.

Everything had happened so fast that there was no time to think. I was sending my two little sisters, Hana and Nadia, away from the fighting in the city. I had no idea what the girls' fate would be, nor did I know what would happen to those of us who were left behind. In all the confusion, the only thing clear to me was my unshakeable sense of responsibility to my siblings.

'I don't want to go. I don't want to leave you,' Hana sobbed.

It was heartbreaking and I felt like screaming but I knew that that would only frighten her more. I looked into her eyes and tried to sound reassuring. 'Listen to me. You will be fine.' I held her hand and kissed it.

'Why are Nadia and I the only ones who have to go?' she muttered.

'Hana, there isn't enough room on the bus for all our family. We had to make up our minds quickly this morning whether we were going to take the last two seats on the bus, or lose them. You and Nadia are big enough to go by yourselves.' I wiped her tears and put my arms on her bony shoulders. The straps of her schoolbag were digging into her dark blue cashmere sweater. At twenty-one, I was the eldest of ten and, of all my siblings, Hana and I were the most alike. Our shared enthusiasm for learning and our similar personalities closed our nine-year age gap.

'You'll be back soon, you'll see.' My voice trembled but I tried to sound encouraging. 'Listen, Hana, once you're on the bus you'll be OK. I'm sure you and Nadia will find one of Dad's friends and they'll help you get in touch with Mum. If you hear gunshots during the trip, put your heads down. Do you understand?'

Hana nodded obediently, her face frozen with fear.

'You might be away for a while, maybe even two or three weeks. It will probably be hard, but no matter what happens you have to remember how much I love you. Promise me you will be brave.' I smiled at her and through her tears she smiled back at me, revealing the two dimples in her cheeks. I pulled her closer.

The bus engine started and the door opened. A man standing outside the door hastily called out names from a list in his hand. My whole body started to shake. I looked back at Hana and hugged her tight.

'I'll miss you.' A large lump in my throat was choking me.

'Atka, Hana,' I heard Nadia calling from across the crowd. 'They've called our names, we'd better go.'

With her short dark hair and her jeans and sneakers, Nadia looked boyish. She was just fifteen. We had already said our goodbyes, so I stretched my arm up as high as I could and waved to her. She was in tears but waved back at me, blew me a kiss and climbed on to the bus. Then, as if someone had pushed a mute button, all the noise around me faded and I heard myself saying, 'Come on, Hana, you'd better go now.'

I walked behind her and pushed her through the crowd. She turned around and we hugged again.

'Atka, I'll be brave if you promise me that you will be too,' she said, adamantly.

'Yes, I'll be brave just like you.' I looked straight into her eyes and hugged her for the last time.

'Come on everyone, hurry up. If we get spotted they'll shoot at us,' someone shouted.

I pushed through and walked Hana to the front of the bus. As she stepped on, something inside me died and I was overcome by a terrible sense of dread.

'Be careful and remember to duck down,' I shouted as I forced my way through the wailing crowd and walked beside the bus, not taking my eyes off my sisters. I watched as they walked almost to the back and sat down. Hana pushed her face hard against one of the large windows and I could see she was saying something but I couldn't make out what it was. Nadia's tearful face peered out from behind her. I raised my arm and put my hand on the window. Hana slowly put up her hand as if to touch mine, with only the thin glass separating us. We looked at each other in silence.

The bus started to move slowly and I walked along with it, still holding my hand high up to the window. The bus sped up and I stepped away. I could see only two blurred figures in the window. Crying, I waved until the bus reached the bottom of the street and disappeared around the corner. Then everything started to spin, and for a moment I thought I would collapse. Someone tapped me on the shoulder and offered me a cigarette. I inhaled deeply and, after a few puffs, started to calm down.

I wiped my tears away with the sleeve of my shirt and looked around. The people left behind, mostly men, were smoking and talking amongst themselves.

'It's good that they're getting out,' an old man commented. 'But they'll be back soon . . . This bullshit that the Serbs have brought upon us surely can't go on.'

'The world won't stand by and ignore what they're doing. It's so uncivilised, surely there will be a military intervention,' someone else said. A ripple of agreement ran though the crowd.

'It's easy to shoot at the city from up there in the hills, knowing that we're unarmed. You'll see, when the Americans intervene, all those heroes in the hills will be smaller than a poppy seed,' the old man said angrily and spat on the ground.

I threw away my cigarette butt, took a deep breath and walked down towards my house, taking care to stay close to the side of the street. Walking in the middle was dangerous and I would be an easy target for snipers from the hills around our city. I felt slightly sick as if I'd just woken from an anaesthetic.

My grandmother, two sisters and three brothers were standing in the doorway of our large red brick house, waiting for me to return. Both the girls, Janna and Selma, had long dark hair and, being of school age, were just big enough to understand what was happening around them. Grandma was in her mid seventies but despite her age remained active and strong. She was holding Tarik by the hand. He had blond hair and green eyes and had just turned four. The two-and-a-half-year-old twins, Asko and Emir, were making silly faces at each other, blissfully unaware of what was going on.

'Atka, we saw the bus and waved goodbye.' The girls spoke quietly and sadly. We walked into the hallway and I gathered them all around me and hugged them.

'Half of our family's gone, it's only us now.' The younger of the girls, Selma, lowered her head and, with her skinny shoulders hunched, burst into tears. 'When are Mum and Lela coming back?' she lisped.

'I don't know, Selma,' I answered, pulling her closer to me. 'Now that the Serbs have blocked the roads, no one can get into the city.' Our mother, who'd been working for a humanitarian aid organisation, had been sent as a delegate by the Bosnian government to Vienna to collect aid for Bosnia. Lela, our sixteen-year-old sister, had gone with her to help. They had left in the first week of April and two days later the Serbs opened fire on Sarajevo, completely blockading the city. The last we'd heard from Mum, she and Lela had been waiting in Vienna for the roads or the airport to open again.

'Will the Serbs kill us?' Janna was scared.

'No. Don't you worry, little ones. Everything will be fine, Grandma and I'll take care of you all.' I knelt down and hugged them again. The girls wiped their faces, trying to manage a little smile.

'Mesha will come and save us. He's a soldier,' Tarik declared. Mesha was our nineteen-year-old brother. A year ago he had been drafted into the JNA (Yugoslav People's Army) for his military service, which was compulsory for all men over the age of eighteen. Yugoslavia was united and at peace at that point and he was sent to Montenegro. But since then, the Serbs had taken over the JNA and attacked Slovenia, Croatia and, most recently, Bosnia. Mesha was now trapped on the side of the enemy. The last time he'd phoned us was at the beginning of this month, just a day before our main Post Office building was shelled, shutting down the switch-board and most of the phone lines in the city. He told us that he wanted to escape from the JNA barracks and return home. We had had no news of him since. It was crazy to think that the army of which we had been so proud was now attacking us.

'Oh, our dear Mesha,' Grandma patted me on the back. 'Come on, I'll make us some coffee.'

We went through to the living room where Dad was putting on his shoes.

'Did Hana and Nadia get away all right?' he asked. His brown eyes looked dull and he rubbed them as he spoke.

'Yes, Dad, they've just left,' I said, sadly.

'At least we've managed to get two of them on the bus. They have Mum's number in Vienna, if she's still there. I gave Hana a big list of all my friends and contacts in Croatia as well. I'm sure that they'll be able to stay with someone for a few days until they can come back. This fighting won't last very long.' He stood up then straightened his shirt and jacket. He was tall, just like his two brothers.

'I'd better hurry to Mayka. I'll probably have to stay the night again,' he said.

Mayka was his mother. She was in her eighties and lived alone. She'd been a widow for ten years and, like the rest of us, was terrified of the shooting. It usually took twenty minutes to walk to her place from our house but since the fighting had started the walk had become very dangerous. We never knew how long it would take or if we'd make it at all. The children kissed Dad and he left.

I sat on the couch, put my face in my hands and closed my eyes for a moment. *It would be so nice to curl up, go to sleep and forget about everything.* A little voice at my side shook me out of my thoughts.

'Atka, can you make pancakes for us?' It was Emir. The twins had been born prematurely and they were still so delicate and fragile. I was not in the mood but then he looked up at me with his big brown eyes and said in his sweet voice, 'Please, Atka.'

I couldn't resist. 'All right, I'll make some pancakes.'

His eyes lit up and he leapt with joy into the middle of the room shouting, 'Pancakes, pancakes.' The other children joined in, jumping up and down. We had been eating dry pancakes for days now and I was amazed that, as far as the children were concerned, the novelty still hadn't worn off. I watched their joy and felt an overwhelming sense of hope. I couldn't help but smile.

The Bus Trip

Hana

We got onto the bus and they moved us to the back. In tears, I pushed my way to the window on the side where Atka was standing. I couldn't open it, which made me cry even harder. 'Atka, Atka,' I sobbed. These were the only words that I could think of, though there was so much more to say. I wanted to tell her how much I loved her and that she was my best friend. Atka stepped closer to the bus and put her hand up, as if to touch mine. Tears streamed down her cheeks. I put my hand against the glass.

The bus started moving. I stood with my hand fixed to the window until we turned into another street and I could no longer see my sister. I knew how much she loved me and that I had to keep my promise to her to be brave.

On the bus no one spoke. We were too stunned.

'Kneel down on the floor and stay still,' the co-driver yelled. We obeyed. 'Don't let yourselves be seen through the windows. It's safer that way,' he shouted.

The gap between my seat and the seat in front of me was wide enough for me to squeeze into. I sat there, frozen for a few minutes, too scared to do anything. Nadia held my hand tightly and she seemed just as scared as I was.

It took a while before I mustered up enough courage to lift my head and glance towards the front. Being so close to the floor, I couldn't see very far, but then I spotted the dark ponytail of a girl in the row across from me and realised that it was my friend from next door. She lay curled up with her back to me. A woman with short blond hair was kneeling down on a seat in front of her. It was my friend's aunt. Seeing an adult made me feel safer.

I looked up towards the window. We were driving fast and the rooftops of the grey Communist-era apartment blocks came into view then quickly disappeared again. Since the beginning of April, the heavy shelling and bombing had kept us all confined to the school shelter across the street from our house. I hadn't been to school in over a month. Today was the first time I'd ventured beyond the now closed-off world of our street.

There was no sound of city trams or any cars. The eerie silence was broken only by sporadic gunfire. I didn't know what was happening to us. It was only this morning that Dad had found out that a UN convoy was taking a small number of women and children out of town, to the safe parts of the coast of Croatia. He told Nadia and me that the bus was leaving in less than an hour. I felt sick when I heard that only two of us were going. I cried a lot. It wasn't fair. I didn't want to go. I wanted to stay at home with my family. There was no time for long goodbyes. Everything happened so fast. We left with only a small schoolbag each.

The gunshots outside the bus became louder and more regular. I'd never heard them so close before. I was terrified we might get shot. A bullet could easily pierce my skin and kill me. Suddenly the co-driver yelled in panic, 'Fuck, they're shooting at us!' and told the driver to turn into one of the side streets. Screams and sobs erupted through the bus.

Shaking with fear, I begged, 'Please God, don't let us die. Please, please, please.' I squeezed the small piece of paper in my pocket on which Grandma had written a prayer. She told me that it would protect me and to carry it with me all the time. Nadia had one too.

The bus came to an abrupt stop.

'Get up and run across the street into that building!' The co-driver pointed at something outside. I looked up and saw people getting up off the floor. Nadia and I jumped to our feet.

'Come on, quick, quick!' he shouted.

The people in the front ran out first. I heard more gunshots.

'Leave your bags behind, come on, move!' A thick vein stood out on the driver's neck.

I thought that Nadia and I might be left behind. 'Hurry up!' I said, my knees knocking.

'You at the back, come on!' The driver motioned to us in a frenzy.

I ran to the front.

'Duck down and run fast,' his hands shook as he pushed me out of the door.

I couldn't see which way I was meant to run. I could hear adults' voices but I couldn't see them. Finally, I spotted them standing at the entrance of a grey building, beckoning me towards them. My jaw was quivering when I reached them.

'Go to the basement!' one of them shouted without even looking at me. 'There's a shelter down there.'

I stood at the top of the stairwell waiting for Nadia. I couldn't see her. Frightened and alone, I was about to start crying again, but she ran in a few seconds later and grabbed my hand. We hurried down the stairs, leaping two or three steps at a time. I was sure we'd trip and fall over.

The shelter was dark and cool. A heavy dampness hit us

as soon as we walked in through the door. This shelter was smaller than the school one. It was windowless and the walls were grey.

There was a lot of shouting inside. Being shot at terrified everyone. People spoke fast and couldn't keep still.

'How can they shoot at us? Innocent women and children,' I heard a woman say.

'They're not humans, they're animals!' another voice cried.

Their angry comments continued. I knew they were talking about the Serbs when they said *they*. The Serbs had started the war. I was very angry that the Serbs were doing this to us but I was even more scared of dying.

My friend from the bus appeared from somewhere in the darkness.

'Hana, I saw you on the bus. Are you OK?' she said.

'Yes,' I answered, quietly.

'My aunt's with me. Who's with you and Nadia?' she asked.

There was a pause.

'Are you two on your own?' Her voice was lower this time.

I was on the verge of crying, so I just nodded.

'We're going to Pisak when we get to Croatia, my aunt has a friend there,' she told me. Pisak was a small, popular holiday place on the coast.

'And you?' she looked at me. 'Where are you going?'

'I'm not sure,' I replied.

Before we left, Dad had given us Mum's number in Vienna and a list of his contacts in Croatia. Most were business associates who he didn't know very well, but he said to let them know that we were his children and he was sure that they'd help us. I wished we had an aunt or someone else we knew in Croatia with whom we could stay.

My friend smiled. 'Don't worry, we'll be back in a week or

two.' Her voice was gentle and reassuring. She was a bit older than me and I believed her.

The adults were still talking amongst themselves. I don't know how long we'd been inside the shelter when the driver asked us to re-group by the door. We were told that we'd be getting back on the bus shortly and that a UN vehicle would accompany us for the rest of the trip.

A loud sigh of relief spread through the shelter and shortly after that we were on the bus again. The co-driver told us that we didn't have to kneel down any more. I was half expecting the driver to turn around and tell us that the war was over. But instead he drove on.

Not long afterwards, we were on the outskirts of Sarajevo. I turned back and looked at the city behind me.

So much had happened during the day that it wasn't until sometime in the afternoon that Nadia and I realised how hungry we were. I grabbed the *lokumi* from my schoolbag. They were my favourite Bosnian pastries and, when Dad had told us this morning that we were leaving, Grandma made them in a hurry, wrapping them carefully in napkins for us. I felt grateful to her as we ate them.

Grandma's outlook was pragmatic even in the worst of circumstances and since the beginning of the war she had instinctively known what to do in these dire times. She had lived through the Second World War and knew how to cope in times of hardship.

People seemed a lot calmer now than earlier in the day and were chatting softly to each other. My eyes followed the contour of the undulating hills outside. I became lost in the landscape and gradually fell asleep. When I woke, the first stars were appearing in the evening sky. At first, I couldn't remember where I was. Waking up on a bus away from my home and my family filled me with dismay. Nadia whispered that we were just outside Travnik, where we'd be staying the night. Apparently, we weren't allowed to travel at night. I was not sure if I'd heard her correctly. Travnik was a small town where we'd often had weekend lunches with our parents. I knew it wasn't that far from Sarajevo.

Nadia turned to me and said, 'There were a few stops while you slept. Soldiers came in to check the number of people on the bus and to make sure that there were no men amongst us.'

The news about our bus hold-up had reached Travnik and some of the townspeople were organising lodgings for us for the night. The town was under Serb attack but the fighting didn't seem to be as severe or constant as it was in Sarajevo. Nadia and I stayed with an elderly couple who were very kind and hospitable. The events of the day had taken their toll and we were exhausted and drained. Although I was hungry, I didn't want to eat, knowing that my family in Sarajevo was surviving on minute rations of food. I kissed the paper Grandma had given me and thought of everyone at home until I fell asleep.

We left Travnik early the next morning and headed for the Croatian coast. It seemed as though we were driving through a country of ghosts. The villages and towns were empty and silent. There were hardly any cars on the streets and those that we saw were not moving. Over the last few weeks there had been many power cuts. Whenever we did have electricity, we watched the local news but the reports were sketchy and it was hard to know what was going on in the rest of the country. It was now clear that the disease of war had spread.

The first people we saw were Serb soldiers at a checkpoint somewhere near the small town of Livno.

'People, we're coming up to a Serb army control,' the

co-driver sounded apprehensive. 'Stay in your seats and don't talk to them unless they ask you a question.'

The bus slowed down. Several trucks were parked in front of us to create a barrier to any passing vehicles. More trucks were parked on either side of the road and two burnt-out cars were lying in the ditch. There were a lot of men outside with rifles, dressed in camouflage. I could see that most of them were young and only a few looked to be our dad's age.

As soon as we stopped, two uniformed men came on board. They had long, dirty beards and carried machine guns. They towered over us, smelling of cigarettes and alcohol. I knew they were Chetniks, Serb soldiers. I had heard about the atrocities that they were committing but I'd never seen a Chetnik in person. I put my head down and clenched my teeth, scared that they might shoot us.

'Papers!' they demanded of the driver, brusquely.

'Are there any men hiding on this bus?' one of them asked.

'No, women and children only,' the driver spoke politely.

'Let's see if you're telling the truth,' the other said and started moving down the bus. When they came to us, I felt as though they were staring at me so I lifted my head.

'What are you looking at?' he said as he stood over me.

'Nothing, nothing. I'm sorry,' I said and bent my head down again. I held my breath until I heard him walk away.

They got off the bus and started searching the baggage compartment. The tension on the bus was like a dark, menacing cloud that hovered above us. Everyone sat still, as if paralysed.

A few minutes later, they shouted from the outside.

'It's all right. It's empty.' They waved their arms at the driver and let us pass.

The tight knot in my stomach relaxed a little.

It was another four hours before we reached the Croatian

border and darkness had set in for the night. Croatia had recently become independent and this was the first time I was going to cross into it as a foreign country. We had no passports or documents. A man in a uniform walked on to the bus, demanding the passenger list from the driver.

'So, we have more Bosnian refugees,' he said in a harsh tone. The letters HVO (Hrvatska Vojna Obrana) were sewn across the arms of his jacket, indicating that he was a member of the Croatian Military Defence Force. They were fighting off the Serb attacks inland, but for now most of coastal Croatia was a safe haven.

He pranced up and down the bus, flicking through the list. 'You won't be able to eat any *cevapcici* here,' he said, referring to the popular Bosnian dish.

'Why's he talking about food?' I whispered to Nadia.

'Shh . . . he's mocking us.'

Any joy I had felt about crossing into Croatia was crushed right then. My family had spent every summer holiday on the coast of Croatia and the Croatians had always been so kind to us. I couldn't understand why he was being so rude now.

After talking to the driver for a few minutes, the soldier got off and the bus pulled away.

Several people remarked about his arrogance and the disrespectful manner with which he'd treated us. But I wasn't going to let it get to me and I tried to ignore the tightness I felt in my chest.

Around midnight, we pulled into Split, a busy port town on the coast, where the trip ended. We stopped at the bus terminal, near one of the main wharves in the old city. The town was sleeping peacefully, which I found surprising after the havoc in Sarajevo and the events of the past thirty-six hours. I had imagined that the rest of the world was caught up in the same storm as Sarajevo.

Everyone got off the bus and seemed to disappear. Nadia and I found ourselves completely alone. Darkness and night had always terrified me, even when I was at home. In a strange city without any adults to tell me there was nothing to be scared of, I feared that I would fall into the hands of all sorts of unknown terrors, homeless people, thieves, or even the claws of stray dogs.

An old Croatian woman wearing a long black pleated skirt with her face wrapped in a black scarf came over to us. Black was usually worn by widows and the fact that she might be one made my heart beat faster from fear.

'Do you need a room, you two?' She spoke in the typical coastal dialect. Their accent was different from ours.

'Yes,' I exclaimed, happy that this old woman, who was probably about my grandmother's age, wanted to help us.

'That's a hundred Deutsche Marks a night.'

I was astounded. Dad hadn't had any cash to give us because all the banks were now defunct. We had no money. Overnight, our national currency had become worthless and everyone seemed to be trading in Deutsche Marks.

'We've just come out of Sarajevo! How can you ask us for money?' I cried in anger. I tried to keep my voice down because I knew it was rude to shout at someone older.

'Well, we all have to make a living somehow,' she said, coldly and walked away.

I sat down on a small seat nearby and for the first time since leaving Sarajevo broke down and sobbed loudly.

'What are we going to do?' I asked Nadia in despair. She hugged me. We had been sitting there for more than ten minutes when someone ran towards us and asked if we were from Bosnia.

'Yes,' we replied, not knowing any longer if that was a safe thing to say.

'There's a bus going to one of the sports centres. Over there.' He pointed a few hundred metres ahead of us. 'That's where all the refugees are going,' he said, helpfully.

I'm not a refugee, I thought, *I have a family and a home.* But we needed a place to sleep for the night so Nadia and I grabbed our bags and ran.

The inside of the large hall was dark when we arrived. We were shown to an empty row of seats in the stand. The seats were bare and there were no blankets with which to cover ourselves. We used our schoolbags as pillows. I listened to others breathing and tossing around in their sleep. It took a while for sleep to come, despite our exhaustion. It was not until the morning that I realised there were thousands of refugees here. The stands were full; people were quietly moving around in their rows, amongst their small suitcases and heaps of clothing. I stood up, it all looked too chaotic to me. I liked order and routine.

'Nadia, we have to get out of here,' I said, shaking her. She was still asleep.

I pulled out the list of Dad's contacts from my schoolbag and skimmed down the first page.

'There's a man called Mr Yusic staying in Split. We have the name of his hotel.' I turned to Nadia. 'Let's go and ask someone how far it is.' We picked up our bags.

On the way to the large exit sign at the bottom of our row, we passed dozens of women and many young children and heard the sound of a crying baby. The few men amongst us looked old and frail. An instant sadness came over me; these men were of a similar age to my grandma and I felt sorry that they had to be uprooted like this in their old age.

When we walked to the outside grounds of the centre, the smell of fresh bread and hot cocoa drew us to a large trestle table in the far corner. Someone from the crowd told us that food was being handed out so we picked up a piece of bread and moved to the side. As two young girls on our own, we didn't want to stand out in the midst of too many strangers.

'Excuse me, do you know where the Hotel Split is?' I asked a middle-aged woman in a catering uniform who walked past.

'Not far, just follow the main road.' She pointed ahead of us. 'Bus number 3 goes there. It takes about twenty minutes,' she said and carried on walking.

'Thank you,' I shouted behind her.

Because we had no money Nadia and I decided to walk. We asked for directions along the way and more than two hours later we reached the hotel. There was a large white panel on the rooftop with the hotel's name written in blue capital letters. We had been to hotels before with our parents, but going into this one on our own was intimidating.

We walked up to reception and asked the woman at the desk for Mr Yusic.

'Mr Yusic? He's currently in Germany; he's not due back for another week,' she said. She was a sophisticated-looking woman, with long straight black hair. A name badge on her shirt showed that her name was Mladena.

I looked away and started biting my bottom lip.

'Can I help you with anything else?' She sounded cheerful.

'We've just come out of Sarajevo,' I blurted out. I couldn't keep it in any longer. 'Mr Yusic is an acquaintance of Dad's and he told us to get in touch with him. We have nowhere else to go.'

'Is there anyone else you can call?' she asked as she reached for pen and paper. The way she said it and the speed with which she moved made me realise that she wanted to help us. As far as she was concerned, we were not *just* refugees from Bosnia.

'Yes, we could phone our mum,' I answered. 'But . . . it's an international number. She's in Vienna.' I was scared to say it, expecting her to say that she didn't have permission to dial those numbers without a charge. But she simply handed the telephone to us.

I dialled the number. Waiting for the woman who answered to fetch my mother was nerve-wracking. When I heard Mum's familiar voice, through tears I managed to say, 'Mum, it's Hana. Nadia and I have just got to Croatia.'

I explained the situation to her and told her that the rest of the family was still in Sarajevo. Mum was so relieved to hear that everyone was alive. For the last two weeks she had been trying to contact us in Sarajevo and was devastated that she and Lela had not been able to get back home. After a few minutes, I passed the phone to Nadia so that she could give Mum the names of the contacts from the list. While Nadia was on the phone, the hotel manager came over and started scolding Mladena for allowing us to use the phone.

'This is not a refugee camp,' he shouted. He was a tall, dark man with a face that seemed to be set in a permanent frown.

'But they are family friends of one of our regular guests,' she said in a professional manner.

The manager's demanding tone attracted a man with curly hair in his thirties who came over to reception. He was wearing a press card around his neck and spoke in English. I couldn't understand what he said but a few moments later the manager walked away, leaving us in peace. I was so grateful to this foreigner who stood up for us. We desperately needed help and it was obvious that he was willing to come to our aid. Mladena told us he was a journalist from England and that his name was Christopher.

Nadia hung up the phone and said that Mum was going to call us back. After a few minutes, the phone rang and Mum told us that we were to go to Zagreb, the capital of Croatia, to stay with one of our family friends. The only problem was that they were away for a few days so we'd have to find a place to stay in the meantime.

We stayed and talked to Mladena and Christopher. He wanted to know more about us and the current situation in Sarajevo. Mladena translated. We told him everything that had happened in the last few weeks. Of all the people we met, these two were the kindest. Mladena was non-judgemental and Christopher was very friendly. I felt I could trust them both.

We gave Mladena our contacts list and she picked up the phone, telling us to leave everything to her. I knew the news was good when she finally put the receiver down and smiled at us. We had a plan. That evening, Nadia and I were to take the ferry to Rijeka, on the northern part of the coast, to stay with one of Dad's acquaintances, until we could continue on to Zagreb. I couldn't believe Christopher's generosity when he offered to buy the ferry tickets for us. We accepted with relief. I definitely didn't want to go back to the sports centre; it had been a humiliating experience and I hated the feeling of being unwanted and a burden.

Later, Christopher took us out for lunch. It was the first proper meal we'd eaten since the start of the war more than a month ago. When Mladena finished her shift, she took us to her apartment. She told us she had two sons of our age and couldn't bear to think that someone would refuse to help them should they, God forbid, ever be in a similar situation. I took a shower and stood under it for a while. It felt as though the water was washing away all the horrors of the last few days.

Nadia and I lay down to relax for an hour. The normality of Mladena's life was comforting but also left me with a feeling of emptiness. I longed for the rest of our family to be with us and for life in Sarajevo to return to normal. I just wanted everything to be the way it was before.

Christopher and his colleague accompanied us on the ferry that night. Christopher handed me his transistor radio. A U2 song was playing; it was one of Atka's favourites and reminded me of happier times.

Three days later, our Dad's acquaintance from Rijeka sent us on a bus to Zagreb. A family friend, whom we'd never met before, picked us up from the bus terminal and, as soon as he saw Nadia, he said, 'I recognised you straight away, you look so much like your mother.'

His name was Omer. Once in his car, he said how lucky it was that our mother had managed to get hold of him. He wanted to know what the situation in Sarajevo had been for the last two months and listened with interest as we spoke, glancing at us from time to time in his rear-view mirror.

'I saw your mother on the news a while ago with all those other mothers petitioning for their sons to be released from the JNA. What is she doing in Vienna?' he enquired.

Nadia tucked a strand of hair behind her right ear and gestured with her hands while she explained that Mum's work for the 'Mothers for Peace' organisation had been extended to humanitarian aid. She had been sent to Vienna to receive aid from Caritas.

'So, did she manage to get your brother out of the JNA?' he asked.

'No,' Nadia replied with a sigh. 'They wouldn't let him go and we're not sure where he is now. It's been three weeks since we last spoke to him.'

'Don't worry, girls. I'm sure he'll be fine,' Omer said with confidence. 'And you two will be all right now. You can stay with us until your mother arrives,' he said.

As we drove on in silence, I heaved a sigh of relief. We were safe for the moment.

The Phone Call

Atka

It was the middle of the night and pitch dark. Packed like sardines, we slept on the only couch in the tiny shelter at the back of the basement. The shelter was dug into the side of the hill and was the safest place in our three-storey house. When my parents had built our new home a few years ago they had been required under a new council rule to build an atomic shelter in case of nuclear disaster. At the time we had all laughed at these ridiculous regulations, but now I was very glad to have these thick concrete walls protecting us.

Usually, Grandma and the girls preferred to sleep in the school shelter, which was crowded with our neighbours whose company Grandma enjoyed. But tonight we had all stayed at home. The children were fast asleep, the noise of their breathing steady and comforting.

In the daytime we were able to use the living room and kitchen on the ground floor if the shelling was not too heavy. Grandma's room was off the living room and all the other bedrooms were upstairs but ever since the snipers had started shooting at the upper floors we were too scared to go up there.

The roar of the falling shells reminded me of thunderstorms. I felt bitter. All of my life Sarajevo had been a multicultural city where marriages between Serbs, Croats and Muslims were common. How could the Serbs, with whom we had lived in harmony for so long, turn against us and how could they believe that any place where Serbs lived rightly belonged to Serbia? Most of our Serb neighbours remained in the city, facing the same peril as everyone else. I couldn't understand those who had left to join the Chetniks in the hills.

I touched the cold, damp concrete wall, searching for the light switch. I turned it on but there was no light, just a hollow click; the power had been cut off for weeks but I couldn't resist flicking the switch on in the hope of a small miracle. I was uncomfortably close to the edge of the couch and I turned slowly, trying to get back to sleep. My mind was filled with thoughts that tormented me. It had been three weeks since Nadia and Hana had left on what had turned out to be one of the last convoys out of the city and we hadn't heard from them since. We knew that their bus had made it to Split but the uncertainty of their whereabouts was gnawing at me. We had no idea where Mum, Lela and Mesha were either. Dad spent most of his time looking after his ailing mother, fetching water for her and taking her any food we could spare. His two younger brothers and a sister lived in the new part of town but, with no trams, buses or petrol for cars, walking all the way to Mayka's house under fire was too dangerous. They were rarely able to make the trip. Since the first big massacre at the end of May, when a Serb shell killed twenty-two people queuing for bread, few dared to go out into the streets any more. A brave cellist from the city symphony orchestra played daily in that spot in memory of those who had been killed.

In the darkness of the shelter I could not stop these thoughts running through my mind and, feeling desperately sad and powerless, I cried myself to sleep.

In the morning when I opened my eyes, shafts of lights were visible under the shelter door. The front of the basement had two large windows facing our small backyard where our old garden shed stood. The children were chatting under their blankets. For a split second I was tempted to stay in bed and sleep all day, but I knew I couldn't do that so I ordered myself to get up. I helped the boys to get dressed then took them to the bathroom. We had run out of disposable nappies and the lack of running water made the washing of cotton ones an impossible task. The only solution was to train them out of nappies and luckily they learnt quickly.

Upstairs in the living room, Grandma was already lighting a fire on the potbelly stove. Before the war it had been used only for additional warmth and cheer during the winter but now we had to rely on it for cooking as well as heating.

Grandma was a small but strong woman with piercing blue eyes. Practical, kind and especially caring towards all her grandchildren, she had lived with us ever since our grandfather's death some twenty years ago. We loved her very much and couldn't imagine a time without her.

'I'm going to make some tea for everyone,' she winked, putting the mint leaves she'd collected from our back garden into a pot. Fortunately, we had some wood left over from the previous winter, which we were now using sparingly.

I opened the kitchen cupboard and looked at our food supply. The city shops had been closed or ransacked, the only food we had came from two handouts of humanitarian aid. There was not much on the shelf: half a jar of sugar, a small bag of flour, half a bottle of cooking oil, a good-sized can of milk powder and two cans of sardines in tomato sauce. At the bottom of the cupboard was a large sack of rice, which I had managed to get while the shops were still open. More than half of it was gone. We had been eating rice for weeks. Just looking at it made me feel sick.

'I'll make some *lokumi* for breakfast,' I shouted, grabbing the flour. Grandma's hearing was deteriorating and we had to speak loudly. While we sipped our tea, we ate *lokumi*, taking small bites to make it last longer.

'If it stays quieter today, I'll go and trade my gold for food.' Grandma took out her rings, bracelets and necklaces from her purse. She looked at Janna and Selma. 'We'll have to sell your earrings too . . . but don't worry, I'll buy you prettier ones after the war.' I took off my earrings then helped the girls with theirs. We handed them to Grandma.

'Save that,' Grandma said as I was taking off the gold ring set with three little diamonds that she'd given me for my eighteenth birthday. 'We'll keep that and my wedding ring along with the locket that Grandad gave me. Easy come, easy go,' she said, looking at the small pile of gold on the table. 'As long as we're alive and healthy . . .' She put the jewels back into her purse and asked me to take them to her room. As I walked towards her bedroom, I glanced out of the living-room windows which looked out to the city with Mt Trebevic towering above it.

Our house stood on a small hill near the city centre and I could see hundreds of buildings sprawled across the lower slopes of the surrounding hills and down to the River Miljacka, which flowed through the valley and out of sight towards the new part of town. The Serbs held the high ground and it was easy for them to shoot at the city.

Our kitchen faced the street. The small courtyard in front of our house was relatively protected by the two-storey house next door. This was the only outside space where the children were allowed to play. Men from our close-knit neighbourhood had organised themselves into a defence unit and used our courtyard as their station. There were always two guys on duty safeguarding the street, with the inevitable neighbour or two standing around chatting. All work had ceased except for essential services.

Grandma shook the jerry cans in the hallway outside the living room. The taps had been dry for weeks and the closest place from where we could collect water was the large concrete building on the main street, at the bottom of our hill. The L-shaped building had been the Communist Party Headquarters before the war but now its basement housed one of the few remaining radio stations, Studio 99.

'There's not much water left,' Grandma looked at me with a worried expression on her face.

'Don't worry,' I said. 'I'll go and get it. You went last time. Can you keep an eye on the children?'

She nodded. The girls immediately jumped to their feet, each grabbing a couple of jerry cans. They insisted on helping me since they knew that every drop of water was precious. By now we'd learnt to ration water carefully and we had become accustomed to washing with no more than a few cups of cold water. I packed two jerry cans into a backpack then heaved that on to my shoulders. Grandma handed me two more jerry cans before we left.

The guards were standing outside with some of our neighbours, listening to a transistor radio.

'Any good news?' I asked.

'No, we're listening to the names of people who were killed yesterday,' Bruno replied. He was twenty-five and, like most of us, had lived on our street for his entire life. 'Going to get water?' he asked, looking at the jerry cans. 'Watch out, girls, the snipers have been shooting all morning.'

The three of us ran past the house next door and down the long, steep, stony steps. These steps were visible from the surrounding hills and, scared of being shot, we hurried as fast as we could, instinctively lowering our heads and hunching our shoulders.

Janna and I reached the bottom where we were shielded by tall buildings. As I looked around, I realised there was no sign of Selma. 'Where's Selma?' I screamed to Janna.

'She was just behind me,' Janna replied.

We looked up. Selma was lying on the ground halfway down the steps.

'Selma! Selma!' we shouted in panic.

'My sandal fell off,' she cried. 'I'm too scared to move . . .'

'Get up quickly and run! Leave the sandal,' I shouted.

'Come on, Selma,' Janna screeched.

Selma hesitated but then stood up and raced down towards us wearing only one sandal.

'Selma, you really scared us. You could've been killed because of a stupid sandal,' Janna said before we both hugged her.

We stopped for a moment to calm down then went to join the long water queue. Most of the people standing there were from our area, voicing their anger at what we had been reduced to.

'I queued for three hours yesterday to get water. What sort of a way is this to live at the end of the twentieth century?' said an old man in a suit, staring at the jerry cans at his feet.

I caught sight of one of my neighbours, Hamo, a tall skinny guy with black curly hair and a cigarette dangling out of the corner of his mouth. He was dressed in his usual jeans and black leather jacket. Before the war he had worked as a DJ in one of Sarajevo's most popular clubs. The day the Serbs first started shelling the city, Hamo had put two large speakers on his outside windowsill and played, very loudly, 'Give Peace a Chance'. The voice of John Lennon, smothered by the sounds of whistling shells, echoed through the neighbourhood, but then when the Serbs cut off the power, Hamo's music protest ended. He was now working for Studio 99. Catching sight of me, he came over to talk.

'Hi Atka, what's up?' He pulled a packet of cigarettes out of his pocket, offering one to me. Cigarettes had become a real luxury and I was reluctant to accept one from him but he insisted.

'Thank you,' I said, deciding to save it for later.

'Don't mention it,' he waved his hand. 'Have you heard the latest joke?' The moment he said the word *joke*, people turned to look at him. Once he had everyone's attention he began. 'Two Sarajevans are walking down the street smoking when all of a sudden a shell explodes in front of them. There are bits of shrapnel and rubble flying everywhere. Through the thick cloud of dust and smoke they manage to spot each other.

' "You've lost your ear," one of them says.

' "Fuck the ear," the other one replies, "where's my cigarette?" '

Everyone laughed before turning away.

'You speak pretty good English, don't you?' Hamo asked me. 'So, so.'

'Come on, I know you're pretty good,' he nudged me.

I grinned and thought for a moment. Actually, he was right. The high school that I had attended specialised in arts and languages and was considered to be one of the best in the city. My English class was often called upon to translate movies, books and medical journals and I had continued studying English at one of my classes at university.

'It's not too bad. Why do you ask?' I was curious.

'Well, we're looking for someone to come to the studio at night to listen to *The Voice of America* and translate it for us. Do you think you could do that?' he asked, flicking the ash from his cigarette. *The Voice of America* was a news programme and one of the few sources of information from outside Sarajevo.

'I'll give it a try,' I replied, excitedly. 'It would be great to use my brain again.'

'The studio's a mess at the moment but we're hoping we'll have the equipment sorted soon. If you're still alive why don't you come after curfew one night next week?' He winked at me and touched my shoulder goodbye. Janna and Selma's faces were glowing with pride.

'Are you really going to work at the radio?' Janna asked loudly, tapping the empty jerry can against her knee.

'We'll see.'

We returned home two hours later with full cans and Selma's sandal. We boiled some rice for lunch and afterwards I enjoyed every puff of the cigarette that Hamo had given me, smoking it right down to the filter.

After several days, Grandma traded her gold on the black market for two large sacks of rice and flour, a can of oil, some canned food and a packet of candles, all of which we rationed carefully.

'Atka, we eat rice all the time, are we going to turn into Chinese people?' Tarik asked, curious.

'No, of course we won't,' I laughed.

'Can you make us some meat for lunch, then?' Asko asked. His skinny little body looked out of proportion to his head, which was covered in a giant mop of blond curls.

'Meat! Can you?!' Tarik was excited.

'Sure, I can . . .' I promised.

The girls gave me a puzzled look and giggled. The morning fire had gone out and Grandma lit another one, carefully putting the box of matches back into the pocket of her jersey.

'Atka, put some water on to boil, I'm just going to say my prayers,' Grandma said, adjusting her red headscarf. Grandma held an important role in the Sarajevan Muslim community.

For fifty years she had led the prayers at memorial services, which took place at various intervals after the death of a loved one. At their request, Grandma would visit the house of the bereaved, where family and friends had gathered, and lead them in their prayers. Her firm belief in God gave her the strength to keep going. Both mine and my parents' generation grew up under Communism, which viewed religion as the opium of the people. I'd never questioned her beliefs but our situation angered me and when I asked her how God could allow all these horrors, she simply replied that this evil had nothing to do with God but was purely Satan's work. I admired her unshakeable faith.

The sound of the crackling fire in the potbelly stove reminded me of the nights I would come home from ice-skating and warm myself by the fire with a cup of hot cocoa. I waited for the water to boil then cooked some rice. The children gathered around the stove, looking excitedly at the pot. It saddened me to see how skinny and pale they had become. The girls set the table and the five of them sat down. The boys were too young to know the difference between rice and meat so I thought that a little imaginary game would do them no harm. I shaped some of the rice into small balls and put them on a separate plate. The boys, excited at the thought of eating meat again, were drumming their feet under the table. Grandma came out of her room and joined us.

I served Emir first. 'Here you are, a bit of rice,' I scooped a generous spoon of rice, 'and some meat . . .' I put two rice balls on his plate. His eyes were shining and wide open.

Looking at his food he asked, 'Which one's the meat?'

I pointed at the rice balls.

'Can I eat those first?' He looked at me.

The girls were laughing and I tried to keep a straight face.

I served everyone and by the time I came to Tarik, I only

scooped some rice on to his plate. Seeing that he had no rice balls he looked very disappointed and asked plaintively, 'Where's my meat?'

'Tarik, we're only pretending,' Selma giggled. But he didn't seem to understand so I added two rice balls to his plate. He smiled and straight away started shovelling the food into his mouth.

'The boys will be telling the guards outside the house that we had meat for lunch. The neighbours will wonder where we got it from!' Selma's laugh was infectious.

That night, Grandma stayed at home with the children so that I could go to the studio to work for the first time. I left the house quietly. Grandma sat on the couch, silently praying with her beads. The street was in darkness and it took a few minutes for my eyes to adjust. I heard the guards talking. A small light glowed from one of their cigarettes.

'Is that you Toni?' I whispered.

'Yes. We heard you guys had meat today,' he teased.

'Are you jealous?' I replied. They were very amused when I told them what we had done.

Toni, who had sent his wife and two small daughters out of the city on one of the last convoys, said, 'Children are great, so innocent and naïve . . . I miss mine a lot.'

'Any news from them?' I asked.

'No,' he sighed.

'Just like us,' I remarked.

'I'm glad you came out to chat,' the other guard said.

'No, not to chat. I'm going down to Studio 99.' I was in good spirits. 'They've asked me to translate the news report from *The Voice of America*. I know it's after curfew but can I go anyway?'

'Sure,' he waved me on, 'it's just down the hill.'

'Good for you,' Toni said with admiration in his voice. 'When you come back, do bring us some good news. Hopefully the world won't stand by much longer and watch us suffer.'

'Hmm, we'll see,' I said and made my way to the top of the steps.

Before the war, the shimmering lights of the city at night had always charmed me but now everything was plunged into complete darkness and the rumble of shells frequently landing nearby filled me with fear. Flashes of artillery fire lit the night sky. Someone had mentioned that the snipers used night-vision goggles, which enabled them to see in the dark. I could see only a few steps at a time and, trying not to stumble, felt my way to the bottom of the hill. My heart was racing. It was the first time I'd ventured outside alone at night after curfew and I felt as though I were walking through some kind of surreal world.

When I reached the entrance of the studio building, I knocked on the small square window of the guard's office. He checked my identity card before letting me in, then led me down the stairs by the beam of his small torch. It was cold and damp. We came to a long corridor and I saw light coming from underneath one of the doors; the studio was powered by a generator from the UN Headquarters building next door.

'Here's the studio.' The guard shone his torch at the heavily padded door and opened it for me. Hamo was sitting in the corner right by the door, turning the volume button on the stereo, the inevitable cigarette hanging out of his mouth. He had his headphones on and put his index finger to his lips when he saw me. A large black console divided the small smoky room in two and a familiar voice was speaking into a microphone at the other end of the room. It was Fazla, one of the city's popular radio personalities. As soon as he'd finished speaking, Hamo played a song. Taking off his headphones, he turned to me. 'Atka, I'm glad you've come.' He looked at Fazla and said, 'This is the girl who's going to translate for us.'

We acknowledged each other. I had expected Studio 99 to be much more sophisticated than this but I didn't say anything. Instead I asked Hamo, 'Is this live?'

'Yep,' he said, checking his watch. 'I have four minutes before I'm back on air. Come on, I'll show you what to do.' He led me to another room, not much bigger than the last. In this room there was a desk, a few chairs, a TV and mountains of technical equipment. Hamo pulled a chair up to the desk then plugged the headphones into one of the tape recorders.

'First, record the news then you can take your time translating it.' He handed me a pen with a sheet of paper from a drawer and showed me how to use the equipment. He headed to the other room but then turned back and put two cigarettes on the desk in front of me.

'This is your pay,' he joked. Once he'd left I looked around, fascinated by this world of light and music. The TV was on and although it was muted the flickering images from the screen gave me a sense of normality. Suddenly, the troubles in the city above seemed remote. I adjusted my headphones, ready to listen to the radio. The news had not come on yet so just to make certain that everything was working, I made a practice recording. Everything was fine. There was a phone on the desk so I picked up the receiver and was pleasantly surprised when I heard the dial tone. The phone lines had been down since the bombing started. I dialled a few numbers but none of them were working. Then I tried calling Tidja, my maternal aunt, and was completely amazed when I heard it ring. Her voice was drowsy when she answered but within seconds she was completely awake. She lived on the lower slopes of Mt Trebevic and even though we could see each other's houses across the city, we hadn't been able to communicate for the last two months.

I told her that Hana and Nadia had left and that we had not heard any news from Mum or Mesha. She told me how worried she was for her own sons. The older one, who was an electrician, was on duty almost all the time, even during heavy shelling, trying to repair damaged cables around the city, while the younger one had been mobilised. Before I hung up I gave her the studio's phone number, which I read from a list pinned to the wall in front of me, and told her I would call her again as soon as I could.

It was time to listen to the news.

'This is *The Voice of America*,' a deep voice announced and I pushed the 'record' button. I listened and, with a growing sense of bitter disappointment, wrote down the following: *President Bush rejects a personal appeal from the President of Bosnia and Herzegovina to use military force against Serbian forces to end the Balkan war. Bush instead calls for a combined international effort to ensure the delivery of humanitarian aid. Both Italy and France promised to increase their participation* . . .

When I finished the translation I stared at the words. There was to be no military intervention and no help from outside. I was shattered. I walked to the other room and handed the translated text to Hamo, who swore aloud after he'd read it. Fazla announced the next song and Hamo pushed the red button indicating we were off the air.

'They don't give a flying fuck,' Hamo said, bitterly. 'If we had oil, someone would be here in a flash.'

'The idiots at the UN should lift the arms embargo so that we can at least defend ourselves,' Fazla shouted from his corner and, swearing, threw a tape across the table.

'I can't be bothered with this bullshit,' he said. 'Hamo, give us a song to soothe the soul.' Seconds later, the unmistakable voice of Bob Dylan filled the studio. We sat there listening to music until late.

Over the next weeks, our small pile of wood diminished, together with the rice and flour. Food was scarce but Grandma picked stinging nettles and dandelions from our back garden and taught me how to make a pie and a salad with them. One of the neighbours devised a recipe for 'cheese' using a mixture of milk powder, vinegar and oil. The children's favourites by far were bread 'schnitzels' and a bitter 'dessert' mixture made from water and two teaspoons of cocoa powder. We were constantly hungry and couldn't stop talking about food. At night, in the darkness of the shelter we listened to our rumbling stomachs, trying to work out whose was the loudest.

One afternoon in late June, the children held a song contest in the living room. Janna, wearing her usual denim overalls, was singing loudly and boisterously in front of the others. Selma, sitting next to the boys, was giggling in her pink dress. When her turn came to sing, she was too shy to stand up but Janna and the boys cheered her on so she covered her face and sang quietly from her seat. The children had been so good and obedient since the start of the siege. Their pure innocence and delight in the smallest things was a strong tonic to counter the hardships that came with taking care of them all under these awful circumstances. I was about to join the contest when a thunderous crash pierced the air. Another one followed. The glass in the windows shattered and smoke filled the room. For a second none of us moved, then the children started screaming. I was dizzy, the ringing in my ears was painfully loud. The children were terrified.

'Is everyone OK?' I was shouting but I could hardly hear my voice. 'Quick, go to the shelter.'

Janna and Selma grabbed the boys and ran down the stairs. Through the smoke I saw Grandma lying on the living-room floor, her eyes wide open. I thought she was dead but then she blinked and shouted, 'Even I heard that one.' She seemed more amused than frightened.

I helped her up and we went downstairs to the shelter where the children huddled on the couch.

'Atka, will they hit us?' Emir whispered through tears.

'No, not a chance. The concrete walls of this shelter are so thick they could throw ten bombs directly at it and still we'd be safe.'

The noise outside was getting louder and louder. It was as though thunderbolts were landing all around us.

'What if a hundred bombs hit the house?' Tarik shouted.

'They couldn't destroy the walls,' Janna yelled back.

'What about millions and millions?' Tarik stood up and started kicking the couch.

'Millions and billions, they still wouldn't hurt us. Please sit down and behave.' I pulled him down beside me. I was still shaking. 'Be good and I'll tell you a story when the shelling stops.'

Every time a shell crashed down with a deafening roar, the children trembled and Grandma and I hugged them close. Grandma prayed, holding her beads in her hand.

As the weeks had passed, we'd learnt to recognise the difference between the sounds of the various killing machines and their proximity. The sound of exploding shells didn't frighten us much any more, unless they landed close enough to shake the house.

After a while, the shelling ceased but we remained in the shelter in case of a second round of attacks.

I was telling the children a story, when we heard a loud banging upstairs.

'What's that?' Selma said in a small, frightened voice.

'I don't know,' I said and rushed upstairs. To my surprise, Hamo was standing at the front door. He was coughing and trying to catch his breath.

'What are you doing here? Are you trying to get yourself killed?' I was astounded.

He grabbed me by the hand and pulled me outside. Gasping for air, he told me that Mesha was on the phone at the studio.

Shocked by his words, I didn't know what to do.

'Run, before we lose the connection,' he yelled. 'I'll follow you after I've had my heart attack.'

'Tell Grandma I'm going,' I shouted to him as I made my way around the corner. I hurried down the steps, stumbling, almost falling, with the sound of shells exploding in the distance. When I reached the studio building, the guard let me in. He ran with me, lighting the way.

A few people were at the studio. Across the room, two guys were talking into the microphone. They were on air.

'Is it *your* brother on the phone?' someone whispered in my ear.

I nodded.

'Go to the other room.'

I tiptoed in and picked up the receiver from the desk, hoping that Mesha was still there. I took a deep breath and spoke. 'Hello? Mesha?'

There was nothing but silence at the other end.

'Mesha?' I repeated.

'Atka, is that you?'

When I heard his familiar voice on the line I started to cry. A few people gathered around me. 'Yes, where are you? We've been so worried.'

'I've been trying to call everyone for weeks and finally I

managed to get hold of Aunt Tidja this morning. She gave me this number,' Mesha replied. 'I escaped from the army last month and the only place I could get to was Serbia. I'm hiding in Belgrade with one of Dad's friends but I want to come home.' His voice sounded casual and calm.

'No, you can't come back. Don't you know what's going on here?' I was shouting. 'We're completely besieged and no one can get in or out of town.'

'That's not what the Serb TV is showing here. They're saying that they are the victims. I've been told there are buses from Belgrade to Pale and Grbavica.' Mesha sounded determined. Pale was a small ski resort near Sarajevo and Grbavica was a suburb under the slopes of Mt Trebevic.

'I don't know anything about buses from Belgrade. The Serbs have taken Pale, it's their headquarters now. And Grbavica . . . the Serbs are holding it too. They have expelled almost all the Muslims and Croats from there. Mesha, I know it's hard for you to understand but we are being shelled and shot at by the Serbs every day. We have no water, food or power and almost all the phone lines are down. If you get on that bus the Serbs will catch you and we'll never see you again . . . I can guarantee that. Please don't come back.' I spoke rapidly and with urgency, fearing that the line could be cut off at any minute. It was obvious that the Serbs' propaganda had painted a distorted picture.

'Aunt told me the same thing, she urged me to go to our cousins in Macedonia.' Mesha sounded confused now.

'Yes, go to Macedonia, please, but don't come back here until this shit has finished! Trust me, if you try to come back you'll get yourself killed.' I couldn't contain myself any longer and started to sob. Someone handed me half a cigarette and I inhaled deeply. Hamo appeared in the doorway.

'All right, I'll try to get to Macedonia,' Mesha replied. 'But

I'm not even sure if I can make it there. I haven't got any identity papers, they were confiscated by the JNA.'

'You have to try. Whatever you do, please don't come back.' I waited for his reply but now there was only silence.

'Hello? Mesha? Mesha?' I called, but the line had gone dead and, after waiting for a while, I reluctantly put down the receiver.

Everything was a blur. Somebody asked me why I was crying and wondered if I had received bad news. I couldn't speak. I was waiting for the phone to ring again.

I heard Hamo telling the others, 'It's her brother. He was serving in the JNA when the war started . . .'

I wiped my eyes and explained, 'He's escaped, he'll try to get to Macedonia.'

'He's best to stay away from here,' someone remarked.

'I know, I'm just worried.'

Trying to cheer me up, Hamo said with a grin, 'Mesha owes me for this one! I've lived on that hill for more than thirty years but I've never ever run up those steps. I thought my heart was about to jump out through my nose.' He put his arms on my shoulders. Looking me straight in the eye, he said, 'Don't worry about your brother. He's a smart guy.'

In Zagreb

Hana

P arts of Croatia were engulfed in fighting but its capital
city, Zagreb, and most of the central areas were safe.
Omer, his wife and their two children lived in a modest
two-bedroom apartment in a residential complex near the
airport on the outskirts of the city. The noise of planes flying
overhead constantly droned in the background and I watched
them, knowing some of them were carrying humanitarian
aid to Sarajevo. Two weeks had passed since Nadia and I had
left home. We had thought that we would have been able
to go back by now but the Serb attacks had become more
intense and more Bosnian refugees were arriving in Croatia
every day. Despite Omer's wife telling us to make ourselves
at home it was still a bit awkward staying with people we
hardly knew. I didn't touch anything without asking first,
even if it was just to look at a book on one of the shelves.
Most days we stayed at the apartment and watched reports
from Sarajevo on the TV.

'How long do you think we'll have to stay here?' I asked
Nadia as we were watching the news one afternoon.

'I don't know, the war's getting worse and worse. Maybe
another two or three weeks . . .' she said, turning the TV down.
'We'll see what Mum says when she comes here.' Mum had
phoned us from Vienna. She and Lela were staying in a centre
that had been set up for Bosnian refugees and they had run

out of money. Their situation was dire. Mum was desperately trying to find a place for Lela to stay, so that she could come and be with us, but she didn't know when that would be.

When we had left home, Nadia and I had taken only a pair of jeans and a couple of T-shirts with us, so Omer's teenage daughter, Maya, gave us some of the clothes that she had outgrown. She also shared her tiny bedroom with both of us and Omer managed to fit an inflatable mattress on the floor for Nadia and me to sleep on. At night, we often lay awake talking quietly and wondering about the fate of our family and Sarajevo. We had left home without any photos and I tried to imagine their faces in my mind's eye. Somehow, this made me feel closer to them. Although we tried phoning every day, we couldn't make any contact with them and didn't even know if they were still alive. It was the same with our extended family who, as far as we knew, were all still in Bosnia. I missed them all.

One afternoon while Maya and I were chatting I thanked her for letting us share her room.

'Not at all, don't worry,' she said, waving her arm to dispel my awkwardness. We sat and looked at the dozen or so posters on her bedroom walls: Freddie Mercury, AC/DC, Guns N' Roses and several of our national singers. 'Do you like any of these bands?' she asked.

'I like Oliver,' I said, glancing at the image of the Croatian singer. 'He's very popular in Sarajevo.'

'Oh, really! He's my favourite too,' she said, putting one of his cassettes into her pink stereo. She sang along and, although I knew the words, I felt too shy to join in. When the song had finished, she rewound the tape, then sang along again, this time with the volume much louder.

'You're so funny,' I laughed.

I wasn't so relaxed with Omer and his wife or their ten-year-old son, Vedad. Most evenings, we ate dinner together but because I didn't want to be in the way, I didn't talk much. They never made any remarks about the length of our stay with them but I felt uncomfortable. The economic situation in Croatia was hard because of the war and I knew Nadia and I were two extra mouths to feed. I was aware that Maya's brother loved his food and was always the first to finish. One evening, while we were eating meat and roast potatoes, I caught sight of him eyeing everyone else's food. Letting out a big sigh, I said, 'Oh, I'm so full. Would anyone like to finish mine?' His chubby face lit up as he piled the food on to his plate. We all laughed. I felt happy to be able to give something to him, even though it wasn't really mine to give in the first place.

Careful not to disrupt anything around the apartment, I was horrified one afternoon when Omer's wife returned from work to discover that there was no hot water. I had accidentally switched off the hot water cylinder after my shower. Feeling completely stupid, I worried all evening that they might tell the two of us to leave. But neither of them mentioned anything and eventually I relaxed.

In the mornings, Omer and his wife went to work and Maya and her brother went to school. I was angry and frustrated that the war meant I couldn't go to school but still believed that soon we'd return to Sarajevo and life would go back to normal again. Most days, after tidying the apartment, Nadia and I followed the daily news bulletins. It was hard to hold back our tears when reports from Sarajevo were screened. So many people were being killed and wounded. Countless homes had been destroyed. I hoped that my family was safe and that none of the bombs had dropped close to our house. I missed them but, not wanting Omer or his wife to think I was ungrateful or feeling sorry for myself, I always rinsed my face with cold water before they returned home, to disguise the fact that I'd been crying.

In mid-June, on the first day of their summer holidays, Maya and her brother rushed through the front door and threw down their schoolbags, hardly able to contain their excitement. It was a hot day and from the kitchen window I could see a few children playing together. Maya was on her way outside when I finally mustered up enough courage to ask, 'Can I come with you this time?'

'Of course you can. I didn't want to ask you before because I didn't think you'd want to . . .' she said, tying her hair back into a ponytail.

We put on our shoes and ran outside. Her friends were playing with a ball but as we approached they stopped and looked at us. A girl in blue shorts folded her arms and said, 'Maya, who's this?'

'The refugee from Bosnia that I've been telling you about. Can she play with us?'

No one answered. I stood there in the pink T-shirt and shorts that Maya had given me, feeling as though I had an extra eye and four legs. Finally, the girl with the ball in her hands asked, 'What's your name?'

'I'm Hana. You?' I looked at her.

'I'm Petra,' she said, tossing the ball to me.

I caught it and threw it to a boy with fair hair.

'Good pass,' Maya said and we began to play. Later, we sat on the curb outside Maya's building. Petra asked me if the war in real life was the same as it looked on TV.

'It's more scary,' I replied. 'I remember the first sirens when a couple of JNA jets flew low over the city. My friends and I thought it was so exciting to see jet planes that we ran up and down the street shouting, "*Top Gun*, Tom Cruise." But the next day the Serbs started shelling the old city and we could see our National Library burning in the distance. The Serbs bombed houses, museums, churches and mosques, even the hospitals. One of our neighbours was killed. The worst times were at night when we had to sit in the dark shelter hoping that the shells wouldn't land too close to us.'

'There were sirens in Zagreb last October when the JNA planes bombed the main government building,' Petra said. 'They were trying to kill our president but that's the only time that Zagreb's been attacked.'

'I know, we saw the news and watched the reports of Serbs attacking Vukovar and Osijek, but we never thought it would happen in Bosnia,' I said.

'If all the Serbs want to live together, why don't they all go to Serbia?' Maya said. Everyone agreed.

At dusk the streetlights came on and Maya's mother called us from her balcony to come inside for dinner.

'You'll have to tell us more tomorrow,' Petra said as I got to my feet.

'Sure,' I said, then ran after Maya back to the apartment.

Two days later our mum walked in through the door of Omer's apartment, carrying a blue travel bag. 'Mama, Mama,' we cried as we ran towards her.

'I'm so happy to see you at last,' Nadia sobbed. Mum hugged us both and I burst into tears. The skin on her hands didn't seem as soft as it used to be, her hair was greyer and longer but now that she was with us again, all my worries melted away.

'You have lovely daughters,' Omer and his wife remarked when they greeted her.

Mum thanked them for looking after us, telling them how

lost and bewildered she felt in the chaos and confusion that the war had brought.

'Hopefully, it won't last long,' Omer said, leading Mum to the kitchen. Nadia and I sat next to her and told her everything that had happened to us since she had left home. Mum listened and later, as she dipped a sugar cube into her coffee, she told us what she and Lela had been through. Unable to return to Sarajevo with the aid that she had been sent to collect, Mum had no choice but to remain in Vienna where she helped at the refugee centre where they were staying. Not knowing how long it would be before we could all return home, Mum had managed to leave Lela with a family friend in Vienna. We were sad that she wasn't here with us.

That evening, Mum insisted on cooking dinner and made our favourite meal, *krompirusha*, filo pastry with potatoes. Long into the night, she sat in the kitchen talking to Omer and his wife about the war and politics.

'I saw you on TV last year in front of the JNA Headquarters in Belgrade, when you and all the other mothers were demanding that your sons be released from the army,' Omer said. 'Did anything come of it?'

'Nothing. There were five thousand of us from all over Yugoslavia, none of us knew what was happening to our sons. They locked a few hundred of us up inside the headquarters for twenty-seven hours, with the threat that our sons would pay if we continued protesting. There were some reporters with us but they were thrown out. On the second day, a JNA solider who sympathised with us came in with a warning that he'd overheard two generals planning to stage a riot so that they could open fire on us. When we heard this we left of our own volition. I fear for Mesha now. I can't even reach him at the barracks in Montenegro. Who knows where he is . . .' Mum's voice was shaking and she started to cry. 'And God only knows what's happening to them in Sarajevo . . .' she frowned and lowered her head.

It was late when we all went to bed. Maya slept in the living room so that Mum could sleep in the same room as us.

In the morning, as Omer and his wife were leaving for work, Mum thanked them again, telling them that we would find alternative accommodation as soon as we could. We tried calling Sarajevo but again had no luck so we went to one of the Red Cross Centres in town from where we were told we could send a message. Even though we were warned that it might not reach its destination, we filled in one of the forms anyway and wrote a message home. On the way back, we bought a newspaper for Mum to check the job advertisements. We had no money and desperately needed some. There was an advertisement for a house-keeping job, which under normal circumstances Mum would never have looked at, but because board was provided she decided to apply. She called the number and made an appointment for the next day. Her interview was in the city centre, which was a forty-minute bus ride away. Nadia and I went with her. From the bus station, we walked up one of the main streets, looking for the address.

'Zagreb's so flat,' I remarked. 'I really miss the mountains.'

'Me too,' Nadia replied.

'The centre of Zagreb looks like Vienna,' Mum said. 'That's because the Austro-Hungarians ruled here.'

'Yes, these buildings remind me of the ones that they built in the centre of Sarajevo. But I don't think Zagreb has the charm of Bascarsija,' I added, thinking back to the old part of Sarajevo with its old mosques and narrow cobbled lanes cluttered with small craft shops. I missed the smell of grilled meats and roasting coffee emanating from the little cafés and restaurants.

'Well, that's because Sarajevo was ruled by the Turks and

Zagreb never was,' Mum explained as we walked up to the address. I liked having Mum back with us – she always knew so much.

We rang the doorbell of a grand house with big arched windows. An immaculately dressed woman with her hair pulled back into a bun opened the door and led us into the large garden at the back. I'd never seen a garden of this size in the middle of a city before. We sat down at the table on the carefully mown lawn and Mum and the woman started talking. The woman explained that she was the wife of a government minister. Mum told her that she had never worked as a housekeeper but certainly loved to cook. I interrupted their conversation, saying that Mum's food was delicious. It was strange to be listening to my mother applying for a cleaning job. The woman seemed impressed with her and before long she and Mum were talking about the current situation. They got on well but it turned out that she couldn't employ a refugee because there could be complications with our status. When we left, I felt better – even though Mum didn't get the job, at least we were doing something to help ourselves. Mum said she would try somewhere else, but if nothing came of it, she would contact the Croatian branch of the humanitarian organisation that she'd been working for, hoping that through them we might be able to find a place to stay.

After a few days Mum started volunteering at the 'Mothers for Peace' Centre. At first, she only worked for a couple of hours at a time but then began to stay longer and longer, sometimes for the entire day. She received donations of food and clothes for her work and was happy to be able to bring something back to the apartment. Nadia and I saw her only in the evenings or if we went to some of her meetings. We didn't want to stay at the apartment all the time because our presence made it very crowded and, lately, Maya and her brother had started fighting, even in front of us.

During Mum's meetings, Nadia and I sat quietly at the back. The rooms were always crowded, with hundreds of refugees all looking for help. No one seemed to be leading these meetings and to me they appeared very disorganised. However, at the end people would always approach us to tell us how helpful Mum had been to them and their families.

One hot afternoon, Mum took us to the women's hospital in town. A nurse showed us to the garden where a young girl was sitting on a bench under the shade of a large tree. Her long hair was hanging loose and her skin was as pale as the gown she was wearing.

We introduced ourselves and Mum sat down beside her. Nadia and I sat on the grass, listening as they talked. The girl clasped her hands together and with her head bowed, told Mum that she was sixteen years old and came from a small village in Bosnia. She spoke in a low voice. We couldn't hear her very well so we moved closer to the bench.

'The Chetniks came through the village.' Her voice was hardly audible. 'Two men raped me in front of the other girls. More Chetniks arrived and they took turns with the others.'

The word *rape* made me feel sick. I shuddered. Nadia and I glanced uncomfortably at each other.

The girl shrugged her shoulders, then paused. Mum put her arms around her. The girl took a deep breath and through her tears said, 'Afterwards, they mockingly told us that they were spreading the Serb seed.'

Her story disgusted me. I felt desperately sorry for her but remained silent. We stayed with her for a while. She was pregnant and needed help so Mum promised to try to find her a place to stay. I felt so fortunate that nothing had happened to Nadia and me while we had been on our own. On the way back, we couldn't stop talking about her.

Two weeks passed. Aware that we were crowding Omer's apartment, Mum tried to look for accommodation in Zagreb but, without money, our only option was to go to one of the temporary centres which were already packed with refugees. Omer suggested that we stay put until we find something better.

Late one night, while Nadia and I were lying in bed, I turned to her and said, 'Why is Mum doing all this work for other people? What about us? Who's going to help us?'

'Don't ask me,' Nadia responded, raising her eyebrows. 'She can't go home. I guess she feels useful doing something. There are a lot of people who need help.'

'I know,' I said, kicking off my blankets. 'But we're not exactly at home here. Mum's not getting paid and I wonder how much longer these people can tolerate us! I just wish this stupid war would end soon so we can go back home.'

We chatted until we heard the front door open. Mum was back and she had some good news. She had arranged for us to go to Primosten, a small, safe town on the coast.

'Why Primosten?' I asked, confused.

'Hana, believe me, it's the only place I could find,' Mum replied. 'You remember Marko, Mesha's friend from the JNA? He's living there with his family in refugee accommodation,' she said.

Last year, while serving with Mesha in the JNA, Marko's home-town of Vukovar, in eastern Croatia, was attacked. He had lost all contact with his family and didn't know if they were dead or alive. For weeks he was desperate and often called us in the middle of the night, threatening to blow up the army barracks and himself. Mum spent days on the phone talking to the Croatian Red Cross until she finally found out that, although his family had been thrown out of Vukovar, they were alive and safe. Marko had escaped from the JNA in January and stayed with us in Sarajevo for a few days until Mum managed to organise his safe return to Croatia. Before he left he said he'd never forget our family's kindness.

'He's managed to secure a room for the two of you,' Mum explained.

'What do you mean, the two of *us*? Aren't you coming?' I asked.

Mum said she felt more useful volunteering, so she had decided to remain in Zagreb and stay with one of the women from the humanitarian agency. My heart sank. The thought of going somewhere new by ourselves again was scary. Although I understood why Mum felt more useful here, I was angry that we had to go away again on our own. With tears in my eyes, I walked out of the room.

Anger towards the war and the Chetniks overcame me. Why did they have to start the war and force us to leave our home? The same feeling of helplessness I had experienced when we left Sarajevo choked me and again I felt totally alone.

The Uncles

Atka

The crooked little plum tree in the small garden below our house had never borne so much fruit and its gnarled branches were bent under the weight. It was encouraging to see that something could flourish under these circumstances. The children and I picked the ripe plums and I made our first ever batch of jam. It was a delicious and exciting addition to our bland and relentless diet of rice and flour. These few jars, which we carefully stored in the cupboard, were the only improvement we could make in our lives. Our wood supply had dwindled to nearly nothing so we removed the door from one of the bedrooms and chopped it up for firewood.

As the siege of our city stretched into its fourth month, every day seemed like a year. Carting jerry cans up the hill took us most of the day, since the only source of water now was from the brewery in the old part of town, which was a fair distance from our house. Large shipping containers lined up across the streets provided some protection from sniper fire. Abandoned dogs strayed through the city, picking through rubble and piles of uncollected rubbish. The main city cemetery was too exposed and too dangerous for any burials to take place there, so the city parks and soccer fields that had once been packed with cheerful crowds were rapidly filling with freshly dug graves. The glass in the window frames had been shattered and the buildings were riddled with bullet holes. A number of buildings had partially collapsed under the constant barrage of mortar and shellfire. People's faces were worn and anxious.

However, after months of hiding, people had begun to venture out, resigned to the fact that being wounded or killed seemed to be a matter of fate. The main bakery and the local daily newspaper were still functioning, showing defiance in the face of war. The UN had taken control of the city airport, allowing their planes to bring food aid into city but the flights were often suspended due to heavy shelling. We received minute rations of flour, oil, cheese and canned fish. But the black market was flourishing and food prices were astronomical; the few vegetables and canned food that were available now cost twenty times more than before the war. These prices were simply out of our reach. I'd heard that most of this food had been stolen from aid parcels intended for Sarajevans and I despised these black marketeers for making fortunes out of our misery. All our bank buildings were closed and abandoned, everyone's savings had gone. Like most people, my father no longer had any work and we had no income.

Foreign journalists seemed to be the only people allowed in and out of Sarajevo on the UN flights and they'd become our only means of communication with the outside world. In the middle of July, we had received our first good news in a long time when a French journalist delivered a message to us from Mum written on a small piece of paper. In English, I asked him where and when he had seen my mum but he shrugged his shoulders, then showed me the bunch of letters he was carrying in a small plastic bag. 'I came across hundreds of refugees when I was in Zagreb the other day. So many had asked me to take messages to their families . . . I'm sorry, but I can't remember which one was your mother,' he explained. We thanked him before he rushed away. Mum had written that Lela was still in Vienna, while Nadia and Hana were with her in Zagreb but would soon be going to a refugee centre in Primosten. Scribbled on the paper were everyone's addresses.

Mum said that she was involved in a lot of humanitarian work, helping to place refugees from Bosnia in England and Austria. She wrote that she loved us and thought of us all the time. The message was short and it was difficult to tell how they were coping away from home. After almost two months of worry, at least we now knew where they were and that they were safe. Every time I thought of her message, I felt a sense of relief and not even the heavy shelling, which started later on in the day, spoiled that.

Over the next few days we sent several letters to them, some through the Red Cross and some through foreign journalists. As a sign of affection, the children drew their hands on the letters that we sent, and Dad and I hoped that at least one would reach its destination.

The last week of July claimed the first victim from our family. Our uncle Nako, one of Dad's younger brothers, was killed by a sniper. We were all devastated. Nako lived in Dobrinja, a suburb on the outskirts of town right on one of the frontlines. The suburb was connected to the city by a short stretch of road, which was always under fire. Dobrinja itself was a siege within a siege, it was far too dangerous for any of us to go there to comfort his wife and their two young children, let alone attend his funeral.

One hot day, almost a week after my uncle was killed, I was lying curled up on the couch – the pain in the right side of my lower back was unbearable and I clenched my teeth in agony.

The children were looking at me, confused and worried. I wanted to smile, to reassure them that I was fine, but the look of pain on my face only frightened them. Grandma was looking impatiently out of the window.

'Here she comes,' Grandma said, and went to open the front door.

My friend Sabrina, who lived a couple of doors down from us, came in carrying a bag over her shoulder. She was good-looking with a cheery face and worked as a nurse at one of the makeshift ambulance centres that had been set up at the local school. She looked concerned when she saw me and asked, 'Where does it hurt?'

I pointed to the area and she gave it a sharp jab. The pain was so intense I thought I was going to faint.

'It must be your kidney,' she said. She opened her bag and handed me a couple of pills. 'The best I can do is give you these strong painkillers while I still have some left.'

Selma jumped to her feet and brought me a small glass of water. I swallowed the pills immediately.

'It's either a kidney stone or an infection,' Sabrina said, 'but it's hard to tell without an ultra-sound.' We looked at each other, knowing that my kidney could not be attended to. The hospitals were flooded with the wounded and dying, and often they had no water or electricity.

'I'll leave some pills with you and the pain should ease soon. You'll be all right.' She rubbed my shoulder. Turning to Grandma, Sabrina asked loudly, 'Shall we have some coffee?'

Grandma smiled and replied apologetically, 'My child, I would make you some if I had any but I haven't smelt or tasted coffee for a long time.'

Sabrina pulled out a handful of coffee beans wrapped in a

handkerchief and handed it to Grandma. 'I'm not asking you if you have any, but if you'd like some,' she smiled.

Grandma beamed at her and took the coffee. She lit a fire in our trusty potbelly stove.

'Is your grandma using doors for firewood?' Sabrina said. 'I've heard that leather shoes and jeans burn well too.'

'Yes, I know, we've burned one or two pairs already,' I replied.

Sabrina handed a few sweets to the children and instantly their faces lit up. The noise of their contented sucking filled the room.

It took a while for the water on the stove to boil and by the time the coffee was ready, the pain in my back had subsided enough for me to be able to sit up a little. The strong aroma of dark coffee wafted around us, lifting our mood.

Sitting down next to me, Grandma carefully poured the coffee into small cups, apologising for the lack of sugar. Sabrina offered me a cigarette. We smoked and sipped the hot liquid.

'I heard about your uncle Nako. I'm so sorry. What happened?' Sabrina asked.

I took a deep breath and said, 'He was shot by a sniper while crossing the street. His wife and two children saw it all from the window of their apartment.' My voice broke and I wept.

'Oh, what a tragedy, poor children. Did you go to the funeral?' she asked.

'No, they live in Dobrinja . . .' I replied, unable to hold back the tears.

'Your poor grandmother. So, how did you find out that Nako had been killed?' she asked.

'I was at Studio 99 translating. Dad's youngest brother Zoran managed to get hold of me and told me what had happened. I had to tell Dad when I got home. It was awful.' I paused for a moment, remembering the look of horror on his face. 'He just stared at me in disbelief and, as I went to hug him, he turned away. The next day we went to tell Mayka.'

'You don't have to talk about it if you don't want to,' Sabrina said, lowering her head.

'Actually, it makes me feel better talking about it to someone.' I blew my nose and wiped my eyes. 'Zoran and Aunt Azra were at Mayka's house when Dad and I arrived. They had told Mayka what had happened. She was beside herself. Azra tried to comfort her while the rest of us just sat there most of the day stunned and powerless. What else could we do?' I looked at Sabrina and shrugged my shoulders in defeat.

'How's your dad coping?'

'I'm not sure, we hardly see him. He spends a lot of time at Mayka's or working with his friends. They've all come together, writing letters of appeal to world leaders for help. Because some government officials believe that their work could be worthwhile, Dad has been exempted from army duty. Whenever he's home, he sits for hours writing letters. He even believes that Margaret Thatcher will somehow help Sarajevo, even though she's not prime minister anymore. I think he's in a state of shock,' I explained, sadly.

'Who isn't? It's hard to remain sane,' she said. 'That's why a few of us from the street get together at night at the school shelter to play the guitar and sing . . .'

'I know – anything to take your mind off it. I go down to the studio whenever I can,' I said, pointing at my newly issued Studio 99 press card on the table. 'I've been reading and trying to study for my university exams as well.'

'What, exams in the middle of the war?' she sounded surprised.

'I know, who would've thought! One of my friends and

I went to the university the other day just to see what was going on. We found a few professors who are still there and they told us we could come and sit some of our finals whenever we could.'

Sabrina laughed. 'There's no escape from study. I'm surprised that anyone was there.'

'The university is not actually functioning. The building is full of hundreds of refugees from the villages. They have to cook on fires outside and are forced to share the few amenities available. Without any water, you can imagine the stench . . .'

'How miserable, at least we're still in our own houses.'

I extinguished my cigarette and shuffled down on the couch. The pain had gone and I was feeling sleepy. I yawned and soon drifted off to sleep.

A few days later, it poured with rain so we collected the rainwater from the downpipe and strained it through a sieve. Although this water wasn't drinkable it was fine for washing dishes and clothes.

Thick plastic wrapping taped to the window frames replaced the shattered glass in the living room. There was a large blue UNHCR sign printed across it. The rain had leaked through the sides of the tapes, so I placed towels on the windowsill to soak up the water.

The pain in my kidney was almost gone and I felt much better so I decided to make use of the rainwater and wash some of our clothes. Sometimes our humanitarian aid included a bar of soap, a large brown brick with a waxy texture. It had an odd smell but it was effective and washed the clothes well. I divided the soap into smaller parts to ration it.

I soaked the clothes in the cold water and started to wash them. As always, Janna and Selma came to help. I gave them each a small piece of soap and showed them how to use it sparingly. Janna started singing loudly and Selma frowned as she concentrated on washing one of her dresses. I stepped back and looked at the two of them wistfully.

'Atka, is this all right?' Selma said, lifting the dress she was washing.

'It's perfect, Selma. We'll give it a rinse and then put it on the washing line later.' The girls were so young but they helped me all the time without being asked. They often played with their little brothers, and read them stories. They never complained about anything.

We spent most of the day washing clothes, and later on, when the rain had stopped, we hung them out to dry. Both Grandma and I praised the girls' efforts and they beamed with pride. We made some tea and I spent the afternoon reading and studying. It was a quiet day, with the silence broken only by occasional gun fire.

A couple of days later I went to see Mayka. I had lived with her for two years after my grandfather died because she'd been so grief-stricken and we became very close. Dad was spending a lot of time with her and the rest of the family dropped in to check on her as often as they could. The loss of her son Nako had shaken her badly; she was very frail and sad.

I was glad to see Zoran at Mayka's house. He was her youngest son and my favourite uncle. When I was little, Zoran was still a student and I vividly remembered the times when he played his guitar and sang to us. Back then, his hair was long and I thought that he was a pop star. He taught me his favourite songs and carried me around Mayka's rose garden on his shoulders. Later on, as an electrical engineer, his job took him and his family abroad and they had returned from a posting in Iraq just before the war started. The whole family loved Zoran because of his calm and cheerful nature and seeing him always made me feel happy. He always encouraged me in my studies and when I told him that I had recently passed three exams, he congratulated me.

He had brought some food and a newspaper for Mayka. While she browsed through the paper, we went to check the small vegetable patch in the garden that he'd planted.

'How's my big brother?' Zoran asked, looking at the plants before us. He and Dad were very close.

I rolled my eyes and sighed. 'I don't know. He writes appeals all day long, he wants to save the whole of Bosnia.'

'You know what he's like, he wants to help everyone. He's done a lot for all of us, but I know what you mean. He's like an aviator, always with his head in the clouds,' Zoran said, softly. He knelt down and started weeding around the onions and potatoes and I bent down to help him.

'He's very lucky to have a daughter like you. It's not easy looking after small children at the best of times,' Zoran said, looking straight at me.

His praise slightly embarrassed me, so I changed the subject. 'Are these vegetables ready to eat?'

'They will be soon, in another week or so. When they're ready we'll share them amongst us.'

'I don't remember the last time we ate potatoes; the kids will love them.' Talking about food made my mouth water. We finished weeding and picked some cherries from a tree in the corner of the garden. Zoran cut a few roses to take to his wife. We went back inside and divided the fruit between us.

Mayka had finished with the paper. There was not much to read in it anyway – it was now reduced to a few pages, most of them taken up with death notices and reports on the fighting. Mayka folded the paper and looked at Zoran.

'Was the bombing of Baghdad as bad as this?' she asked.

Zoran and I looked at each other in surprise. We hadn't heard Mayka asking about anything lately and I thought her curiosity was a good sign.

'No Mum, nothing like this,' he answered.

'I used to worry about you so much. Every day I prayed to God for your safety and look at us now, worse than Iraq.' She shook her head.

'Yes, it's much worse.' Zoran reiterated. Carefully, he packed the cherries into the plastic bags and placed them on the kitchen table. Mayka sighed and clasped her hands.

'I lived through the Second World War here. I don't remember the bombing being so intense. Will humans never learn?'

'That's a movie we'll never see,' Zoran laughed cynically. He wrapped the roses in the newspaper.

We talked for a while and I was glad to see Mayka holding a conversation without bursting into tears at the smallest mention of her dead son. Zoran left before me and I walked him to the door. He gave me a kiss and as he was leaving said to me, 'Don't worry about your dad. Just keep studying and doing what you're doing, it will all work out.'

I stayed with Mayka for another hour, reading to her until she drifted off to sleep.

It was a Sunday and Sabrina's day off, so I popped down to see her. Her dad had taken the battery out of their car and attached it to the radio in their living room, so they were able to listen to the news. I froze when I heard an announcement. *At just before noon today, enemy shells were fired into a long queue of people waiting for bread in the Square of Solidarity. It is believed that approximately fifteen people were killed and more than twenty injured.*

Zoran lived near the square and it was possible that he could have been in the queue. 'I have to find out if my uncle's all right,' I said to Sabrina. 'I'm going to run down to Studio 99 to ring him.'

'You can call him from here,' she said. 'Our line's working at the moment, can you believe it!'

I dialled the number and asked for my uncle. In Zoran's building there were more than fifty apartments, but because of the war everyone had to share one phone line on the ground floor. I waited nervously until at last I heard my little cousin's voice on the other end.

'Hello, Haris, it's Atka here. Are you all right? Where are your mum and dad?'

In a weak and confused voice he replied, 'Mum's crying. We don't know where Dad is. He went to buy bread and he hasn't come back yet.'

I was terrified. 'Don't worry, Haris. I'm sure everything will be fine. I'll call you again later.'

There was nothing to do now but wait. As she walked me to the door Sabrina tried to reassure me that I was probably worrying unnecessarily and suggested I come back later and call again.

When I returned to our house I was surprised to hear a gurgling noise coming from the taps. We always left one tap on so that we would know if the water supply had been turned back on and although we had heard this sound before, water had never flowed. This time however, a thin trickle of muddy brown water started to drip. I couldn't believe my eyes. I ran to turn all the taps on and water gushed from them. We rushed around the house grabbing all the jerry cans, buckets, pots, jugs and cups that we could find and once the water started to flow clear we filled them all. After so many months, we finally had running water and I hoped that it was a small sign of better things to come. I made the most of this opportunity to give the children a quick shower and soaked a large pile of dirty clothes in a tub. I had never thought that having running water could cause so much excitement.

After a short time, the pressure died down and then the water stopped running. Still, we were pleased to have collected enough water to last us for the next few days. The nagging pain in my kidney was still troubling me and it was a relief to know that we could take a break from the never-ending necessity of collecting water.

Having been so preoccupied with the water, I had forgotten about the news that had been broadcast earlier. A loud knock on the door brought everything back to me.

Standing in front of me was a man in a fireman's uniform. It was Zoran's brother-in-law, Mesko. He'd never come to the house before and I feared the worst.

'Is your dad at home?' he asked.

I nodded and opened the door wide to let him in. The children were excited to see a man in uniform in our house and Tarik asked him if he carried a gun. He didn't reply.

Dad was sitting in the corner of our living room, writing.

Mesko approached him and Dad got up to greet him. As they were shaking hands I heard Mesko say, 'I'm sorry to have to tell you this . . . our Zoran was killed today.'

His words were like a blow to my gut. Dad started shouting at Mesko in disbelief, accusing him of telling lies. Mesko glanced at us and abruptly left the house. Dad walked down to the basement, slamming the door behind him. I couldn't move. My knees gave way and I fell back onto a chair with my head buried in my hands.

'What's happened?' I heard Grandma asking. Tarik told her. The girls were sobbing. I felt Grandma's hand on my shoulder. I was in a daze.

Is this what hell feels like? I thought. I couldn't believe he was gone. I thought of Mayka. Zoran was her youngest – this would break her.

I went downstairs to check on Dad. He was staring at the wall. I tried to talk to him but he didn't reply; his silence frightened me and I didn't know what to say or do. I stood there for a while hoping that he might make some sound. As I turned around to go upstairs, Dad said to me, 'My Zokica . . .' he called Zoran by his nickname. 'Atka, I don't know how to tell Mayka, this will kill her. You'll have to do it for me.'

I ran upstairs and straight into Grandma's arms. The children were still crying. We huddled on the couch and occasionally one of us checked on the soundless figure downstairs.

Having heard what had happened, Sabrina called in to see how we were coping and brought some sedatives for Dad. Janna made sure he took them.

I was so sad, torn and worried that I hardly slept at all. The next morning, I caught sight of my face in the mirror. I looked so old. Hoping that Dad was a bit better this morning I made some tea and took it to him. He was asleep and didn't respond when I called him. I shook him but he told me to leave him alone.

Someone had to go and tell Mayka the awful news but I didn't want it to be me. The load I had to bear was suffocating me. *How do you tell someone that they have lost their second child in the space of a month?* I thought. Somehow I had to bring myself to do it.

Sabrina came again. She gave me a hug and I asked her if she would come with me to Mayka's house. On the way there, we agreed it would be wise to give my grandmother something to calm her down before I told her the terrible news, bearing in mind her age and fragile state of mind.

In all the times that I had visited Mayka, I had never seen her standing at her courtyard door but there she was. It was as if she sensed something was wrong. Before she could see us, we ducked into a nearby yard to hide and to share a cigarette. My hands were shaking and I felt sick. I stole another glance at my Mayka's doorway. She was no longer there. I leant against the concrete wall and listened to the sound of the birds.

If I were a bird, I thought, *I could fly away*. When Sabrina agreed I realised I had said it out loud. We sighed and with a sense of dread made our way into Mayka's courtyard.

I knocked on the large kitchen window where Mayka always sat. When she saw me I waved and walked around the house to the veranda where she welcomed us.

'How is my girl?' She smiled and opened her arms. Her hair was pulled back and I could smell the familiar sweet scent of her lemon eau de cologne. Even in these hard times, she still tried to maintain her elegant appearance and dignity. I hugged her tight and we walked inside. After some small talk, Sabrina offered to take Mayka's blood pressure. It was easy to convince her that it was a little high and that she needed an injection to stabilise it. Mayka was pleased that she was receiving some medical attention and a long overdue check-up. Sabrina gave her the injection, then went outside.

Now I was on my own. I sat on the couch next to Mayka and held her hand. The minutes passed but still I couldn't speak. She sensed something was wrong, and at that moment her eyes widened and a look of horror crossed her face. When I lowered my eyes, she said, 'Who is it? Is it Zoran?'

When I heard his name I shivered. I couldn't answer. I squeezed her hand tight.

She let out a sound which seemed to come from the depths of her being and screamed his name. She pulled at her hair, moaning like a wounded animal. I held her arm and cried with her. I kissed her hands and stroked her head.

We hung on to each other for a while. Mercifully, the sedative started to take effect, her moaning quietened and she soon fell into a deep sleep. I feared that my lovely Mayka would not be able to cope in this world much longer. I sat there just looking at her and listening to her breathing until my aunt Azra and her two daughters arrived, their faces twisted in pain. Together we grieved for the man we all loved so much. He was buried the next day at the old Lion Cemetery. The cemetery was exposed and it was too dangerous for all of us to go to the funeral so Dad went alone. He came back a wreck. The funeral had to be cut short when snipers opened fire on the mourners.

More than a week passed. Early one evening, Dad came home with a postcard from Mum, which she had sent from London. It had been left at the reception at the Holiday Inn hotel, where most of the foreign press was based. A short message on the back said that she missed us and that she was in London for a few days with the humanitarian organisation 'Mothers for Peace'. Tarik asked where London was and I told him that it was where the King and Queen of England lived. He said they might come and rescue us.

Dad sat down to write more letters of appeal. Since Zoran died, he had given hundreds of them to foreign journalists to post.

'Dad, why are you writing all those letters?' I asked him. 'Do you really think anyone will help?'

'No.' He paused for a moment, looking at me. 'But I want the rest of the world to know that the spirit of this city is not dead.'

Dad had always had visionary ideas. Twenty years ago, after

he'd quit his job as a director of a government company, he started writing mathematics textbooks and formed his own publishing company. Everyone thought he was crazy. Establishing a private business under Communism was incredibly difficult and very few people believed he would be successful, but despite the system, Dad persisted and his business flourished. The numerous textbooks he wrote proved very useful and were used by students at schools and universities all over the country. Over the years he had sold several million copies.

Now I sighed as I watched him. He was so engrossed in his writing and seemed to pay scant attention to what was going on with us. I realised I'd have to get by without relying on him.

The next day, Dad asked a number of us to gather at the Museum of the City of Sarajevo, in the old Turkish part of town. Dad's behaviour was becoming increasingly strange. He wanted to take photos of us dressed in traditional Bosnian clothes so that he could add them to the endless piles of letters for help that he was sending to world leaders and royal families. I thought his appeals were a complete waste of time but I went along with his wishes anyway because I felt so sorry for him.

It was a beautiful sunny day with only sporadic shooting. The museum was a large rectangular building with a lovely rose garden in the middle. The curator showed us around and gave us complete liberty to choose whatever costumes we wanted.

Mira, one of my university friends, was with us and we discovered a small room where the clothes the Austro-Hungarian Archduke Franz Ferdinand and his wife Sophia were stored for safekeeping. Ferdinand and Sophia had been assassinated by a young Serb during their visit to Sarajevo in 1914, an event widely believed to be one of the sparks that led to the First World War.

We looked at the clothes in amazement, not sure if they

were authentic or not, but Ferdinand's uniform was still stained with blood. Mira put on the beautiful lace dress that had once belonged to Sophia. It fitted her perfectly. I settled for a traditional costume and Sophia's large hat. Dad wore Ferdinand's uniform.

The others found dresses of various national costumes. We all walked into the courtyard and posed for the photo. My dad looked ridiculous in Ferdinand's short, tight uniform and we all laughed hysterically. It was strange and surreal, we looked like a group of lunatics let out for the day. We heard artillery fire in the distance, followed by loud explosions. The shelling had started again. The all-too-familiar whistle of bullets above our heads sent us rushing back to the building. As we ran for cover I heard Dad shouting, 'Run Ferdinand run! The Serbs want to kill you again.'

Everyone laughed and for a moment I was reminded of the way he used to be.

The Refugee Hotel at the Seaside

Hana

We were dropped off just outside the hotel, a gleaming white building nestled against the hill, surrounded by pines and bay trees. What struck me most as we got off the bus was the deafening sound of cicadas. In the sweltering heat, the scent of pine needles and acorns was intoxicating. For a moment, I was reminded of the long summer holidays I had spent at the seaside with my family.

'Let's go and find Marko,' Nadia said, picking up her bag, which contained the clothes Maya and her friends had given us.

We walked into the cool foyer, where Marko was already waiting for us. I recognised him by the freckles on his face and his curly red hair. At the sight of him, Nadia started to cry. 'Don't be such a coward,' I said to her under my breath.

'Welcome, Sarajevan girls,' he said, walking towards us with a big smile. It was lovely to see a familiar face. He patted us on the back and before I knew it, he had taken our bags and was carrying them towards the reception desk. Nadia and I followed. We didn't know him well but he was our brother's friend, which was enough for us to trust him.

While he was checking us in, Nadia and I walked onto the nearby balcony. From there, we could see the Adriatic Sea and the small stony beach below. It was soothing to hear the sound of the waves lapping at the water's edge. Looking at the water, I said to Nadia, 'I wish everyone were here too. Can't you just see Tarik running around the hotel?'

Nadia looked at me. 'And Grandma would probably chase after him, telling him to slow down.' We laughed.

'I think about them constantly,' I said. 'And you?'

'All the time,' she answered with that same wistful look on her face that I had often seen before. 'You know . . .' She was about to say something, but stopped at the sound of footsteps behind us. We turned and saw Marko. In the sun his freckles were more noticeable.

'I'll be your guide for the day,' he said. Nadia and I made a face at each other because his words amused us. We followed him back inside.

He took us to one of the rooms on the ground floor, which he shared with his sister and their elderly parents. The balcony door was open and the room smelt wonderfully fresh. Marko's parents welcomed us and treated us with the same familiarity that I was used to receiving from family and friends.

'Your brother was a very good friend to our son,' his father said. 'And without your mother's help, God only knows if he would've found us.' His words gave me goose pimples. Marko's mother nodded repeatedly in agreement, a serious expression on her face.

Their room was modest with a double bed in the middle of it and two single ones on either side. Some framed family photos stood on the bedside tables and a large cross hung above the double bed. They were Catholics, like the majority of people in Croatia. It seemed as though they had been living in the room for some time and they had tried to make it look like home.

Marko turned to us and said, 'They've made a mistake at reception so you won't have your own room until the day after tomorrow. Do you think you two can squeeze into that bed in the meantime?' He glanced at the single bed near the balcony.

'No problem,' I replied, quickly. I was just pleased to have a roof over our heads and to be amongst people who cared for us.

We sat down to talk and Marko's mum offered us some biscuits while his father told us how they had had to flee from their home in Vukovar. A few months ago, the Serbs had overrun their town and razed it to the ground, burning and plundering everything in their path. I remembered the many devastating reports I'd seen on TV last winter. Vukovar was the only town in eastern Croatia which had fallen into the hands of the Serbs and there were no longer any Croatians living there. It was really sad hearing about their forced flight from home. A few photos and a suitcase of clothes were the only possessions that they had been able to take with them.

For a brief moment it crossed my mind that Sarajevo could also fall into the hands of the Serbs. It was the first time this thought had occurred to me and I shivered. It was too awful even to contemplate.

'So, how did you end up here?' Nadia asked.

'Well, the war has killed tourism and with so many empty hotels on the coast, our government decided to house refugees here. Those of us from Vukovar were a priority because of what happened there. And now here we are.'

Marko's dad paused for a few minutes, and while cleaning his glasses, shook his head and spoke again. 'I fear the war in Bosnia might be a lot worse than we've seen here in Croatia. We pray to God that He will put an end to it all.' He kept on repeating how sorry he was to see what was happening in Bosnia. It surprised me that despite his own hardship he was still concerned about other people.

Marko's mother tried to smile but I couldn't help thinking how sad she looked. We found out from her that the food in the hotel came from UNHCR funding. She thought the UNHCR must have donated some money too, to pay the staff who continued working as usual, although she wasn't completely sure.

Marko got up from the other small bed where he'd been sitting. 'This is all too serious for a sunny afternoon! Do you girls want to unpack and then I'll show you the rest of the hotel?'

'Good idea,' his mother said, approvingly.

I went into the bathroom and changed into a pair of shorts and a T-shirt. Marko's father was lying on the bed asleep when I came back into the room. We left quietly.

The hotel was small and well kept. The sun poured in through the large windows at each end of the hall. While we wandered around, Marko told us about our brother Mesha and how difficult it had been for the two of them in the JNA once the Serbs had taken over. He told us that Mesha had had the good fortune to be assigned to the army photo lab and that neither of them had been sent to the front.

'When I decided to escape I tried to convince Mesha to come with me because I was sure the Serbs would attack Bosnia too. But he didn't believe me so he stayed behind . . .'

We told him that we hoped Mesha had escaped by now.

Later on, Marko took us up to the restaurant on the top floor to show us the view. It was breathtaking. The Adriatic Sea stretched far into the distance in front of us and on the right there was a small town perched on a peninsula.

'That's Primosten,' Marko said. We could see a church tower which stood out above the tiled rooftops of the surrounding houses. 'It only takes ten or fifteen minutes to walk there. It's a quaint little place,' he said.

It did look beautiful in the soft, pink, evening light but all I could think about was that my family wasn't here with me.

'When it comes to food, it's a little bit like the JNA here,' Marko said and chuckled. 'We have fish every Tuesday, Thursday and Saturday, spaghetti Bolognese on Mondays, Wednesdays and Fridays and meat on Sundays. It's a luxury refugee camp,' he joked.

The hotel was full of refugees, mainly from Vukovar, with twenty or so women and children from Bosnia. The war had brought us all here and our individual circumstances needed no explanation. Soon, we settled into our own room, No. 34, and got to know everyone.

Nadia and I befriended four other children from Sarajevo and we spent most of our time with them. One of the girls, Nevena, was the same age as me, and was here with her older brother. He was skinny and his sister liked to boss him around. The other two teenagers, Amela and Kemo, were here with their mother, whilst their father remained in Sarajevo. They left just after we did, but their convoy was held hostage by the Serbs for two days and they barely made it out.

The six of us did everything together: swimming, walking, playing and eating. One afternoon on our way to lunch, I mentioned to Nevena that we had not been in contact with our family in Sarajevo since we'd left.

She stopped halfway up the stairs and looked at me. 'Hana, didn't you know that foreign journalists are able to go in and out of Sarajevo on UN flights?' she said. 'Occasionally, some of them come to the hotel to collect letters from us to take to our families in Bosnia. Last month, an Italian journalist came with a letter from our parents.'

'Really?' I stared at her, filled with hope and excitement.

Then, only a few days later, a journalist did come to the hotel. We had just got back from the beach, and were walking into the foyer, when we noticed a group of people gathered at the reception desk. I hadn't seen it so busy before and ran towards the crowd. Kemo's mother spotted me and called out, with urgency in her voice, 'Hana, this journalist's going to Sarajevo. He'll take letters with him.'

I rushed to our room. Nadia's diary was on the bedside table and I tore a clean sheet of paper out of it. *The letter has to be short,* I thought, afraid that the journalist might leave before I could give it to him.

Dear Dad, Atka and everyone else, I began. I told them where we were and that I missed them a lot. I gave them our address and mentioned that we'd been with Mum in Zagreb. I told them not to worry about us and that I lived for the day we would all be together again.

At the end I signed it, *We love you, your Nadia and Hana.*

I raced back to reception and handed the letter to the journalist, glad that he was still there. 'Thank you,' I said in English. Everyone was in high spirits for the rest of the day.

The daily routine at the hotel revolved around three meals, for which we were given weekly coupons. We always ate all the meals we were given because none of us had any money to buy food of our own. The small amount of money that Mum had been able to give us, we kept for emergencies. Nadia and I checked the amount every night, just to make sure that it was all there.

Between meals we ventured out with the other children, to play and swim at the small beach in the bay. But most of the time, there was little to do and sometimes we just walked back and forth to Primosten five or six times a day. The town was very small and the locals knew that we were refugees from the hotel. Every time we walked past the ice-cream kiosks, we wished we had money to buy ice creams for ourselves.

On really hot days we stayed inside playing cards and Monopoly, always talking about home. Before the war our summer holidays had passed all too quickly, whereas now some days were painfully long and seemed to drag on for ever. One such afternoon, I was sitting inside with a girl who came from Mostar, a town in the southern part of our country. She was two years older than me and she and her younger brother were here on their own as well. Suddenly, while we were playing, she burst out, 'I'm sick of this war,' and threw the game board on the floor. 'Enough, enough!' she screamed over and over, gesturing with her clenched fists. I didn't know what to say so I just gave her a hug. Often I had the same thoughts, but I couldn't voice them because that would mean breaking my promise to Atka and it was too terrifying even to think of what could happen to us or our family. I knew I had to hold on and be brave until we were together again.

Nadia and I took turns cleaning our room. Once a week, we washed our sheets in the hotel laundry. On Sundays, we were given a ration of soap and washing powder to wash our clothes. We washed everything by hand in the bathroom sink, then dried it all on the balcony. Everyone had to do the same.

The TV room was always crowded for the evening news. Every night we watched the news, hoping to hear that the end of the war was in sight. But the reports from Croatia and Bosnia showed that the war was worsening and the situation was becoming more complicated. Afterwards, the room was always noisy and full of smoke, with the adults engaged in heavy discussion and debate. I listened to them because I thought that was the only way to understand what might happen next. They talked of foreign intervention and believed it was imminent.

The common view seemed to be that foreign governments wouldn't tolerate the Serbs' atrocities much longer. Everyone agreed that NATO should be stepping in. I had hoped that foreign governments would intervene and save Bosnia but when nothing happened for weeks I no longer knew what to think. Eventually, I got tired of the same old arguments and started avoiding the news. I got into the habit of walking to Primosten before dinner because sometimes I liked to get away on my own. But I always came back in time to eat.

A stony clay path covered in pine needles led from the hotel through the forest towards the town. Tiny lizards moved swiftly under the trees then disappeared into the holes in the ground. I pretended that the war was over and I was on my way home from school. I imagined talking to my brothers and sisters and could picture it all so clearly. At the end of the forest, the path turned into a quiet little street. I liked it here because there was a row of beautiful houses on one side, all facing the glistening Adriatic Sea. Walking slowly, I imagined being inside each house with my family. I wished for it so much and although I knew it wasn't real, it made me feel better.

At weekends we wandered around the small market in town. There were always a few stalls selling fruit, vegetables and the daily catch of fish. Some of them sold souvenirs and cheap jewellery and one day, for fun, I stopped to try on some of the bracelets. When I looked up, I realised that my friends had gone on ahead of me. I was walking back to the hotel on my own when a girl with long brown hair stopped me. She was standing in front of a large house and wearing a green T-shirt with Benetton written across it.

'Are you from the hotel?' she asked.

'Yes, I'm staying there for the moment,' I replied. I had heard some of the older locals making derogatory comments about refugees and I was scared that she would mock me. But she didn't – she was just curious. Her name was Ivana and she was from a town near Primosten. I told her I was from Sarajevo. The house behind her belonged to her grandmother where Ivana spent every summer holiday. She was very friendly and talked a lot. I liked her because she seemed kind and we decided to meet and play the next day.

'You have so many books,' I said to her the following afternoon while admiring her grandmother's extensive book collection.

'Most of them are my dad's,' she said. 'He grew up in this house and likes to keep them here. You can borrow one or two if you like.'

'Really?' I pulled out a book called *The Gathering of the Young Seagull*. 'Is it all right if I take this one?'

'Yes, of course. And when you finish that one, you can borrow another.' There were no books at the hotel and I couldn't wait to start reading.

The sweet smell of baking drifted up from the kitchen and we went downstairs to see Ivana's grandmother. She was very kind and wanted to hear about my parents and family. It was pleasant, for a change, to talk about them, rather than about the war. A radio was playing in the background and a light breeze wafted through the windows. Ivana's grandmother cuddled her and plucked her cheek. Ivana was embarrassed, joking that she was not a baby any more. I liked it though because it reminded me of my own grandmother, who was very affectionate and liked to tickle us until we screamed for mercy.

Ivana introduced me to her local friends and we played football together on the field near the hotel. Sometimes, boys played against girls, but most of the time those of us from the hotel played against the locals. Our team didn't have a name but eventually the locals decided that *Refugees* was the most accurate. It was light-hearted and no one took any offence.

One Sunday after playing soccer with the locals we sat down for dinner but Nadia's seat at the table was empty. I wasn't sure where she was and wished she'd hurry up or she'd miss her meal.

'Has anyone seen her?' I asked, slightly concerned.

'I saw her coming back from the football field. She must have stopped by your room,' Amela said as she reached for the bread.

Nadia came up a few minutes later, slightly short of breath.

'Where were you?' I asked, annoyed but glad to see her.

She flopped down on to her seat. 'I've been at reception talking to Mum on the phone.'

I was about to take a mouthful but put my fork back on the plate. 'What did she say?' Mum called us whenever she could and the last time we'd talked to her she was helping with the transport of a group of refugees to Austria.

'She's back in Zagreb,' Nadia said, pouring herself a glass of water.

'Is she going to come here?' I asked.

Nadia shook her head. 'No, but she wants to bring us to Zagreb. She's thinking of going back to Sarajevo.'

'What?!' I said, not believing what I'd just heard.

'She doesn't think the war's going to stop any time soon and she wants to try to get home.'

'Dear God, what is she thinking?' I said. It was all over the news that people were desperate to get out of Bosnia and trying to get back was very risky and dangerous. The Serbs controlled most of the territory and if Mum were caught trying to get into the country, especially with her Muslim name, she would probably be killed. But then I thought of all my little brothers and sisters and I could only guess how Mum felt being away from them all.

At the beginning of September, with the summer coming to an end, many of the local shops and restaurants closed for the season. Ivana and some of the other children had gone back to their home-towns for the new school year. Primosten was empty. Everything around us was moving and changing, but we were at a standstill. We were still waiting to hear whether or not we would be going back to Zagreb. Mum was trying to arrange for us to go to a refugee centre there. No one seemed to know how long the hotel would be used as a refugee centre or even if the Croatian government would continue helping Bosnian refugees. Several families from Vukovar had left the hotel for Zagreb where the government had arranged some housing. A few Bosnian women who had been granted permission to seek refuge in Norway had left with their children. Others were trying to get visas for Germany and Sweden, whose governments were also accepting refugees. I feared that the hotel might close and that we would be left on the streets.

Nadia and I were in our room when we heard a loud banging on the door. Amela was standing outside and urged us to go to reception. A foreign journalist had just returned from Sarajevo and had brought letters with him. One of them was for us. We raced to reception without even locking the door behind us. I recognised Atka's writing on the blue envelope which he gave us. Carefully, we opened the letter and moved away to read it. Others were reading their letters and some newspapers from Sarajevo which the journalist had brought.

Atka had written the letter at the beginning of August. She told us they had received our message and that everyone was very relieved to hear that we were safe. The situation in Sarajevo was horrific and they didn't know when it would end. She told us to stay in safety and that they all loved us and thought of us a lot.

Then she wrote that tragically Uncle Nako had been killed by a sniper. Nadia and I just stood there, shocked. We looked at each other and, holding each other's hands, started crying. We felt so alone and far from home.

Kemo, whose head was buried in the newspaper, raised his voice, 'Hana, Nadia, are you related to a man called Zoran? He has the same surname as you.' I saw the look of shock on Nadia's face, she'd heard it too.

Why is he asking? I thought, panic enveloping me.

I walked towards Kemo and recognised the death notice section that he was looking at. It showed photos of people who had been killed. At home, I had always skipped reading that part, because I thought it would bring bad luck. My eyes were immediately drawn to the black and white photo of my uncle Zoran. I didn't have to look at the name. He had been killed a few days earlier.

Nadia put her arm around me and, weeping, we slowly made our way back to our room. Sobbing, we collapsed on our beds. I knew innocent people were dying, but I couldn't understand how Nako and Zoran could both be taken away. It was impossible to imagine that we would never see them again. I thought of all my cousins who no longer had fathers.

Stairways

Atka

Whilst exploring the dark, narrow corridors of the basement next to the studio, Hamo discovered a small room full of books. He shared his discovery with me and a couple of colleagues who were working that night.

'There are hundreds of books in the back there,' he said, dropping a couple of heavy volumes on the desk.

I pulled one of the books closer to me and flicked through the dusty pages. 'This one's about Stalin,' I said, dismissively, closing the cover with a thud.

'Isn't there anything more contemporary than that?' one of the guys joked.

'No, it's all Marxist crap. They must have been left behind and forgotten. Remember, this used to be the Communist Party Headquarters.' Hamo lifted one of the books from the desk and tapped it. 'I wonder how well they'd burn.'

'Do you think we should take some home for firewood?' I asked without hesitation.

'Who's going to miss them?' Hamo replied and shone his torch back towards the room. We followed him, giggling, grabbed a few books each and took them home.

'The hard covers of *Das Capital* were so slow burning, I managed to bake a whole loaf of bread,' I told Hamo at the studio the next evening.

'Lenin burns well too. Finally the old Communists are contributing something to society,' Hamo remarked.

'I was so bored, I tried to read some of the books last night,' one of our colleagues said. 'No wonder the system collapsed, I couldn't get past the first few sentences.'

'First few sentences,' Hamo exclaimed. 'Not a bad effort, I don't know anyone who's got that far.' He walked towards a large travel bag, which was sitting on the cluttered desk. He unzipped it and tugged a long cable from it.

'What's that for?' I asked.

Hamo inclined his head and, squinting from the smoke of his cigarette, replied, 'I'm connecting the cable to the power here and I'm gonna run it up to my house.'

Hamo lived just up the hill. Thick bushes separated his house from the studio. I couldn't believe that he was going to run the cable all the way up there.

'Are you serious?' I said, incredulously. 'How are you going to do that? The power comes from the UN next door!'

Hamo shrugged his shoulders. 'So what? Fuck the UN!' he scoffed. 'By the time they make any decisions we'll all have carked it.' With that he hoisted the coiled cable over his shoulder and, leaning slightly under the weight of it, strode out. We thought his plan ridiculous and returned to our work, laughing.

I sat behind the desk and concentrated on translating the news. The UN was trying to negotiate a ceasefire but every time an agreement was reached, the Serbs would renege on the deal and continue fighting. To make things worse, the Bosnian Croats had recently started fighting the Bosnian Muslims in central Bosnia. The rumours of the Serb concentration camps in northern Bosnia had finally been confirmed by foreign journalists. The chilling reports of the torture and starvation of thousands of civilian prisoners was starting to emerge. It was painfully obvious that the war would drag on into the harsh Balkan winter.

I finished my translation and handed it in. Hamo hadn't returned yet and the image of him lugging the cable through the bushes made me grin.

Tonight I didn't have to rush home to look after the boys. After almost six months under siege most of our neighbours, resigned to their fate, had stopped going to the school shelter. Grandma and the girls were no longer sleeping there either. I walked home through the balmy evening. The sky above the darkened city was glistening with stars and the sweet scent of linden leaves surrounded me, taking me back to those carefree late summer evenings spent in the company of my friends. How things had changed. How strange it was to think that all we had to worry about in those days was which bar to go to and what to wear. It was another life.

The next morning the entire neighbourhood was gossiping about Hamo. The news that he had connected the power to his house had spread like wildfire. I really had to go and see for myself. Strings of extension cords hung from house to house like empty washing lines. Hamo's plan had worked. He had dragged the cable to his house and his next-door neighbours connected the power to their houses. Hamo warned everyone to use only a few small appliances at a time so that the power supply would not become overloaded.

'Turn off your TV,' one of the neighbours shouted to another out of his window. 'You've had yours on all morning. Give us a turn!' It made me smile to watch Hamo's immediate neighbours trying to organise the use of their newly found source of power.

Later in the day, one forgetful old woman turned on her oven, which overloaded the system and killed the entire operation. Annoyed but unfazed, Hamo fixed the problem. I envied them their little luxury and wished my house was closer to his.

Busy with work and household chores, I had little spare time, but I went to see Mayka whenever I could. She was silent in her mourning and her only solace was in prayer. She barely spoke when I visited and had lost all interest in food; I worried about leaving her alone. The only thing I could think of doing to comfort her was to tuck her up under her blanket before I left.

Walking home after one of my visits, I was saddened to see the ruined facades of the buildings on the familiar route; not even the large orphanage building had been spared. Some of the children from the orphanage leaned on the fence asking for money and cigarettes but I had nothing to give them.

I could hear the thud of shelling in the distance, it was continuous, only varying in its intensity and, like everyone else, I had become used to the constant danger, running for cover only if the shells started landing close by.

As I walked, hands deep in my pockets, I started thinking about my ex-boyfriend. We'd been together for a few years but had stopped seeing each other months before the war began. When he'd heard about the deaths of my uncles, he hitched a ride from Dobrinja to come and see me, despite the danger. I was surprised and touched that he'd made the effort but we found that we didn't have much to say to each other any more. It was strange to realise that instead of the war bringing us closer together, we had drifted even further apart.

I was nearing home when someone called my name from across the street. It was a family friend of ours who lived near the orphanage and I walked over to greet her. She looked concerned and told me that she'd just heard from someone that Zoran's little son, Mirza, had been wounded in the leg the day before and taken to the hospital near my house. Horrified, I raced to see him.

The front of the nine-storey building, formerly a military hospital, was riddled with massive holes due to the constant shelling from the hills. When I arrived, I enquired at the desk and was told that Mirza was in intensive care. The receptionist said that all the patients and medical staff were now confined to the lower floors of the hospital, where it was relatively safe. I searched through the crowded ward until I saw Mirza's mother, Merima, standing in one of the corridors, smoking. She looked anxious and drained. How unfair and cruel it was to see her here with the soil on her husband's grave hardly settled. She was a beautiful woman in her mid-thirties who, like her late husband, always seemed to have an air of composure about her. I walked towards her and we embraced. She took me by the hand and together we went to see Mirza.

The odour of antiseptic and warm air mingling in the windowless room was overpowering. Rows of beds were lined up on either side. Mirza was lying in one of them, covered by a sheet. His hair was wet and drops of sweat covered his pale little face. I looked at him nervously, wiped his forehead and kissed him. His eyelids fluttered, he mumbled something then drifted back to sleep. It was so awful to see him like this that I couldn't hold back the tears.

'Is he going to be all right?' I whispered to Merima.

'He has gangrene, the doctors have told me they have to watch him carefully.'

'I wish Zoran were here,' I said without thinking.

She pursued her lips and nodded. We stood silently, looking at Mirza. He was only twelve and already looked so much like his father. I stayed with them for a while and promised to come back the next day.

Selma and Janna cried when I told them about Mirza and Grandma prayed for him through the night. I thought of Zoran and begged him to take care of his little boy. Fortunately, Dad was staying with Mayka that night and I was relieved that I wouldn't have to face him just yet.

The next morning I went back to the hospital. When I arrived, I saw Merima sitting in a chair by Mirza's bed, watching over him as he slept. Her eyes were red and puffy and she looked tired. She was dressed in yesterday's clothes and I assumed that she had stayed at the hospital all night. When she saw me, she signalled to me to wait for her outside the room.

'Is he all right?' I asked as she came out through the door.

'He's out of danger now, but they had to amputate his leg just below the hip.' She looked at me in anguish.

I gasped in horror. I put my arm around her, not knowing what to say. We stood there in silence. Heaving a deep sigh, Merima moved away and walked back towards the room. At the door she turned with tears in her eyes and whispered to me, 'Atka, he doesn't know yet, I haven't got the heart to tell him.'

Mirza was crying when I saw him again the next day. He had learned the truth. One of the boys in his room had accidentally blurted it out. Mirza kept telling us that he couldn't believe it because he could still feel his limb. Merima stroked his head. I sat with my little cousin, holding his hand.

With some of the few drugs the hospital still had, they tried to keep his pain under control for the next few days. Soon he started to feel a little better. We chatted and although he was drowsy, he cheered up when I mentioned his favourite movie, *Rambo*. He knew the lines off by heart and recited a few in

English for me. He had attended international schools when Zoran worked abroad and spoke the language fluently.

'You're a real hero, saving your brother's life like that,' I said to him. 'Do you remember anything about it?'

Looking away, he spoke slowly, 'We were playing in the entrance of our building when I heard an explosion. I pushed Haris to the floor. There was smoke and everything went silent. My leg felt warm. I looked at Haris. He was pale and huddled in the corner. I tried to go up and tell Mum what had happened but fell as I tried to make it up the stairs. Then I must've blacked out . . .'

Mirza was still in the hospital when Merima and Haris moved into the basement of her brother Mesko's house where they thought they'd be safer.

The autumn leaves had fallen. The branches of the trees were bare and without their cover we felt even more exposed to the enemy. The weather was becoming wetter and colder, forcing the children to huddle under their blankets for warmth. Whenever we lit the fire to cook, all five of them sat around the stove to warm themselves. Janna and Selma had started to attend the 'war school', which was organised at the apartment of one of their teachers who lived in the neighbourhood. The lessons lasted only for a couple of hours at a time and the girls were happy to go whenever the shooting allowed.

The small rations of food we received were distributed sporadically by the UNHCR. We talked about food all the time and looked with longing at photographs of food in Mum's cookbooks. Some days there was nothing to eat and we were weak with hunger. The children were malnourished and their teeth were decaying. Tarik's long blond hair had started falling out in clumps so we shaved off all of it. His bald head made him look like a little old man. Dad had lost so much weight that his clothes hung loosely off his usually broad frame. In desperation, Grandma urged me to go to the local Muslim centre where she was well known, to ask them for food. Now we were reduced to begging.

The people working at the centre were reluctant to help, explaining to me that the food was reserved only for the families of fallen soldiers. I pleaded with them, mentioning Grandma's name. It was only on hearing that she was my grandmother that they relented and gave me a small packet of flour and a bottle of cooking oil. We survived on thin slices of flatbread for the rest of the week. All we had to spread on the bread was vitamin powder, which had been given to Dad by a doctor from the children's hospital. I mixed this powder with water and spread it onto the children's bread. It smelt musty and tasted disgusting but I encouraged the children to eat it, telling them it would give them lots of energy and make them grow. They held their noses and screwed up their faces every time they ate it.

When he wasn't looking after Mayka, Dad tried to visit as many of his friends as he could to see how they were coping. On one occasion he brought back a large parcel of food for us, given to him by a friend who worked at the synagogue. We unpacked flour, rice and the usual staples and were thrilled to discover luxuries such as coffee and chocolate.

From time to time we had power and water. Having electricity transformed the house into a warm and cheerful place. If we had flour, Grandma and I were able to bake, while the little ones watched their favourite cartoon videos. We had water more often than power and when it flowed from the taps we filled every available vessel. Unfortunately, these occasions were few and far between and usually short-lived.

Dad came home one grey afternoon with a letter from Nadia and Hana, which had been delivered to the Holiday Inn. It was only the second one we had received from them even though they wrote that they had sent a few. We sat down and everyone gathered around me to listen. Tarik interrupted, 'Is there a war where they are?'

'No,' I replied briefly and continued reading.

But Tarik kept interrupting me. 'Can I go to the seaside and see them? I've had enough of this war!'

It was the first time I'd heard any of them complain and all I could do was stare at him. I knew that the government was still trying to evacuate some women and children on UN-escorted buses but so far the Serbs had allowed only one or two buses to leave the city. More and more Sarajevans were trying to flee by running across the deadly airport runway at night. The runway led to Mt Igman, the only mountain on the outskirts of the city that had not fallen into the hands of the Serbs. Those trying to escape were regularly shot at by Serb snipers and, if caught by the UN soldiers patrolling the airport, were inevitably ordered to turn back. None of us had any intention of leaving and anyway any attempt to escape along with five small children would have been suicidal. On top of that, anyone who wanted to leave the city had to provide proof of sponsorship from abroad and we had no one who could do that for us. It had never occurred to me to leave Sarajevo. This was my city, my home, my identity. Our roots went deep. Even as children, my friends and I sang songs of love and loyalty to our home-town.

Before I could reply, Janna put her hand on her hip and, turning to Tarik, said, 'Are you stupid? Can't you see that we're surrounded?'

Tarik drew his knees up and rested his chin on them. The

sad look on his face made us take pity on him. Patting her leg, Grandma beckoned to Tarik to come and sit on her knee. She hugged him close to her and said, 'I promise, when this war is over I'll take you all to the seaside.' She adjusted her headscarf and smiled.

Cheered, Tarik said, 'The Chetniks have been shooting so much, they'll run out of bullets for sure and then there'll be no more war.'

I wished I could believe him.

Early the next morning the heavy shelling forced us to the shelter. The dank room in the basement felt like a prison cell. We'd been there for hours and I had run out of new stories to tell the children.

'Can you tell us about Snow White again?' Asko asked.

'All right,' I replied and reluctantly plunged into the familiar tale once more. The children listened wide-eyed as though they had never heard it before. When I came to the part where Snow White meets the dwarves for the first time, Emir tugged my sleeve and asked, 'Atka, what are dwarves?'

'They're short people with beards who live in the forest,' I answered.

Clapping his hand to his forehead he exclaimed, 'Oh no, are they Chetniks too?'

We all laughed uproariously. I couldn't finish the story because every time I started telling it again Janna and Selma burst out laughing.

The shelling eased later in the afternoon and we were able to go upstairs. It was getting dark and drizzling with rain. Grandma fetched the candles that she always kept stashed in her bedroom, to make sure we had light once the dark set in. The box of matches she kept in her bra.

The children, eager to play, chased each other in the hallway. Grandma and I had just started to light the fire to cook a handful of rice for all of us to share when we heard a scream. Within seconds Selma ran into the living room, shouting that Asko had fallen down the stairwell on to the concrete floor of the basement.

I climbed down the stairs into the pitch-black darkness, calling his name. There was no answer but I could hear him whimpering. I felt my way around until I found him. Carefully, I picked him up and carried him up the stairs. His head was covered in blood. I took him into the living room and put him on the couch. Blood was streaming down his face. I yelled at Janna to grab a towel. She didn't move and I yelled at her again. She brought a towel back to me and I wrapped it around Asko's head, trying to soothe him. The children stared at us in silence.

Grandma hurried to the window and yelled for help. The shelling became louder again and Janna pushed the children back into the hallway. Soon, one of the guards from the courtyard ran into the living room and looked at Asko's head.

'Head wounds are the worst, they bleed like mad,' he said while removing the blood-soaked towel. I couldn't look.

'That's quite a gash on his forehead, he needs to go to the hospital immediately.'

He lifted Asko up and rushed outside, calling for me to hurry. The other guard ran to get a car and soon a rusty van pulled up in front of us – it was the only vehicle in the street that still contained any petrol.

The driver, known to everyone in the neighbourhood as 'Uncle', beckoned to me. I got into the van, taking Asko into my arms, and Uncle stepped hard on the accelerator; we drove down the hill at high speed. I leaned over Asko's slight body.

He was shaking. The noise of the explosions was deafening. It was the first time that I'd been in a car during heavy shelling and I was petrified that the rickety vehicle would be hit.

Even though the hospital was close the short ride seemed like an eternity. Uncle drove straight to the rear entrance and, with a screech of brakes, we came to a halt. Two men in white coats raced to us and opening the door, asked, 'Shrapnel?'

'No, he fell,' I said in a shaky voice, handing Asko to one of them. As we ran inside I told them what had happened. Asko was moaning quietly when they took him into the doctor's room. I wanted to go with him but they wouldn't let me and told me to wait outside. I managed to wave to Asko before the door closed.

There were a few people in the dreary waiting area, some of them with bloodstains on their clothes. A woman hunched in the far corner was sobbing loudly, her long hair hiding her face. A man in a black jacket had his arms around her. I looked away then noticed blood on my own clothes. I tried to rub it off.

Suddenly, I heard loud screams echoing down the main corridor. Doctors and nurses rushed frantically towards the wave of wounded being hurried in through the door. A man, soaked in blood, was wheeled in on a gurney, staring in horror at his missing limb. Someone else ran in, carrying a small child in his arms, yelling for help. I didn't know where to look. It was chaos. Thunderous explosions shook the building. My head was spinning and my back hurt. Moving to the corner, I leaned against the wall and closed my eyes. I was exhausted and found myself weeping uncontrollably. Then the sweet face of my sister Hana came to me. I remembered the promise we'd made the day she'd left Sarajevo, that we would be brave for each other. Strangely, that thought gave me strength.

After a while, a tired-looking doctor called me into his surgery. Under the large bandages, Asko's ashen face looked so small. He was frightened but perked up when he saw me.

'We'll keep him here for a few hours, just to make sure that he's not concussed.' The doctor patted Asko's hand. ' You're a good boy. Your sister's here now,' he said as he rushed away.

I sat on Asko's bed. 'It's all right, I'll stay with you, Asko.'

Soon he went to sleep and I curled up next to him. Over the next few hours the nurse hurried in and out to check his condition and towards midnight she told us we could go home. Although Asko weighed almost nothing, I wondered how I was going to carry him all the way home on my own. We could still hear the faint thudding of shelling in the distance.

To my surprise, Uncle was standing in the corridor.

'Fuck, did you see how many wounded they brought in tonight?' he said, angrily.

'Yeah, I saw them,' I replied, shaking my head in resignation.

It was dark outside; the only light came from the hospital windows.

'I can't believe you waited here all this time,' I said as I climbed into the van.

'Did you think I'd leave you here on your own?' His eyes crinkled under his bushy eyebrows.

With Asko on my lap I sank thankfully into the back seat. Every bone in my body ached. We drove back slowly with the headlights off, so as not to attract snipers. Dad was at home and he kept a watchful eye over Asko throughout the night.

The next morning my friend Samra, who lived just down the street, came to see us bringing her last bottle of homemade beetroot juice.

'I kept this for emergencies,' she said. 'It's full of vitamins.

Give it to Asko, he'll need it.' I couldn't thank her enough.

When the stiches were ready to be taken out, Sabrina came and removed them. We told Asko that the large scar across his forehead would always be a reminder of what a brave boy he had been.

The Barracks

Hana

At the beginning of autumn, a small group of friends from the hotel came to bid us goodbye. One of them sang 'Don't You Cry' on his guitar. Although fate had dealt us a cruel hand and separated us from our families, it had in turn given us these new and strong friendships. Nadia and I were on our way back to Zagreb to join Mum and Lela, who were now staying at the refugee barracks there. Once the bus left Primosten, we chatted excitedly for most of the drive.

'It's been almost six months since we last saw Lela,' Nadia said, as she counted on her fingers. 'I wonder if she's changed,' she continued. The two of them had always been close.

I leaned my forehead against the window and watched as the glittering Adriatic receded into the distance. Hours later, the arid land gave way to gently rolling hills and once we reached the flat plains, I knew we were nearing Zagreb.

It was dusk when we pulled into the main bus terminal. The crowded platform was well lit and I recognised Lela's green sweatshirt, which Mesha had given to her before he'd left for the JNA. Lela was a pretty girl with long brown hair and striking green eyes. Nadia saw her too and jumped up from her seat.

'There she is, I can see her!' she cried excitedly and headed for the exit. I tried to follow but the man in front of me took his time leaving the bus and by the time I reached the platform Nadia and Lela were already hugging. They were both crying. I ran towards them and when Lela saw me, she stretched out her arms to me. The three of us stood under the sign, embracing one another.

'Oh, it's so good to see you at last,' Lela sighed.

'Where's Mum?' I asked when we'd calmed down.

'She had to go to Austria with "Mothers For Peace" but she should be back in a few days,' Lela replied. I was sad and disappointed that Mum wasn't here with us.

The air was cool and I pulled out the only jumper I owned and put it on. Carrying our small bags, we hopped onto the crowded tram. Lela and Nadia were busy talking and every now and then their voices rose in excitement. I looked away, pretending that I wasn't with them. Our accent was different from the Croatians' and I didn't want anyone around us to know that we were from Bosnia. Primosten was small and all the refugees stuck together, but being in the big city of Zagreb was intimidating. I was embarrassed to be part of this huge influx of refugees and felt as though we were intruders. It was dark when we got off the tram and walked towards the barracks.

'Is this where we're staying?' I asked Lela. Large reflector lights lit the area, which resembled a construction site. Several long barracks stood in the middle of the site, with two smaller ones on the right-hand side. A tall, brown wooden fence encircled the entire compound. The ground was bare and I looked around in disbelief. The place looked so bleak that I wanted to run away, back to Sarajevo or even Primosten. Anywhere but here. But there was nowhere else to go, so reluctantly I followed the girls into one of the barracks.

Inside, rows of army bunks stretched from one end of the room to the other. There were a few women and children there. Some were sitting on their bunks playing cards, whilst others stood talking. We walked across the creaky wooden floor towards the two free bunks that Lela had managed to keep for us. We put our bags down on the hard mattress. 'Is this barracks for women only?' I whispered hopefully.

To my relief, Lela nodded. Nadia and I unpacked and put some of our clothes on the bunks.

'Where are you girls from?' the elderly woman across from us asked. I didn't really want to talk and was glad that Nadia answered her.

'Who's here with the three of you?' the woman continued.

'Only our mum,' Nadia replied. 'The rest of our family's still in Sarajevo. What about you?' Nadia asked.

'I'm here with my daughter-in-law,' she said. 'The Chetniks came through our village and told us we had to leave. They let the women and children go but detained all the men. My husband and two sons were taken away.'

I glanced at her in horror. She was dressed in a colourful pullover and the thick woollen socks typically worn by people from the countryside.

'Do you know where they are now?' Nadia asked.

The woman shook her head. 'We don't even know if they're still alive.' She rocked from side to side. Her sunken eyes were full of sorrow.

'Poor woman,' Nadia whispered to me under her breath.

I looked around the barracks, wondering how many of the women here had been through the same ordeal. I realised that there were others whose situation was much worse than ours and I made a decision never to complain.

Lela took us to the canteen where several women sat smoking. After we'd cooked some pasta we sat down at an empty table in the corner. We'd only eaten a few mouthfuls when a couple of women came over to us and started talking. Everyone was keen to talk about their own ordeals and to find out news from each other. Their horrendous stories made me fear for my own family. None of us felt like eating anymore and we pushed our plates aside.

That night there was no hot water left in the communal bathroom and Lela told me that we'd have to wait until the morning to shower. The lights were switched off at 10 p.m. and there was nothing to do but go to bed. The coarse blanket made me itch. Tired, I closed my eyes. Most people were still awake, whispering in the dark. After a while, there was silence, broken only by quiet weeping and the occasional cough or snore. A million thoughts crossed my mind and then, out of nowhere, I found myself praying. I was reciting the words of the only prayer I knew, the one that Grandma had taught me. I prayed for the safety of my entire family and that soon we would be together again.

The nearest registration centre for refugees was at the only mosque in the city and in the morning we went there by tram. I looked at the passing streets; they were busier and wider than the ones in Sarajevo. Grand, classical buildings lined the roads and, although I craned my neck through the tram window, it was impossible to see the rooftops. We drove past several churches. There seemed to be more of them here than at home. Swarms of people jostled each other as they made their way along the congested footpaths and long lines of vehicles honked at each other. Although we'd been in Zagreb only a few months before, the city still looked unfamiliar and its seeming vastness was daunting.

The modern, white exterior of the mosque with its oddly shaped dome surprised me. The stone mosques in Sarajevo had been built hundreds of years ago and none of them resembled this one. A man standing outside directed us to the building adjacent to the mosque and we walked into the noisy lobby which was packed with people. The lines at the two registration tables were already long and we joined the queue. Without refugee cards we wouldn't be able to collect any aid or go to a doctor so we waited patiently. After we'd been standing for over an hour, I turned to Nadia and said, 'By the time our turn comes, we'll be pensioners.'

I must've said it loudly because the woman behind us remarked, 'The lines are long because people are trying to get papers to go abroad.'

'Where are they going?' Nadia asked.

'Sweden, Norway, Germany . . . whoever'll take us,' the woman shrugged. 'We're going to put our names down.'

'Do you know where you'll be staying when you get there?' I asked her.

'We've been told that the governments of these countries will provide for us. It doesn't matter where we go, as long as it's far away from here. I don't think there will be an end to this evil for some time.'

It took us all day to register. With our refugee cards we were given our rations and told to return for more in a couple of weeks. The parcels contained flour, sugar and oil, along with several cans of tuna, pasta, peanut butter and packets of pre-cooked bread. We were given a toothbrush, toothpaste and some soap as well. The packaging looked very out of date and we joked that the parcels must have been left over from the Second World War. Even though we'd spent our whole day at the mosque I didn't mind because it kept us away from the refugee barracks.

The barracks was stuffy that evening and we couldn't open the door because the elderly women complained of the draught. Climbing into bed, I pulled the thin pillow over my head to block out some of the noise. I thanked God for the day and prayed again as I had done the night before. In all this chaos, I started to feel that prayer was my only comfort.

★   ★   ★

Mum returned to Zagreb at the end of the week. 'Thank God you're here. We missed you,' Nadia said as we hugged one another. Thrilled that we were all together again, we sat on our bunks, talking. No one had heard from our family in Sarajevo for over a month and the reports of continuous heavy bombardments constantly worried us. Mum was anxious and looked thinner. She told us that her work with refugees was keeping her sane.

'Will you be taking more refugees away?' I asked her. She said that in a few weeks she was going to accompany a group of women from the barracks to England. To our horror, she told us that they had been raped and tortured by the Serbs. A TV station in England wanted to make a programme about them.

Lela wondered if there was any possibility of us going to one of the foreign countries, but none of their governments accepted unaccompanied minors and Mum, wanting to stay near Bosnia, had no intention of seeking refuge abroad. There was some good news, though. Mum had managed to track down our Dad's half-brother, Damir, who lived in Zagreb. We'd met him only once before, a few years ago. Mum said he was working as an apprentice at the Fine Arts Studio and she'd visited him twice. She said he'd love to see us. Hearing that cheered us up a little and Mum promised she'd take us to meet him when she had time.

The street outside the barracks was busy and cars constantly drove past but life in the barracks stood still. There was nothing to do; there was no school to attend, nor any programmes for refugees. Our futures were so uncertain. Everyone was waiting for something. While Mum was busy volunteering, the three of us wandered through the city and paid visits to the friends we'd made when we'd stayed with Omer. In the evenings, we returned to the barracks, just to cook dinner and sleep. Mum usually came to bed much later than us. I overheard her telling

Nadia one night that she wasn't sleeping well. She kept herself busy. Every morning, her bed was empty by the time we awoke.

That week it was my thirteenth birthday. We treated ourselves to a couple of pieces of cake in a local café. That was all we could afford. There were no birthday candles, presents, friends or a party. But I made a wish anyway, that the war would soon be over.

'Pack your bags,' Nadia shouted as she rushed into the barracks. 'Mum's found us a place to stay.'

Confused, I threw our stuff into bags and ran outside. A middle-aged man wearing a brown coat was waiting for us next to his car. 'Where are Mum and Lela?' I asked Nadia as I got in.

'There,' she pointed through the window at the little office where they were signing us out.

Mum and Lela got into the car and we took off. The man was an acquaintance of Mum's from Zagreb. She'd helped some of his extended family from Bosnia to go abroad. Knowing that we were trying to leave the barracks, he'd found us a small place to rent.

'Most landlords are reluctant to take refugees because they can't afford to pay the rent,' he explained as he drove. 'But I've known these people for a while and I told them I'd vouch for you.'

'Thank you so much,' we replied, grateful for his kindness.

'I can pay your rent for the first month but after that you'll have to cover it yourselves. I wish I could help you more but I have a lot on my plate.'

Mum assured him we'd manage somehow.

He drove us to a lovely suburb on the other side of town where large houses and neon-lit shops lined the main street. He turned into a side street and parked outside a small, single-storey brick house. Squeezed in between two large houses, it looked tiny. Inside there were two small rooms and a bathroom. There was a stove in a cupboard in the hallway and some plates and cutlery stacked on the shelf above. In the front room there was an old wooden table and a chair, and in the other room at the back a double mattress lay on the floor. It was simple but clean and I was glad that we didn't have to share it with others.

'That's where your landlord lives,' our friend said, pointing to the house next door. Only a narrow path separated the two dwellings. Turning to us, he said, 'I have a small café in town and could give a job to one of you. Are any of you girls willing to work?'

I didn't say anything because I wanted to go to school but Nadia spoke out, 'I've never worked before but I will now.'

'It's just waitressing. It's easy,' he said. 'I'm not really supposed to employ refugees so I'll pay you in cash.' Nadia wrote down the address and said she'd be there to start next week.

Lela said she'd look for work in one of the cafés she'd noticed on the way here.

'Come on, we'll go and buy some food,' our friend said, looking at Mum and they walked outside.

'Just as well he offered,' Nadia said as she closed the front door. We had no money and it would have embarrassed us to mention that we needed food. We would have gone hungry rather than ask.

The house was already tidy and it didn't take long to unpack. All we had in our bags were some clothes and our diaries and we placed them next to the mattress. 'Our own bathroom!' I yelled out to the girls from the hallway. They were in the bedroom making up the mattress with sheets that had been donated to Mum.

Mum returned soon after, carrying a bag of food in each hand.

We rushed to help her unpack. She had bought salami, cheese, fresh bread, and even meat and eggs. 'We haven't had food like this for ages!' Nadia exclaimed. 'It reminds me of home.'

The mouth-watering smell of food filled the rooms. Since there was only one chair in the house, we couldn't eat at the table, so we spread a sheet on the floor, sat down and ate our meal together.

Although small, the heater in the room worked well and it was warm when I woke up the next morning. The girls, lying to my right, were still asleep. Mum wasn't in bed and I heard her moving around in the hallway. Moments later, the familiar smell of coffee made its way into the bedroom and she walked in carrying a small tray.

'Coffee's ready,' I said, nudging the girls awake. Coffee had always been a morning ritual and our parents and grandmother never started the day without it. Nadia and Lela opened their eyes and slowly sat up.

'It smells good,' Nadia said, smiling. 'Just like Grandma's.'

Mum poured the coffee and passed the cups to the girls. Taking their time, they sipped it and chatted.

'I had a really good sleep, despite all your kicking,' I said to Nadia. The four of us had slept squeezed together on the double mattress.

'I'm glad to hear that, I kept on sliding off the mattress,' Nadia spoke through her laughter.

Mum had just starting telling us that she was going to the barracks today to help, when we heard a knock at the door. Puzzled, we looked at each other. No one knew that we were here except our friend. Mum answered the door and came back with a woman we'd never seen before. She had short, dark hair and was dressed simply in a pair of black trousers and a brown jumper.

'Sorry I've come uninvited,' she said. 'I just wanted to check that you've settled in OK.' Her name was Danica and she was the landlord's wife.

'Sorry we're not up yet!' we apologised, embarrassed that we were still in bed.

'Oh, don't worry. I'm like a rooster, always up very early,' she smiled.

We talked to Danica about where we were from and how we had come to be in Zagreb.

'There's a Red Cross refugee centre in our neighbourhood,' she said and explained to us how to get there. Looking at me, Danica asked, 'How old are you?'

I told her I was thirteen.

'My daughter Andrea is a year younger than you. Why don't you come in and meet her this afternoon when she gets home from school?'

'I'd love to.' I was excited to meet someone my own age.

We chatted for a little longer. On her way out, she turned and said, 'If anyone needs to get hold of you, you can give them our telephone number.' She wrote it down and added, 'And I have an old vacuum cleaner, which you can use . . . Come and see me if you need anything else.'

After breakfast, Mum left for the barracks and Lela went for a walk around the neighbourhood to look for café work. Nadia and I found the Red Cross building, which was not far from the house. It was busy inside. We wanted to find out if we could send letters to Sarajevo from here and if we had to register again now that we were staying in a different suburb. 'You can give me the letters and, of course, you'll have to re-register,' the woman at the counter said. We handed her our refugee cards.

'You can help yourselves to some clothes, if you need any,'

she pointed to the room at the end of the hallway. It was so crowded that we decided to come back some other time.

Early that evening, I called in at the landlord's house to meet Andrea. A tall girl with blue eyes and short blond hair opened the door. She was wearing light denim jeans and a bright pink jersey with green stripes.

'Come in, come in, it's cold outside,' she said, opening the door wider. Behind the front door of their new three-storey house lay a tiled hallway decorated with plants and modern furniture. 'Shall I make us some hot chocolate?' she asked, leading me to the kitchen.

'Yes, please,' I nodded at her enthusiastically.

We sat at the kitchen table dipping biscuits into our hot drinks. Andrea couldn't stop talking about her school and friends. Listening to her reminded me of my own friends and my life back home before the war. I missed it and was keen to get back to school.

'Can I walk to school with you one morning?' I asked.

'Sure, I usually leave about 7.15,' she said. 'And come and watch TV with me any time.'

Mum was sitting at the table writing in her organiser when I went back to our house. I told her about the landlord's daughter and that we'd talked about school.

'I'd really like to go,' I said, determined. 'Can you try to enrol me?'

Mum was doubtful that they'd accept a refugee but said that she'd try. With her upcoming trip to England, she said it would have to be done in the next day or two. The thought of a new school made me nervous but very excited.

The four of us sat down that evening, each writing a letter to our family. We didn't know which letter would reach them and so we included our new postal address and the landlord's telephone number in all of them, just in case they'd be able to call us somehow. I finished the letter by saying how much I missed and loved them.

Nadia and I slept in the next morning. It was cosy under the sheets so we stayed in bed, talking for a while.

'Mum and Lela are at the barracks,' Nadia said, spotting a note next to the mattress. 'Let's take the letters to the Red Cross and see if we can find some warm clothes.' Our sneakers were falling apart.

We strolled through the neighbourhood, amazed at the number of small boutique shops along the main road. The fashionable clothes displayed in the windows were beautiful but now completely out of our reach. The surrounding houses were grand and some had wooden balconies and window frames which made them look like luxury ski-lodges. Nadia and I wondered who lived in them.

The woman we had spoken to the day before was seated behind the counter at the Red Cross and she smiled as we handed her our letters. The clothing room was busy with people searching through the piles on the tables. We found some fluorescent green winter jackets; they were the only ones that fitted us and we knew that they would have to do. We picked out some long trousers, jumpers and winter shoes. Stepping out of the building on to the street, I lowered my head. Although we didn't know anyone there, it was embarrassing to walk out of a Red Cross Centre. There was a phone box nearby and I ran to it to call a girl from Zagreb whom I'd met in Primosten over the summer. The phone call was brief.

'Did you speak to her?' Nadia asked.

'No. Her mum answered. She asked me where I was from and when I told her I was Bosnian she told me not to call their number again. It was so humiliating.'

Nadia grabbed me by the hand and waved her other arm. 'Don't worry, Hana,' she said. 'I ignore things like that. In one ear, and out the other.' She smiled. Nadia and I spent the rest of the afternoon writing in our diaries.

The next morning, Andrea showed Mum and me the way to the school. It was only a short walk and soon we found ourselves in front of a white three-storey building with rows of classroom windows that faced the street. A few birch trees stood tall in the large yard.

The principal agreed to see us even though we hadn't made an appointment. He welcomed us into his office, which was full of books, and lowered himself into his leather armchair behind the desk. He was very tall and authoritarian. 'Madam, it's difficult for us to take in refugees, especially as you haven't got any of Hana's school records to show me,' he said in a deep voice. I had always been a good student but as we had left Sarajevo in a rush, there were no school reports to prove it. 'Refugee cards aren't sufficient proof of identity for us to take people in either. We need a birth certificate or . . . something more.' He was adamant and I was scared he'd refuse to accept me. Mum then mentioned to the principal that Dad had supplied this school with his maths books. The principal looked slightly puzzled and, getting up from his chair, told us he'd have to confirm that with the maths teacher. He left the room and we waited nervously.

'It seems you are right,' he said when he returned, speaking in a much friendlier tone. 'The maths teacher spoke highly of your husband's books,' he said and added, 'I apologise . . . we have to follow procedure, you understand.'

The principal agreed to enrol me, provided that Mum found a way to pay for my school lunches. Mum assured him that she'd arrange that through one of the charitable organisations.

'In that case, you can start next week.' The principal smiled at me and shook Mum's hand as we left.

'Thank you so much, Mum,' I hugged and kissed her once we were outside.

Danica was standing by the kitchen window as we approached our house and invited Mum in for coffee.

Later on, I heard Andrea calling out to me from the side windows of her house. I stepped on to the narrow path between our two houses.

'I hear you're starting at my school,' she exclaimed.

'Yes!' I jumped up, flinging my arms in the air. 'I can't wait.'

She giggled. 'Do you need school books?'

I nodded.

'Our neighbour was in your grade last year and he'll give you his old books. I'll drop them off to you later. I've got to go now and have dinner,' she said and closed the window with a bang.

'Thanks!' I waved at her and skipped back inside.

That weekend Mum left for England and so on Monday I had to go to school on my own.

'Good luck,' Nadia said. 'Sorry neither of us can go with you but we have to go to work.' Lela had started working at a café in the neighbourhood.

'I'll be OK,' I said, but I was nervous.

Andrea was waiting for me in front of the house. Dressed in my best clothes, a pink jersey and a pair of grey trousers, I walked to school with her. It was raining and she let me share her umbrella.

The form teacher met me in the hallway and took me to my classroom. I stood next to her desk in front of the blackboard, facing rows of desks with unfamiliar faces staring at me. The walls were covered with maps, student drawings and images of people that I didn't recognise. My heart was pounding.

'This is our new student, Hana, from Sarajevo,' the teacher introduced me to the class and then showed me to a desk at the back. As I walked to my seat, I heard some students whispering and I felt very alone and uncomfortable. I kept my head down during the class, pretending to write but I couldn't concentrate. That day we had five different classes and teachers and, each time, I had to introduce myself. My face and ears were burning. In the English class, a couple of girls at the back whispered, '*Bosnicka.*' It was a derogatory name for a Bosnian, but I pretended not to have heard them. All I wanted to do was sit at the back and learn. I didn't want anyone to talk to me.

It was a relief to hear the sound of the bell ringing to mark the end of school. A few of my classmates said goodbye to me. *I survived the first day,* I thought, walking back to the house. I promised myself I'd focus on my studies and work hard. The school year had started six weeks earlier and there were a lot of lessons to catch up on. I studied until Nadia and Lela returned from work. It was almost midnight.

'How was work?' I asked Nadia.

'Long. I almost spilt a cup of coffee on a customer,' she answered, rubbing her eyes. Lela cut a few pieces of bread and spread butter and jam over them. 'Our friend's told all his regulars that I'm a relative of his and no one's giving me a hard time about being a refugee,' Nadia added. 'At least, not yet. How was school?'

'Oh, you can imagine. I'm the only Bosnian in the class.' I shrugged my shoulders.

'You'll prove yourself to them,' Lela said. 'You've always been a nerd. I'm off to bed, I've got to work tomorrow.'

There was no alarm clock in the house and, scared that we might sleep in, we kept on waking up during the night.

★　★　★

Lela and Nadia worked long hours every day, doing both morning and evening shifts. With their tips we bought food to make sandwiches and saved enough to buy an alarm clock. During the day I was at school and spent the afternoons studying. We saw little of one other, catching up only in the early morning or late at night. I didn't like being in the house by myself at night and could never go to sleep until they came back.

One night I heard the front door unlocking and seconds later Nadia and Lela walked in. They were soaking wet. 'It's pouring outside,' Nadia said, taking off her jacket. Lela put her clothes next to the heater to dry and went into the bathroom. 'I'm so hungry,' I could hear Nadia from the hallway.

'There's not much food left,' I yelled out. 'We'll have to go to the Red Cross on Tuesday and collect some.'

'Can you do it? We haven't got time.' Nadia walked into the room, drying her hair with a towel.

I didn't really want to go by myself but I nodded. The girls got into bed and wrote in their diaries for a while. There was a little more space on the mattress now, with only the three of us sleeping on it. I didn't want to ask them to turn off the light; they'd been working so hard all day and writing in their diaries was the only time they had to themselves. Pulling the blanket over my head, I said my prayers and fell asleep.

The day Mum returned from England was cold and wet with large puddles forming in the streets. But the dreary weather couldn't dampen our delight at the news Mum brought us. She had found out that our brother Mesha was staying with distant relatives in Macedonia. We were ecstatic.

'How did you find him? Tell us everything,' Nadia demanded, excitedly. She was so happy, she squeezed and kissed my hand every few seconds as Mum told us how she had managed to track him down. While in England, she'd called the few relatives and all our family friends she could think of, who lived in Serbia and Macedonia, hoping to find out if any of them had heard from Mesha. She hadn't been able to call from Croatia because the phone lines to Serbia and Macedonia weren't working. Mum was relieved when an old family friend in Belgrade told her that Mesha had stayed with her for several days in May and was now in Macedonia. She gave Mum Mesha's number. He couldn't believe it when Mum called. It was such a relief for all of us to know that he was alive and safe. He said that he would remain in Macedonia for as long as he could and he was happy that at least some of us were out of danger.

'I feel as though someone has lifted a huge load off my back,' Mum said.

It was the first time I'd seen her smile for a long time. I thanked God for listening to my prayers.

Later on, when Mum was unpacking, she came across a piece of paper with the name and address of the English journalist who'd helped us in Split. Surprised, I looked at Nadia, then at Mum.

'Coincidentally,' Mum said, looking at us, 'he found out that the group of women I was helping had arrived in England and that one of the women involved had the same surname as you two. Curious, he came to meet me. He was very pleased to find out that *I* was your mother and that we'd been reunited.'

'I can't believe that you saw Christopher!' Nadia exclaimed as we sat down to write him a letter of thanks. 'It's such a small world,' she said, shaking her head.

Mum unpacked her bag and gave each of us a small Union Jack flag along with a box of mint chocolates. The chocolates were Lela's favourites and we put them on her place on the mattress.

It was late, but Mum rolled up her sleeves and cooked some

pastry for dinner. Nadia and I rubbed our stomachs, singing one of our favourite songs in chorus. We were keen to help her but the space around the oven was too small for more than one person at a time. The pastry smelled of freshly baked bread and we ate it with jam as we sat on the floor.

Mum's description of her trip to England was interesting and I asked if she was going to go there again. Moving her plate away, she lowered her head and told us that she had found a way to go back to Sarajevo. A UNHCR convoy was leaving from Split to go to Sarajevo in less than a week. She had put her name down.

Nadia stopped eating midway through a bite, and with a frightened look said, 'You can't go. It's too dangerous! The Serbs will shoot you if they catch you.'

Mum didn't seem to hear.

'You think you can go back just like that?' I was enraged. 'Everyone there is dying, and you want to go back. Are you crazy?' I started to cry.

'Wait until the situation calms down,' Nadia pleaded. But Mum was adamant. Now that she knew where Mesha was, and that we three were safe in Zagreb, she was determined to go back to Dad and our younger brothers and sisters. She didn't want to be away from them any longer. She wanted to make her way home before the bitterly cold winter set in.

Nadia and I looked at each other, shaking our heads in disbelief. Mum had made up her mind and there was nothing we could do or say to change it. When Lela returned and found out, Mum and the three of us cried in bed, cursing the war for bringing this upon us.

Early the following Saturday morning, Nadia and I went to the main bus terminal with Mum. Lela wanted to come but she had to go to work. Mum kept patting our heads and caressing our faces. She was crying but repeated over and over again that she had to leave and go back to the rest of our family. It was a horrible feeling watching her go, especially as we didn't know if we'd ever see her again. *Please God, don't let anything happen to her,* I prayed through tears as we watched the bus drive off into the distance.

'How are we going to cope on our own?' I asked.

Wiping her tears, Nadia said, 'I don't know. We'll just have to manage somehow. We've done it before, Hana, we can do it again.'

The Interview

Atka

To protect themselves from the freezing November sleet and driving rain, the guards moved from our courtyard to a makeshift wooden sentry box outside the school. The skies were leaden. Our shelter was bitterly cold and we couldn't bear to go down there any more. Heavily padded in layers of woollen jerseys, hats and gloves, we slept on the four pull-out couches in our large living room. It was warmer than the shelter and safer than sleeping upstairs.

The echo of sniper fire reverberated through the air. I lingered in bed, loath to leave its warmth. Then, summoning up enough courage, I got up and put on another jersey. The children, already awake, were counting the number of gunshots they could hear. I jumped up and down to warm myself a little and Emir laughed at me and dived under his duvet. These days, the children stayed in bed for as long as they liked. There was nothing to get up for.

Grandma was busy tearing up books and a pair of my old jeans to burn in the potbelly stove. Dad had left early to light a fire for Mayka. Fortunately, there was still some coal left in her garden shed. At least she was being kept warm.

The water in the jerry can was partially frozen, so I shook it to break the ice and splashed my face with the slushy water. My hands and face stung from the cold.

'Atka.' Someone was calling me from the front door. It

was Aida, an acquaintance of mine who was working as an interpreter for a foreign news agency. I was taken aback because I hadn't seen her for months and was even more surprised when she told me that the journalists she was working with wanted to interview our family.

'Why us?' I asked, shivering in the doorway.

'They're looking for human interest stories. I told them about your family,' she said, 'and how you and your grandma have ended up looking after your brothers and sisters because your mother can't get back home.'

After a short chat we agreed that she'd bring the journalists to see us that afternoon. I was quite excited at the thought. This could be quite an occasion!

The prospect of visitors lifted everyone's mood.

'Foreigners coming to our house?' Selma exclaimed. 'Janna, let's tidy the house especially well,' she said, dressing herself hurriedly under her duvet.

Grandma fretted. 'How can we have guests when we've nothing to offer them, no coffee or cake?' Hospitality was an important part of our culture; it would be shameful to welcome guests empty-handed.

'Don't worry, Grandma. We'll offer them tea, it'll be fine,' I tried to reassure her.

'Tea is not enough! At least I can make them a nettle pie.' For her it was a question of pride and she was adamant. I nodded in assent.

Janna spread a large crocheted tablecloth on the table and Selma placed a heavy crystal vase in the middle of it. I kept glancing anxiously at the door all morning, hoping that Dad wouldn't turn up. I was worried that he'd confuse the journalists with his obsessive ideas of getting help for Bosnia, which even I was finding hard to comprehend. Fortunately,

Dad was still out when a white jeep with a large press sign on the bonnet pulled up outside the house. Aida and two men wearing winter boots, jeans and flak jackets came into the hallway. They were about to remove their boots, as was customary, but Grandma, shaking her hand, told them not to bother.

'Hi, I'm David,' the tall blond man said in an American accent. He shook my hand firmly.

The other man, with a couple of cameras hanging around his neck, extended his hand to me and said, 'Hello, I'm Laurent. Thank you for letting us come to your house to talk to you.' He was French.

I replied in English and introduced them to the family. Grandma shook hands with them and promptly busied herself in the kitchen making tea. The children, lined up on the couch, were giggling and whispering amongst themselves. David and Laurent removed their heavy flak jackets, we sat at the table and Aida offered everyone a cigarette. We started to discuss the war and the hardship of our situation.

After a while, Aida stood up from the table. 'Atka's English is so good, you don't need me,' she said. 'I have a friend who lives nearby. Do you mind if I go and see him? I'll be back in an hour or so.'

David nodded and Aida saw herself out. He flicked through his notepad until he found an empty page. Looking at me he said, 'Shall we start?'

'Yeah, sure,' I said with that familiar feeling of nervousness that used to creep up before exams.

'Tell me, why are you and your grandmother alone with the children? Where are your parents?'

I had to think for a moment, unsure of where to start. I told him that with the outbreak of war in Croatia, the Serbs took over the JNA with all its mighty weaponry. My brother, like many others, was doing his compulsory military training at the time, and found himself serving under the enemy. Mothers from Croatia and Bosnia actively campaigned for the release of their sons. This had led to my mother's involvement with 'Mothers for Peace' and she had become one of their leaders. David listened carefully and wrote as I talked. Soon, the words came easily and everything that had happened to us found its way into David's notebook. The words tumbled from my mouth. I couldn't stop talking to these outsiders who were so keen to report to the rest of the world what was taking place here. They remained silent and I continued my story. 'Since the death of my uncles, my dad spends most of his time with his mother, she's not well. So it's left to my seventy-five-year-old grandma and me to manage on our own.'

As I talked, Grandma brought us cups of tea along with a large plate of stinging nettle pie. With her hand on her heart she apologised. 'Please excuse us, this is all we have to offer.'

'It's a nettle pie, help yourselves. Please do, Grandma will be very offended if you don't,' I said.

They hesitated. They were clearly uncomfortable taking food from us but Grandma insisted and with my encouragement they took a small piece each. Grandma tapped David on the shoulder and he smiled at her.

'I'm glad they like it,' she said, pleased. She took another plate of pie to the children. We paused to eat. When we'd finished David offered me another cigarette. He lit it for me and I inhaled deeply. It was such a long time since I had smoked that two cigarettes in a row made me light-headed.

'How do you manage with all these children?' he asked. 'They must miss their mother.'

'They do but they're fine,' I replied. 'They've got me and Grandma.'

David then asked me how we coped from day to day.

'We live, eat and sleep here in the living room. It's the only room we try to heat, but it's hard to keep it warm with only plastic covers on the windows,' I said, pointing to them. He glanced at me from time to time as he wrote. I told him about Janna and Selma and their brave efforts collecting water, which they sometimes did even on their own.

The girls heard their names being mentioned and Janna asked curiously, 'Are you talking about us?' They nudged one another and Janna, hoping that David would notice her, said loudly, 'I hope that soon all our family will be together again. I'd be happy for the rest of my life.' I translated this to David. He winked at Janna and wrote it down.

Laurent asked if he could take some photos of the girls holding their jerry cans, so Janna and Selma took him outside to show him the long steep flight of steps which we had to climb every time we went to fetch water.

I was interested to hear what was happening in the rest of the world but apart from Bill Clinton being elected as the new US President, which I already knew, David couldn't think of much else that was significant. Soon, our conversation turned back to the war. We agreed that the newly formed and poorly armed Bosnian Army, which consisted mainly of untrained civilians, was nowhere near a match for the heavily armed Serbs. Repeated attempts by the Bosnian Army to break through the Serb lines encircling the city inevitably failed and ended in numerous casualties.

'This UN arms embargo on Bosnia is so unjust. The Bosnians should be armed.' David tapped his pen on the table as he spoke. 'That way at least you'd be able to defend yourselves.'

'I agree with you. The irony is that when the Serbs started attacking they had all the weapons from the JNA, while we were totally unarmed. So the UN arms embargo, which was imposed to "promote peace and security in the region", simply enables the Serbs to continue with their killing. We can't defend ourselves, we have no weapons,' I said bitterly. 'If the UN were actually protecting us it would be fine but all they do is record the number of mortars fired into the city each day, as if we can't count them ourselves. No one has any respect for that organisation. We call them the Useless Nations.'

We both turned as we heard the living-room door open.

'How are you getting on?' Aida asked as she walked in with Laurent.

'Great, we've just finished,' David replied, putting his notebook away.

'Come on then, let's go,' Aida gestured to the door. David and Laurent thanked us and promised to bring us a copy of the finished article. As they were leaving, Aida mentioned to me that sometimes she needed an interpreter and asked if I would be willing to help.

'No problem,' I replied eagerly. 'Any time.'

A few days after that interview, we received a message from Mum through a ham radio operator – these days their transmissions were our only form of communication. We learned that she was on the outskirts of Sarajevo, trying to get into the city by crossing the airport runway on foot. My heart sank. I knew that countless people were being killed every night trying to cross that deadly strip. I looked at Grandma anxiously.

'Don't you worry, Atka. I'll pray for her.' She reached for her beads and went to her room.

The children, unaware of the risks that Mum was taking, welcomed the news with excitement.

'Mama, Mama,' Tarik shouted and jumped up and down

with his arms in the air. The twins copied him. Janna and Selma kissed and hugged each other. Their excitement rubbed off on me and I grabbed Emir under his arms and spun him around.

'Me too, me too,' Tarik and Asko shouted. I spun the two of them around and laughed as they staggered in giddy circles around the room. They couldn't stop talking about the delicious food that Mum might bring. But my only thought was that she might not make it past the snipers who had the entire runway in their sights. Later I went to see Samra and her boyfriend who tried to calm me down with a small glass of cognac and a chat.

We were up early the next morning and every time we heard a noise outside the house the children ran to the door to see if Mum was coming. Out of desperation, I ran to see Aida and David whose office was close to our house, to ask them if they could contact the UN at the airport and plead with them to escort my mother across the runway. The two of them tried but none of the UN officials at the airport were prepared to listen, let alone help. Gutted, I went back home. The rest of the day dragged on as we waited anxiously. At nightfall the children, one by one, slowly surrendered to sleep. Grandma and I waited until well after curfew and eventually fell asleep ourselves.

Dad had been with Mayka for the last couple of days and he didn't know anything about Mum's attempt to return. *If she doesn't turn up tomorrow, I'll have to tell Dad what's going on,* I told myself.

The next day there was still no sign of Mum. By early evening the children had stopped looking out of the window and I felt ill with worry and feared the worst.

No one heard Mum coming in. She appeared like a ghost at the door of our candle-lit living room. Her dark silhouette frightened the children but the moment she called to them, they recognised her voice and ran into her arms. The five of them surrounded her in an instant and Mum, trying to embrace them all at once, kept kissing their little heads. Grandma and I stood apart, crying and watching them. I leaned over the children and hugged Mum as tight as I could. Grandma wiped her tears with the corner of her scarf. 'I thank dear God that you made it. I prayed for you all the time,' she said.

Mum's once dark hair was now completely grey and she looked thin and worn. I helped her with her large, heavy bag. She looked around the room and sank on to the couch with a tired sigh. Emir sat in her lap, not letting go of her hand, and Asko snuggled up against her.

'Where's Dad?' she asked.

'He's with Mayka,' Grandma replied.

'You must've brought us lots of food,' Tarik said and clapped his hands in excitement. 'Did you bring any salami?' he asked, unzipping the bag. Selma and Janna joined him and carefully they unpacked its contents.

'Look at all this, there's coffee, beans, rice, soap and hundreds of letters,' Janna exclaimed as she passed the items to Selma who placed them in neat piles on the floor.

Grandma's face brightened. 'May God grant you long life for bringing us coffee! I'll make some straight away.' She patted the packet.

As Grandma spoke, there was an explosion in the distance and Mum jumped to her feet to try to find cover. The children giggled.

'Don't worry, Mum, that one wasn't close,' Janna dismissed the danger with a casual wave of her hand. Mum sat back down on the couch, looking bewildered.

Selma sat at her feet. 'When you hear a heavy thud, that's firing from tanks. The shells whistle as they fly,' Selma said.

In spite of being frightened, Mum seemed amused at all this information coming from her small children.

'I think that's an anti-aircraft machine gun, Mum.' Tarik, unsure of himself, looked to me for approval. I listened to the repetitive bursts and nodded to him. 'I'm the youngest soldier,' he said. Proudly, he struck a pose. Mum looked at him fondly.

'Mum, the snipers are the worst,' Selma said with a little frown on her face.

'Yeah, I hate them,' Janna said, scowling, 'especially the weekend ones.'

Mum looked at me for an explanation.

'They're men from Montenegro and Serbia who have normal jobs during the week and come here in the weekends to shoot at us,' I said. Mum looked at me in horror.

'Mum, don't ever walk down the middle of the street,' Janna warned her. 'Always stick to the sides. The houses and buildings give good cover.'

The children were explaining matters so earnestly, it was as though they were talking about the rules of a game. Asko sucked his thumb and Emir still wouldn't let go of Mum's hand. Sipping coffee and gratefully enjoying every single bite of the food that Mum had brought, we listened as she described her ordeal to us. Under normal circumstances, the trip from Zagreb was an eight-hour bus ride but it had taken her almost a month to zigzag her way through the complex web of front lines and areas of heavy fighting. Unable to get on a UNHCR convoy from Split, Mum waited for a few days before she decided to take the risk and try to make her own way. She'd hitched rides with black marketeers and sought shelter with strangers she'd encountered on the way. Miraculously unharmed, she finally reached Mt Igman and stayed with an old friend who lived in the foothills. She waited there for about three days until an opportunity arose to cross the dreaded runway with a small group of men who regularly smuggled food into the city.

'It was dark when we set out,' Mum continued. 'We hid behind a small mound on the mountain side of the runway, then crawled into a long muddy ditch which was surrounded by barbed wire. My arms were numb with cold and sore from dragging my bag behind me. The man leading us knew the way and took us to an opening in the wire. Eventually, when he thought it was safe enough, we crawled out of the ditch and lay flat on the ground waiting for the group behind us to catch up.'

'So, there were other groups?' I asked.

'Yes,' she said. 'Altogether, there were four that night. We were about to cross the runway together but all of a sudden a UN armoured personnel carrier spotted us and shone its light in our direction. They drove up to us and some of the men fled in panic. The rest of us were ordered to get into the back of the vehicle.' Mum paused for a minute and cleared her throat.

'In the confusion of the night the UN assumed that we were trying to escape from Sarajevo, so they drove us to the city side. We were dropped off at a Bosnian checkpoint in Dobrinja where I spent the night. Finally, just an hour ago, I managed to hitch a ride into the city.'

'You could have been killed by snipers.' I reached for her hand. 'You have no idea how lucky you are!'

The children, however, were much more interested in hearing about their sisters.

'How tall's Hana?' Janna butted in. 'How long's Nadia's hair? And Lela's?'

'Mum, do they miss me?' Tarik tugged at her for attention.

'I bet Hana has lots of friends at her new school,' Selma said.

It seemed that the girls were getting by in Zagreb, although I was concerned that they were now on their own. We were overjoyed when Mum told us that she had spoken to Mesha, who had found safety in Macedonia.

As I listened to Mum describe her work with refugees, I couldn't help remarking, 'What about the girls? How much time were you able to spend with them if you were travelling so much and looking after other people?'

Mum looked at me and tried to explain that without humanitarian work, she had no other means of survival. Grandma patted Mum on the back. 'You did what you had to do. It can't have been easy for you either.'

The next morning, Mum and the children were snuggled up in bed together. My first instinct on waking was to jump out of bed, but then I snuggled back down, relieved that I no longer had to fill Mum's shoes.

Heavy fog shrouded the city. The thick cover swallowed everything and we could only just make out the silhouette of the house next door. It felt as though we were suspended in a cloud.

Safe in the knowledge that the snipers couldn't see through the fog, I made my way to Studio 99. With the war in full swing and cold winter months ahead, nobody went to university any more and all studies ceased. Since Mum's return I had started working full-time, translating the news and editing local programmes. I received no pay for my work, just the occasional packet of cigarettes or some rice, but I loved being busy.

'Great, here's Atka. She can do it,' one of my colleagues said as I came in through the door.

I looked at him in confusion. 'Do what?' I walked towards him.

'We need a report on the state of the power supply. You can do it,' he said and handed me a Walkman.

'But I've never made a report before,' I said, dismissing the idea. I tried to hand the Walkman back to him but he turned and walked away.

I looked at the other man standing in the room. He was the most experienced journalist there and commanded everyone's respect.

'I have no idea what to do,' I pleaded with my older colleague.

'Come on, why the nerves? We're not CNN,' he teased. 'Just go and find someone in charge who can tell you what's going on.'

'Honestly, I can't do it.' I was adamant.

'Listen, these are the questions that need answering: who, what, when, where, and why. It's as simple as that,' he said.

'OK.' Reluctantly, I agreed to go and put the Walkman in my bag.

'Atka,' he called as I reached the door, 'no one's going to bite your head off if you don't get it right.'

Hoping that I wouldn't encounter any of the stray and hungry dogs roaming the city, I walked through the misty streets to the power company building. After a long wait in the lobby I was shown into one of the managers' offices. The man was brief and businesslike and told me that he was only able to give me a few minutes of his time. I placed the Walkman on the desk, trying to look confident and professional. I had my questions ready and pressed the 'record' button, but there was no sound of the tape moving.

'I'll check the batteries,' I muttered. My hands shook slightly as I opened the battery compartment and saw that it was empty. I felt like an idiot. He reached into a drawer, and took out four small batteries, placing them on the desk.

'Use these,' he said, rolling them across to me. After I had put them into the Walkman, he started speaking.

'Frankly, I know little more than the average citizen. As everyone is aware, we try to keep the power supply available to hospitals and government institutions but even that gets disrupted. Whilst we'd like to provide some power to the whole city, it's impossible. The Serbs are constantly targeting and damaging the transmission cables and shooting at our technicians as they try to repair them. A significant number of our employees has been killed and wounded.'

I understood what he was talking about. Aunt Tidja's elder son, who worked for the company, had recently been wounded while on the job. A bullet which had lodged only millimetres from his heart was considered by doctors to be too risky to touch. Strangely, it was safer to leave the bullet in its place than remove it and my cousin was released from the hospital a few days later.

Even though the interview was hurried and revealed nothing new, it was broadcast that afternoon. I'd done a good job and felt quite proud of myself. The chief editor approached my colleague Amna and me and asked us to devise a concept for an hour-long weekly programme. After some discussion, we decided to make a series dedicated to our peers who had lost their lives. Since funerals had become too dangerous to attend, we thought that the programme could at least allow the victims' families and friends to pay their tributes and bid their final farewells. Our editor supported the idea and we were told to have the first programme ready for broadcast within the week.

Seeing my parents together again was reassuring, although Dad's obsession with writing appeals to world leaders continued. Mum and Grandma took over the care of the children and the everyday tasks so I was free to work more.

I saw Mayka most days. She was like a small child, tucked up on her couch in front of the kitchen window. As an aged and 'at risk' person, she was entitled to receive a meal from the Red Cross every day. Dad collected it for her in a small tin container.

Mirza was released from the hospital after his third operation. His stump was healing slowly. He showed me how he managed to get around by hopping on one leg. Merima felt somewhat safer living in the overcrowded basement that she shared with a few close relatives. Mirza and the family had been interviewed by a foreign TV crew and the story was aired internationally. An American family, wanting to help, had contacted the producer. In a city full of fear and broken hopes, we viewed the prospect of any help from the outside with heavy scepticism.

With the first snows, the temperature fell to well below freezing. At -11°C the cold was bone-chilling and our breath was visible in the icy air. The water in our jerry cans regularly froze overnight. We were so desperate for firewood that in the end Grandma insisted that we knock down the long garden shed which Grandad had built. It was dear to her heart. When I was younger, I used to hide there for hours reading Russian fairy tales. It didn't take long to demolish the old shed; its wood kept us warm for the next few days.

Late one morning David, the American journalist who had interviewed me, pulled up outside our house in his Jeep. Since we'd met I'd translated for him on a few occasions.

'I'm interviewing a ham radio operator from Gorazde. Can you come and translate?' David asked me, and quickly I grabbed my jacket.

While most media reports were focused on Sarajevo, the rest of the country was largely unreachable and almost forgotten. The only means of communication with Gorazde was through ham radio operators. Gorazde was a small, predominantly Muslim, town in eastern Bosnia surrounded by mountains. It was one of the many towns and villages completely blockaded by the Serbs.

The UN convoys attempted to deliver aid but were almost always turned back by the Serbs. No aid was getting through and so far only one or two foreign journalists had managed to reach the town.

From our house, it was a two-minute drive down the hill to the centre of the city. David parked across the road from the Presidency, where he was going to carry out the interview. Two Bosnian Army checkpoints, consisting of large piles of sand bags and barbed wire, had been placed in front of the building. The armed soldiers inspected our press cards and let us pass. Inside, the entrance was heavily guarded and we had to go through another security check. We were then led to a room on the ground floor, which was freezing.

A gaunt older man wearing gloves and a ski jacket was adjusting the knobs on a radio. The noise coming from the box sounded as if the radio were tuned in to a windy storm. 'Hi, I'm Faruk,' he introduced himself. 'Shortly, we'll have Gorazde on our frequency.' He pointed to the chairs beside him and we sat down.

We waited. A waitress, wearing a thick, woollen jersey, brought hot black coffee for us. I liked the special treatment I received when working with foreigners. No one offered me coffee when I worked for Studio 99.

Soon we heard a faint voice through the static. 'Sarajevo, can you hear me?'

'Yes, we hear you, Gorazde. Are you ready?'

'Yes, go ahead.'

'How would you describe your situation?' David asked and I translated.

'What can I tell you?' the voice on the other end said. 'We're on the verge of catastrophe. The town's population has swelled with the arrival of refugees from the villages around here and there is simply not enough food for everyone. The situation is critical. People are surviving on less than a piece of bread a day, if that.' Sometimes, his voice was very faint and I had to concentrate hard to hear his every word. I translated and David took notes.

'Is the shelling heavy?' David asked.

'Yes, the Serbs have been shooting at us with everything they've got: heavy artillery, tanks, mortars, anti-aircraft and machine guns. It's hard to tell what the daily death toll is, the numbers vary each day. The wounded are being treated by a handful of overworked doctors who are performing miracles. The lack of medical supplies and basic anaesthetics makes their job damned near impossible.'

The interview continued for another twenty minutes. Afterwards, we drove to the now deserted and partially shattered building, which used to house a bank. The Associated Press (AP) office was situated on the third floor. As we climbed the stairs, David told me that a group of foreign journalists and photojournalists was about to make the arduous and dangerous trip across the snow-covered mountains down into Gorazde.

'If they don't get shot, they'll freeze to death,' I remarked. 'They're walking straight into a death trap.'

The AP office had power and a small heater on the floor was blowing hot air. Aida was checking the handheld radios. She introduced me to a newly arrived photographer, Mike from Texas, who was sitting scoffing instant noodles. The delicious aroma of the chicken stock was a cruel reminder of how hungry I was.

David sat in front of the computer and started writing. He asked me a few questions relating to the interview and I gave him detailed explanations.

Mike looked at me and asked, 'Where did you learn English?'

'At school,' I replied.

'No shit! I learnt Spanish at school but can only remember a word or two now. The Communist schools must've been tough.' He leaned back in his chair with his long legs stretched out in front of him.

'I guess so,' I replied. 'Do you know much about Bosnia?'

'Well, I imagined dirt roads and people living in huts. I didn't realise that this was such a modern country. You even have cable TV.'

Aida and I looked at each other and rolled our eyes. His comments were typical of foreigners who didn't know much about our country.

'Do you understand much about the situation here?' I asked.

'I'm trying to,' he replied, 'but it's confusing because you all look the same; Serbs, Croats and Muslims, I can't tell the difference.' Mike got up and slung his cameras around his neck. 'I don't understand how you lived side by side for so long and then the Serbs turned against you.' He shook his head.

'It's because Bosnia has become an independent country but the majority of Serbs refuse to recognise it,' I explained. 'It's the same with Croatia. Most Serbs from across what used to be Yugoslavia believe that wherever they live that land should belong to Serbia.'

'Why is the fighting so much worse here than in Croatia?' he asked.

'Well, more than a third of the population in Bosnia is Serb, whereas in Croatia they're only a small minority.'

Aida got up and put on her jacket. 'I used to be married to a Serb,' she said, 'but I left him years ago.'

'Really? Is that because he was a Serb?' Mike asked.

'No, it's because he was an asshole,' Aida replied, dryly. We all laughed.

David was on the satellite phone, talking to his office in Paris. Mike and Aida waved to him and left.

I envied the ease with which these guys were able to call the outside world. David finished his conversation and to my surprise he casually handed me the receiver. 'Is there anyone you'd like to call?'

I looked at him and hesitated, knowing how incredibly expensive it was to use a satellite phone. 'Yes please, my sisters are in Croatia but I don't have their number with me,' I said. 'Can I bring it next time so that I can call them?'

'Of course,' he replied.

Later on, as I was telling everyone at home I'd be able to call the girls from the AP office, we heard a commotion in our garden. Two boys were chopping down our plum tree. Dad chased them away but it was too late, the tree could not be saved. We cut it down to use it for firewood. That tree had been in the garden for ever and I could still recall the taste of the jam we had made from its fruit last summer. The wood, still wet and green, smouldered slowly, hardly giving out any heat.

Unexpected Encounters

Hana

Alone at home, I tried to study, but it was hard to concentrate. I was hungry and my stomach rumbled. We'd run out of food and it was still a few days until our next ration was due. Then, just as dusk fell, I heard the front door being unlocked. It was Nadia and she was carrying a small plastic bag. 'I've bought some eggs and bread!' She took off her jacket. 'Look at all this – I managed to buy it with the money I made from tips today.'

'You're a saviour! I'm starving!' I exclaimed. As I fried the eggs I danced into the hallway, waving the wooden spoon. The eggs would be delicious and even just the smell of food cheered us.

'Sorry about last night,' Nadia said, dipping her bread into the eggs. Nadia, Lela and I always tried to get on with one another, but lately we'd been fighting and arguing a lot. Even the smallest disagreements upset us.

'It's not you who shouts at me, it's Lela.'

'I know, but it's not easy for her either,' Nadia said, sadly. 'There's so much to worry about. Mum, the family, paying the bills, our rent. Going to work without breakfast this morning, I wondered all day if I'd be given enough tips to buy any food for dinner tonight.'

'I wish we were at home,' I said, longingly. 'It would be much easier if we were in Sarajevo together. I worry about

Mum . . . How's she going to get to Sarajevo all on her own?' Mum had called us from Split the night before she had left but that was two weeks ago and since then we've had no news.

Smoothing the creased newspaper she had brought from work, Nadia said, 'Don't worry, I think she'll be fine. Last night, I dreamt about Grandma. She was wearing her red scarf and smiling at me. That's a good sign.'

I wished I could believe in dreams the way Nadia did. We looked at the headlines in the paper. Most of the articles were about the war in Croatia and the escalating fighting in Bosnia. The increasing number of refugees pouring into Croatia was putting a huge strain on the economy.

'What if they throw us out of here?' I said, suddenly petrified.

'If they do, they do. We won't be the only ones,' Nadia said, turning a page.

The thought of moving yet again was frightening. I envied my classmates whose lives were so simple and happy. They lived at home with their families and every part of me longed for just that.

'Any letters from the Red Cross?' Nadia asked, looking up.

I shook my head. We'd checked almost every day but so far there had been no mail for us. We sent letters to Sarajevo regularly, but couldn't be sure if the family received any of them.

'I'll check again on Tuesday when I collect the food,' I said, picking up the plates. 'You relax, Nadia, I'll do the dishes.'

It was almost the end of October when Nadia and I found our way to the Fine Arts Studio where our dad's half-brother Damir worked. The old brick building that housed the studio stood at the end of a narrow alley, just off the main road. With apprehension, we rang the bell and a tall, slim man wearing a painter's smock answered the door. When we told him who we were, he wiped the paint off his hands and kissed each of us on the cheek.

'Welcome, girls. It's great to see you. You've really grown,' he said, stepping aside to let us in. His long face and high forehead reminded me of our dad and made me feel homesick all over again.

'Come in, I'll make some coffee,' he said, leading us up the wooden stairs to the tiny kitchen on the mezzanine. From there we could see down into a large bright room full of canvases and tins of paint. Damir put the kettle on and, as we waited for the water to boil, we talked about the war and the deaths of Nako and Zoran.

'What a tragedy. I only met them once,' he said, setting the cups on the bench. 'I wonder what fate awaits Bosnia. People must be going through hell.' We were silent.

Damir reached for the sugar bowl, which was on the shelf. He'd always been a bit of a mystery in our lives and I didn't think he'd mind if we asked him about his past.

'Damir, no one really told us much about you . . . How is it that our grandfather is your dad?'

He poured the coffee and, turning around, looked at us quizzically, 'Don't you know what happened?'

'No, not the full story,' Nadia answered as Damir stirred his coffee.

Handing her a cup, he gestured for us to sit down on the old couch. He perched on the edge of the table across from us and, lighting a cigarette, said, 'Your grandfather met my mother here in Zagreb while he was working on one of his theatre plays. Despite the fact that he was a married man with children, they had an affair. It was only after he left Zagreb that my mother found out that she was pregnant.' He exhaled and waved his hand to clear the cloud of smoke.

'What happened then?' Nadia asked, taking a sip of her coffee.

'At the time, it was a scandal,' Damir let out a big sigh. 'My mother's parents were staunch Catholics and when they found out that she was pregnant, they turned her out of the house.'

'How awful,' Nadia said.

'It was.' He inclined his head and flicked the ash into a saucer. 'When I was born, my mother couldn't cope on her own and had to put me into an orphanage.'

My jaw dropped. 'An orphanage! We didn't know anything about that.'

Nadia and I looked at each other.

'Did you grow up there?' I asked.

'Yes, I was there till I was eighteen. My mother visited me regularly.'

'Where's she now?' Nadia said.

'She's here in Zagreb. She had a breakdown and never really recovered. I look after her now.' He extinguished his cigarette and immediately lit another one.

'When did you find out that our granddad was your father?' I asked.

'Only eight years ago, when I was sent to do my compulsory military service in Sarajevo. That's when my mother finally told me who my father was and where he was from. After a long search, I found his house and met your grandmother. She told me that her husband had died a year earlier and straight away called your father. That's when I came to see you at your house.'

Nadia grinned. 'I remember that day. When I saw you, I thought our granddad had come back from the dead.'

Damir laughed. 'Yes, everyone told me that of all his sons,

I was the one who looked most like him.' He hopped off the table. 'Come on, girls, I'll show you what I'm working on.'

Intrigued, we followed him down the narrow stairs. I was mesmerised by the colourful images around me and it was as though we were in a different world. Vividly coloured canvases hung on the walls depicting mainly religious themes. On an easel in the corner stood a half-finished painting of Christ.

'This is what I'm working on at the moment.'

I was so impressed by Damir's talent and told him how beautiful I thought his paintings were. He grinned at me. 'I do try. One day I might be Croatia's own Michelangelo!'

We stayed for a while and watched him paint. The light was fading and Nadia and I decided it was time to go. As we were leaving, Damir dug into his pocket and handed us some money.

'Come and see me as often as you can,' he said. 'I wish I could help you more, but an artist doesn't earn much.'

We didn't want to take his money but he insisted. 'I'll be offended if you don't,' he said and saw us to the door.

It was grey and gloomy as we walked to catch the tram.

'Isn't he friendly? I'm glad we've seen him at last,' Nadia said.

The classroom was warm and well lit. We rose to our feet to greet the history teacher, who was in her fifties and had an air of quiet authority about her.

'We're going to revise last week's material,' she said, flicking through the pages of the large green book on her desk that contained the names of each student and their marks. 'Any volunteers?' She looked at us over the top of her reading glasses.

My arm shot up and seconds later I was standing beside the blackboard, facing the teacher. She questioned me in detail about the origins of the First World War. I'd studied hard and, though nervous, answered every question promptly and correctly. Fifteen minutes later, she instructed me to return to my seat.

'Now, there's an exemplary student,' she said to the class. 'That's an A plus.'

I was pleased with myself and, once back at my desk, thought of Atka. I knew she'd be very proud of me. The teacher's praise filled me with confidence and I was encouraged to continue studying hard. The long hours spent glued to my school books resulted in high marks. I was moved to a desk at the front of the classroom to sit next to a girl called Klaudia and my classmates often asked me for help with their homework. I was happy that at last I had friends to play with at lunchtime and no longer had to eat on my own. It was a great feeling to be accepted and to be recognised for my academic ability. I had become fully immersed in school life and had made friends with everyone.

Nadia and Lela worked long shifts and most days after school I was alone in the house. There was no TV or radio and, apart from studying, there was little for me to do. The only sounds came from the rustling of my books and the steady ticking of the small alarm clock on the table. At times, all I could hear was my own breathing. It was strange to be in such an empty house. I missed the noise of home and being with my little sisters and brothers as they played and chased each other around. Although it always used to annoy me, I even missed the sound of Dad's favourite music playing in the background. We had no photos of our family and often I lay on the mattress with my eyes closed, trying to picture them all. I didn't want to forget what they looked like.

Knowing I was frightened of being left alone after dark,

Danica invited me to her place one evening. The moment I walked into their house, I was drawn in by the enticing smell of roast meat drifting from the kitchen. Andrea was sitting at the table with her grandmother, who was busy knitting. Danica introduced me to the elderly woman and she looked up to greet me.

Andrea and I went into her bedroom where we spent the evening playing cards and talking. She didn't have any brothers or sisters and remarked how lucky I was to have a big family. We talked about our favourite foods and when I told her that I liked chocolate pancakes, she asked her grandmother to make some for us. Later in the evening, when Andrea's dad returned from work, he came in to her bedroom to say hello. I felt so safe and wished I didn't have to go back to our house. From then on, Andrea and I played together every evening and we got to know each other really well.

My parent-teacher interview was coming up and once, when I was at their house, I asked Danica if she could go instead of my sisters who were working that day. She said she'd be more than happy to.

One bleak Friday after school, I dropped in to the Red Cross to see if there were any letters from Sarajevo. The queue was long and as I waited I recognised a few familiar faces.

'What a curse it is to be a refugee,' I overheard an older man saying bitterly. As the war dragged on, people were becoming more irritable and less friendly.

I handed my refugee card to the woman behind the counter. She searched through the pile of letters on the shelf behind her and pulled out a blue envelope. I saw our names and recognised our dad's distinctive handwriting.

When Nadia and Lela returned from work, we read the letter together. Dad wrote about their trials. The boys were very skinny now and weren't growing much. Dad had lost a lot of weight. Selma and Janna occasionally attended the temporary war school which was held in one of the apartments in the neighbourhood. Atka had stopped studying but she was still working at the radio station.

Included in the letter were diary entries that Janna had written. Nadia started to read one out loud.

Zoran is no more. He went to buy bread outside his house. At that moment, you could hear a shell and people screaming. Some time later, someone came to tell Merima that Zoran was killed. I don't know how Merima could bear that moment but I know it was hard. Mirza and Haris without a father. Sad, isn't it?

With tears in her eyes, Nadia handed the letter to Lela. 'You read the rest, I can't.'

Lela continued.

You people who started the war,
You people who are killing our dearest,
You people who are burning our homes,
Throw down your arms,
Throw away the beastly things that no one needs,
You'll never separate our hearts from the people who died,
Because they always live in our minds.

'Our little Janna . . . She doesn't sound like a nine-year-old, does she?' Nadia shook her head.

Although it was a very sad letter, at least we knew that everyone was alive. The hope of seeing them again kept us going.

At the end of the month, Nadia and Lela received their wages. After we had paid our bills and rent, there was enough money left over for us to prepare a food parcel for our family. We bought packets of rice, flour, sugar, coffee and pasta and, in a separate envelope, we sent fifty Deutsche Marks which Lela had managed to save from her tips. We posted it all to Split.

Mladena, the receptionist at the hotel there who had taken care of us, told us that she'd send it on with one of the foreign journalists. At last we were able to do something to help our family.

The tapping on the window frightened me. It was dark outside and I froze for a second, convinced that it was a burglar.

'It's Danica here. Is anyone home?' Relieved to hear her voice, I ran to the front door.

'You gave me such a fright,' I said as I let her in.

Danica smiled. 'I've just come back from your parent-teacher interview,' she said, standing in the hallway. I'd been waiting in anticipation to find out what the teachers had to say about me and was thrilled to hear that they were very pleased with my work. 'The teachers have nothing but praise for your high marks and good behaviour. Keep up the good work.'

I thanked her for going.

'I was hoping to speak to one of your sisters,' she continued.

'They should be back from work in an hour. Can I give them a message?'

Danica told me she thought that because I was still at school and doing well, it would be better if I moved in with her family.

That night in bed, I talked to Nadia and Lela. It was strange discussing Danica's proposition and, even though it was hard, we agreed that it was a good idea financially because then the girls wouldn't have to worry about providing for me anymore. Lela mentioned that she wished they could have gone to high school too but without any school records, no one was the slightest bit interested in enrolling them.

'Anyway, we'll have more room on the mattress without you,' Nadia joked.

'I'm only going next door. We'll see each other all the time.'

A few days later, I moved my clothes and books to our

landlord's house. Andrea had already emptied two of her drawers for me. There was no room for another bed in her bedroom so we put a single mattress on the floor. We played in the snow in the backyard and built a big snowman. Andrea's grandmother gave us a carrot and an old pot to use as his nose and hat.

That evening, I heard footsteps beneath the window of Andrea's room and saw Nadia unlocking the door of their house. She turned towards me when I called her and as we were chatting, Danica came into the room carrying a small saucepan in her hands. She lowered this out of the window down to Nadia.

'I made stew for dinner and there's plenty left for you two girls. Would you like some?'

Gratefully, Nadia took it from her. 'Thank you,' she said. 'It'll be lovely to have some of your home-cooked food for a change.'

Andrea's family treated me as one of their own and I felt at ease with them. At least once or twice a week, Danica gave the girls pots of hot food. Sometimes she baked them a cake. Every now and then, as I was getting ready for school, I'd find Nadia and Lela in the kitchen, drinking coffee with Danica. They worked so hard to pay the rent and buy food, it was nice to see they were being looked after too.

The branches of the apple tree in the front yard were dressed in a layer of fresh snow. The white winter blanket transformed the entire neighbourhood into a magical sight. I was telling Andrea about the mountain views we had from our house in Sarajevo when the phone rang.

'Hello?' I said, picking up the receiver. There was a crackling sound.

'Hello?' I heard the person at the other end saying. 'I'm calling from Sarajevo. I'm trying to get hold of my sisters.' I recognised Atka's voice straight away and I signalled to Andrea to get my sisters.

'Atka! It's Hana here. How are you?' I was overwhelmed with joy to hear her voice after such a long time.

Atka was calling from a satellite phone and had to be brief. We spoke quickly and urgently and our voices echoed in the background. Life in Sarajevo was tough for them and they were just surviving on small amounts of food, but everyone was still alive and, to our relief, Mum had made it home. The weather was freezing and it was hard for them to keep warm. Sadly, they had not received the food parcel that we had sent them but, strangely, they did receive the money. I was shattered to hear that Mirza had been seriously wounded. Atka was just telling me about the people who had been killed when Lela ran in.

'Here's Lela,' I shouted. 'Speak quickly, Atka can't stay on the phone for long,' I urged, handing the receiver to her.

'Atka, I can't believe it's you,' Lela said bewildered, her eyes filling with tears. 'Is everyone alive?' she asked.

I stood listening to her while she asked all the same questions that I had asked. Then her face fell, her voice quivered as she gripped the receiver. 'How was he killed?' she asked.

Alarmed, I stared at Lela. With a blank look on her face she handed me the receiver.

'I've got to go,' Atka's voice echoed. 'We love you. Look after yourselves and I'll try to call you again.' The line went dead before I could say anything.

'Lela, who was killed?' I grabbed her by the arm.

'Senad,' she said, stunned, 'a sniper shot him.'

Senad, her boyfriend, was only a year older than her.

'When?'

'Don't ask me anything,' she shook her head and ran out of the house.

'Oh,' I groaned, before chasing after her.

I found her in the girls' bedroom sobbing, her head under the pillow. I didn't know what to do. 'Don't cry, don't cry,' I kept saying, but she didn't hear me.

'Mirza's wounded, they're all getting killed. In the end, we'll be the only ones left,' she wept.

'Don't say that,' I was scared and tried to calm her but she didn't respond. I gave her a glass of water with some sugar in it. Grandma used to give this to us sometimes when we hurt ourselves playing. Lela didn't even look at me. Feeling helpless, I sat on the edge of the mattress and waited for Nadia to come home. When she heard what had happened, she lay next to Lela and spoke to her gently. I couldn't hear what she was saying, but after a while Lela's sobbing quietened and Nadia stayed with her until she fell asleep.

The next day on my way to school, I went to check on Lela. Nadia was getting dressed. She said Lela was a little better this morning and had gone to work already.

At school, I tried to pretend that nothing was wrong but I couldn't stop thinking about Lela and as soon as the bell rang, I ran home to see how she was. The front door was unlocked. Lela was alone, lying on the mattress. At first, I thought she was sleeping and then panic struck me when I realised I couldn't hear her breathing. 'Lela, Lela,' I shook her and shouted. She was motionless. Then I spotted an empty bottle of pills on the floor. I felt sick. I raced next door to Danica's house but there was no one there. My hands were shaking as I dialled for an ambulance. When I returned to Lela, she had not moved. I kept shaking her and calling for her to wake up until I heard the siren of the ambulance. The medics came in and carried her out on a stretcher and told me to call the hospital in a few hours.

In tears, I curled up on the mattress, praying that she would survive. Hours later Nadia came home and hurried straight to the hospital. Back at Danica's house, I lay awake, tossing and turning until late into the night when I heard Nadia whistling under the window.

'She's in a stable condition,' she said, 'but they'll keep her for a few days. She took a lot of pills . . .'

Thank you, God, I thought. *Thank you for not letting her die.*

On her return from the hospital three days later, Lela looked drained and her striking green eyes stared out from her pale face. She remained in bed for some time, not speaking much and eating very little. Slowly, she started to recover and eventually some of her usual chirpiness returned. She never talked to me about that day and I never mentioned it again, afraid that it might upset her.

In Croatia, Christmas was the most important festival of the year, whereas in Bosnia, New Year's Eve was the biggest celebration. Wrapped up warmly, my school friends and I strolled through the main square eating hot roasted chestnuts. The bustling square and the city streets around it looked like a scene from a fairy tale. Carefully placed pine trees were lavishly hung with sparkling lights and dazzling trinkets. Beautiful Christmas decorations shone in the shop windows; their floors were covered in twinkling snow dust.

Returning home, I found Danica in the kitchen cooking meat and pastries for Christmas dinner. The table in the living room was set with silver cutlery and crystal glasses. The TV was on. I busied myself helping Danica by carrying things through for her. As I was bringing a plate of food from the kitchen, I happened to glance at the screen and almost dropped the platter I was carrying. I grabbed the remote and turned up the volume.

'My cousin Mirza's on TV,' I yelled. Everyone rushed in and we all stood in the middle of the room, looking at the screen.

Andrea put her arm around me and in silence we watched an American journalist interviewing Mirza. My cousin was very articulate and spoke clearly. In the report the journalist took Mirza and Merima to the cemetery. It was heartbreaking watching Mirza on his crutches, visiting his father's grave for the first time. The report ended with old family videos of Mirza skiing. I thought of the last time I'd seen him and remembered how we used to race each other up and down our street. I thought he was brave and I felt so proud of him.

In the New Year, out of nowhere, our brother Mesha phoned us. He was in Zagreb and, within minutes, the three of us were on our way to meet him at the city mosque. Being refugees had taught us to act swiftly and ask little.

The last time we'd seen him was in March 1991 on the platform of the railway station in Sarajevo. Still recovering from the big party we'd had the night before, the whole family had turned up to say goodbye to him as he left us to do his army service. Back then, the JNA was seen as the country's protector and was respected by the whole nation. Our brother was going to serve his country and it was a proud moment for us all. We sang as the train pulled out of the station, totally unaware of the terrible times that lay ahead.

We found Mesha in the foyer of the mosque, standing with a group of people. He was dressed in jeans and a thin brown jacket. His hair was cut short and he looked bigger and older than I remembered him. He hugged Nadia and Lela and hoisted me up in the air and spun me around. Then he pulled the three of us close to him again. In the past, Mesha had seldom hugged us, but now he was in no hurry to let us go. Our lives had been turned upside down since we'd seen each other twenty-two months ago. With our big brother with us, I felt safer and closer to home.

'You look so grown-up,' Nadia remarked tearfully as she stepped back to look at him. Mesha raised his eyebrows and smiled sadly.

'Let's go somewhere where we can talk,' he suggested. Excited to see him, we kept pinching him all the way to the nearest café. It was smoky inside and we settled at a table by the window. Lela ordered drinks for everyone.

Mesha reached for his cigarettes. He leaned back in his chair and looked at us. 'The three of you are real teenagers now.'

'Mesha, it's been almost two years since we've seen each other,' Nadia remarked, grabbing one of his cigarettes.

'You shouldn't be smoking,' Mesha frowned.

'I only have one or two a day, it calms me down,' she answered, defensively.

Mesha listened as we told him about everything that had happened to us since the start of the war and then Lela asked him how he had managed to get out of the JNA.

'When the war started,' he told us, 'it all became very confusing. After a month I realised that the officers in charge didn't know what to do with those of us who were from Bosnia, so one day in May last year I decided to escape from the barracks in Montenegro. I literally walked out of the barracks and hid in the city for a few days with some people I knew. Later, I managed to get on a bus out of town.'

'Were you ever sent to fight?' I asked, scared for him.

Mesha shook his head. 'No, I was working in the army photo lab in the barracks so I was kept behind, but most of the Serbs serving with me were sent to fight in Croatia. We didn't know what was going on either in Croatia or Bosnia.' He shrugged his shoulders. 'We weren't allowed to watch the news. At night, we were confined to barracks but we often crept out. All through the night we could see trucks coming and going, bringing their wounded and dead into the barracks.' He gulped down the last of his coffee and signalled to the waitress to bring him another one.

'What happened after you escaped?' Nadia asked, blowing smoke from the corner of her mouth.

Mesha continued, 'I went to Belgrade first. You know how many friends Dad has there . . .'

'Yes, Mum told us that you'd been there. Was it safe for you?'

'I thought it was,' he scratched his head and continued, 'I had no idea what was happening in Sarajevo. The news in Belgrade always portrayed the Serbs as the victims. I moved around amongst Dad's friends, staying with each one for no longer than a week at a time. I didn't go out, I knew I had to stay out of sight. By June, I'd made up my mind to return to Sarajevo and a few days before I was set to go, managed to get hold of Atka and Aunt Tidja. It was only then that I found out what was really going on.' He picked up his cigarette packet and lined it up with the ashtray on the table. 'They begged me not to return to Sarajevo as it would be too dangerous and Aunt Tidja urged me to go to our relatives in Macedonia, which I did, even though I had no papers.'

Lela bit her fingernails as she listened to his story.

'I took a bus to Macedonia but kept a low profile, hoping to go unnoticed. At the border, we went through passport control. I didn't have a passport or proof of identity, so the cops took me into the border office.'

'Shit, did you get arrested?' Nadia stared at him.

Mesha grinned at us. 'I couldn't believe my luck when I saw my former superior officer from the JNA in the office. It turned out that he'd escaped too. He recognised me and, sympathising with me, let me go through.'

Lela joked that Grandma must have prayed hard for Mesha that day.

'I did too,' he laughed. Mesha spent five months living with our cousins in Macedonia, helping out in their friends' plumbing supplies shop. Fearing that he might be found out by the local authorities, he decided that it was best not to contact us.

'At least I knew you were safe. I always tuned into Radio Sarajevo for daily reports but I had no way of knowing how anyone else was or even if they were still alive. The phone lines to Sarajevo were dead. It drove me crazy, I just knew that I had to try to get home . . .'

'How did you get here then?' Nadia asked.

'I found out that a convoy had been organised to take young men who, like me, had run away from the JNA back to Bosnia. Of course, there was no way we could go there directly because of the war, so we were told that the bus would take us to the Bosnian-Croatian border, going via Zagreb. They put us on a group passport and we left Macedonia four days ago.'

'Why did it take you four days to get here?' the three of us said in chorus. Macedonia wasn't *that* far away.

'It was too dangerous to take the direct route so we had to go the long way round, which took us through Bulgaria, Romania and Hungary. Once we reached the Croatian border the military police escorted us, and will escort us again to the Bosnian border tomorrow.'

Mesha had only twenty-four hours to spend with us before the convoy left. I was so happy to see my big brother but saddened to hear that he had to leave so soon. I sat on his lap and he wouldn't stop tickling me.

Back at the girls' house, we made an extra bed for him using our bags and suitcases, and Danica lent him a blanket. The next morning we were up early and spent the entire day together. Danica cooked a big lunch. She bought Mesha a warm winter jacket. I wished there were more hours in the day. It seemed that he'd just arrived and already he had to leave. We gave him a letter to take home. He shared with us the little money he had left and wouldn't let us come to the bus stop with him.

Meetings

Atka

Around midnight, the Serbs besieging the city marked the arrival of the Orthodox New Year by intensifying their tank and mortar fire. The barrage continued until just after dawn when the Serbs, probably exhausted after their night of drunken revelry, fell silent.

Taking advantage of the lull in the shelling, Mum and I ventured out to collect water from the brewery. On our way, we passed the apartment of Mum's friend Mikana and asked her to come along with us.

'Happy New Year,' Mum said when Mikana appeared at the door. Although Mikana was a Serb, she considered herself first and foremost a proud Sarajevan. She didn't practise her religion but followed her Orthodox traditions for cultural reasons. Like many Serbs, she'd chosen to remain in the city and share the same fate as the rest of us. We headed towards the brewery in the old part of town. Low clouds, hanging above the city, muffled the sound of sporadic machine-gun fire.

'Remind me why your New Year's Eve falls on the thirteenth of January,' I said to Mikana. 'I know it's something to do with the calendar but I always forget exactly.'

'It's because the Orthodox Church follows the Julian calendar which trails two weeks behind the modern Gregorian one,' Mikana told me.

'Oh, that's right, we learnt that at school,' I remembered.

Mikana took something out of the pocket of her fur coat. 'Look what I've got!' she said, showing us a cone-shaped paper wrap, filled with roasted coffee beans.

'Coffee! Is that a present from Santa Claus?' I joked.

'This one's from my secret stash. I want to take you to see a friend of mine and we'll drink it with her. She's good at reading coffee cups,' Mikana said, quickening her pace.

Fortune-telling from coffee cups had been an amusing pastime for my friends and me before the war, but now it seemed ridiculous.

'What could she possibly tell us?' I couldn't help feeling a little cynical.

'It doesn't matter, it's the coffee we want,' Mum remarked with a grin.

We walked past my old high school, then ran hurriedly across a narrow bridge to the other side of the river. Instead of turning towards the brewery, we continued on up the hill and turned into one of the steep back lanes.

'Here we are,' Mikana said, opening the wooden gate into the garden of a two-storey dwelling. A large pile of logs was stacked under the eaves along the front wall of the house. Mikana knocked on the front door.

'Look at all that wood,' I said, astounded.

An elderly woman peered from behind the curtain at the window. An olive-green scarf framed her wrinkled face.

'Come on, open the door, it's me!' Mikana said as she stepped closer to the window. The woman's face softened in recognition and she welcomed us into the house. Soon, we were sitting on the long couch in her kitchen. The windowpane behind the couch was cracked in several places and the glass was held together by strips of wide brown tape. Intense heat emanating from the large rectangular stove across from us enveloped me and I slouched into the couch.

'Where did you get all that firewood from?' Mum asked the old woman.

'I had a few trees cut down,' she replied, pointing towards the window. I looked out at the straight lines of bare trees in the garden below.

'It's lucky you have so many trees,' I remarked, enviously.

The woman shrugged. 'I'll have to get the rest of them cut down before anyone steals them. I'll store the wood in the basement – it'll last me for the winters to come.'

'What do you mean? The war's not going to last for another winter,' Mikana said, dismissing the old woman's comment with a wave of her hand.

'Oh, you young people, you think you know everything!' the woman said. She inclined her head and continued. 'That's what they said about the Second World War but look how long that dragged on.'

Surely things are different now, I thought to myself. *A war in Europe can't possibly last that long. Not in the age of* The Simpsons *and satellite TV.*

Mikana leaned over and put the cone-wrapped coffee on the table. The look of surprise on the old woman's face was priceless. Happily, she reached for the brass coffee grinder on the shelf.

'You're the youngest, you can grind,' she said and handed it to me. She filled the coffee pot with water, then placed it on the stove. I started to turn the handle and looked around. White lace doilies covered almost everything in the room: the TV in the corner, the glass table in front of us and the back and arms of the large couch. The familiar face of Tito, the former president of Yugoslavia, looked down at us from the wood-framed photo on the wall. He'd been the leader responsible for holding the country together for almost forty years. It wasn't long after his death that our Communist system collapsed and various nationalist parties started rising to power. Instead of the prosperity we had all expected from our new democratic system, Yugoslavia, as I knew it, began to fall apart. Although Tito had died more than a decade ago, people remembered him with great respect and his image was still visible everywhere, reminding us of our country's peaceful and united past.

I opened the bottom half of the coffee grinder and smelt the finely ground powder.

'All done,' I said, passing it back to the old woman. She brewed the coffee then placed the pot and four very small cups on the tray and brought it to the table. She spooned the foam from the top of the pot and put some into each cup. Carefully she poured the coffee and we waited for the grounds to settle. The brew was hot and strong and we savoured every sip.

'Do you want me to read your cups?' the old woman offered, guessing that this was probably one of the reasons for our impromptu visit. I finished my coffee and with plenty of grounds still left at the bottom, swirled the cup gently, then turned it upside down on to my saucer. Mikana and Mum did the same.

The small kitchen smelt of spices and cloves and, while we waited for the grounds to dry, I closed my eyes for what I thought was just a second.

'Atka, wake up. It's your turn.' Mikana's voice startled me. I yawned and roused myself.

The old woman was studying the patterns in my cup.

'I can see a bird, just as I did in your mother's cup,' she said, turning it around.

Drowsily, I looked at her.

'This bird's close to your house, I think you may receive some news soon.'

Perhaps we'll get a letter from my sisters, I thought.

'Hmm . . . and there's a long road ahead of you,' she continued.

'Where to? The other side of the runway?' I asked, jokingly.

'I swear, I can see you going far, far away,' the old woman said in a firm voice. But I wasn't really listening any more; I didn't want to go anywhere, just back to sleep.

On the way home we collected enough water to last us for the next couple of days. It was fortunate that we fetched it when we did, because the following morning eight people were killed by mortar fire while waiting in a queue for water at the brewery.

A week later, when I returned home from the studio, Grandma handed me a piece of paper.

'A young man dropped in half an hour ago and gave this to me,' she said with a smile.

It was a certificate of some kind, but the bottom half of the page was missing and I couldn't make any sense of it.

'Well, turn it over,' Grandma said, impatiently.

I let out a cry when I recognised Mesha's handwriting and quickly skimmed through the note. He was with one of the Bosnian Army Brigades at Mt Igman and was waiting for permission to come down into the city. Our whole family was ecstatic about the news. Mesha had sent us a hundred Deutsche Marks with his note. With that money we bought three kilos of partially frozen potatoes and a few cans of food. We would make it last for a few days.

That same week one of Dad's good friends who was involved in the writing of letters of appeal had been killed. His body was discovered buried under snow near his house. He'd been stabbed multiple times and his body set on fire. Dad suspected that someone had used the havoc of war to settle an old score against his friend's wife. She was a judge before the war, but when the fighting started, she fled from the city with their children. Whatever the reason, Dad was devastated.

It was the beginning of February and Mesha still hadn't arrived. Everyone was beside themselves with worry and to avoid the gloomy atmosphere at home, I spent most of my time working at the studio.

'What's on the agenda today?' Hamo asked me. He was always there and I often teased him that he'd become part of the furniture.

'I've got a bit of editing to do. Can I use your earphones?' I asked.

'Help yourself,' he said.

I sat at the desk and started working. The studio was busy with people coming and going but I had a deadline to meet and couldn't afford to be distracted. I was engrossed in my work and didn't pay much attention when someone came and sat next to me. The person nudged me and, annoyed, I looked up. My heart missed a beat when I recognised my brother. He was dressed in his army uniform.

'Mesha!' I screamed and threw off my earphones.

With a triumphant look on his face he exclaimed, 'I made it.'

We stood up and flung our arms around each other. I buried my head in his shoulder for a long time and then looked up at him.

'Thank God you're alive and finally home!' I said, with tears in my eyes. 'It's been three weeks since we got your note. All this time I've been so scared thinking that you might've been killed. Why did it take you so long to get here?'

Mesha sighed. 'It's a long story, I'll tell you all about it later.'

He hugged me closer and I caught sight of Mum's tearful face behind him.

'My son's back,' she kept telling everyone around us. People were asking him questions and it was a while before the three of us were able to get away.

Mesha looked taller and broader than I remembered and the typically mischievous and boyish demeanour he once had was now gone. He seemed older and more serious but his hug was just as warm as the one that he'd given me that day on the platform when he left home to serve in the JNA.

The twins didn't remember him but Tarik, thrilled to see his big brother and deeply impressed by his uniform, clambered all over him. It was a while before all the excitement died down and Mesha was able to tell us what had happened. For hours, we all listened intently, Janna and Selma squeezed in together beside him.

'Three days after seeing the girls in Zagreb, I arrived at Mt Igman,' Mesha explained. 'Because I had no means of proving my identity, I was arrested at the Bosnian Army checkpoint.'

'How ironic,' Mum said. 'After all you've been through, you end up getting arrested by your own people.'

The Bosnian Army, thinking that he could be a Serb spy, locked him up. After two days in prison, he was taken before the Bosnian Army authorities at Mt Igman, most of whom were Sarajevans.

'Amongst them was Kenan,' Mesha said and Dad smiled. Kenan was one of Dad's old friends.

'What's he doing at Mt Igman?' Dad asked.

'He's working for the army as an interpreter. He recognised me and confirmed my identity. Good fortune smiled upon me.'

Mesha was released but because he was of fighting age, he was put on duty, manning the checkpoint for a fortnight. It was only yesterday that he was given a week's pass to come down to the city to see us.

'I tried to cross the runway three times,' he told us, 'and when I finally made it to the city side, I knelt down and kissed the ground. I can't describe to you how happy I was to have made it back, still in one piece.'

He had lugged his heavy backpack full of food through the cold and snow for some twenty kilometres from Mt Igman. As we were unpacking it, he drifted off to sleep. That night, our house was filled with happiness.

The next morning, I walked through the deep snow outside our house, flicking at the long icicles hanging from the eaves of the house next door. It was still snowing and I looked up at the large snowflakes, trying to catch a few on my tongue.

'Let's go,' my friend Armin said, pulling his sledge behind him. In happier times, on a day like this, we would've been at his house listening to Pink Floyd and rearranging his vast record collection yet again. But today, the most pressing task was to collect water.

I tied the empty plastic jerry cans on to my wooden sledge and looked down the street. Normally, the neighbours scattered soot outside their houses to prevent people from slipping, but it was early and the snow was still untouched.

Armin believed that the best time for collecting water was at the crack of dawn. After a few trips, I was convinced too. The guns were quieter at this time of the day and the queues for water were shorter.

'I'll race you,' I shouted to Armin. Pushing the sledge with all my strength, I hopped on to it. I heard Armin laughing as he overtook me. As we whizzed down the hill, my eyes watered from the rush of cold air. We hadn't raced this way since we were children.

Armin waited at the bottom of the hill. The smile on his face revealed the large gap between his front teeth.

'The First Motorised Bosnian Brigade, that's us,' he joked, tossing a snowball at me. I jumped off my sledge and saw his shiny, black leather gloves.

'Hey, that's not fair, I can't fight back. My gloves are woollen, they won't dry till summer if I get them wet!' I put up my hands to show him.

'I'm glad I've got gas heating,' he teased.

'Yeah, rub it in,' I replied. Unlike the electricity, the gas hadn't been cut off. No one could explain why. Unfortunately, our house wasn't connected to the city gas supply.

'That was a low blow,' he admitted, half apologetically and tightened the rope around my loosely tied jerry cans. Pulling our sledges behind us, we walked towards the main intersection and stopped. This is where we had to cross. Shipping containers lined up along the right side of the intersection blocked the snipers' view and afforded us some protection from their fire. We couldn't hear any shots.

'There is no blood on the snow, yet. Let's go!' Armin urged.

'Well, we might be the first ones . . .' but before I could finish he'd started running. I psyched myself up and ran behind him. My mind went blank. I could hear loud thumping in my head and my heart was pounding. We ran until we reached the cover of the buildings on the other side of the road then stopped to catch our breath. Cold air was cutting painfully through my nostrils and throat. Shaking with fear, I stared back at the road in a daze.

'Fuck this sport,' I heard Armin swearing angrily. He pulled me by the arm and we continued walking, sheltered by the tall buildings along the street. These days very few cars were on the road because petrol was virtually unavailable. We continued along the main road and passed what had been an imposing multi-storey dark-blue department store, which was now just a shell. Broken checkout counters and mannequins were lying on the floor covered in large pieces of shattered glass. I looked towards the park on the other side of the road from which great numbers of trees had been cut down. Here and there I could see mounds of freshly dug graves, covered in snow. Next to the park stood a tall grey building, the ground floor of which once housed our favourite café. My friends and I used to spend many hours in one of the corner booths, drinking, chatting and filling countless ashtrays. The waiters knew us all by name.

'Nostalgia is a killer, isn't it?' Armin said, as if reading my thoughts.

I took off one of my gloves and reached for a packet of cigarettes from the inside pocket of my jacket.

'Do you want one?' I dangled the packet in front of him.

He rubbed his hands with delight.

'Where did you get those?' he asked, as he took one. 'Did Mesha bring them?'

'Yes,' I said, 'a real treat.' Everyone in the neighbourhood had heard that Mesha was back.

'He must've had an "interesting" time getting back,' Armin said, lighting his cigarette.

'Yeah, he sure did,' I said and went on to tell him everything about Mesha's long journey home.

'Does he have to go back to the Mt Igman Battalion?' Armin asked.

'I don't know. Mum said she'll pull all the strings she can to get him transferred to a battalion here in town.'

'I can't believe he came back to this hellhole; he should've stayed where he was and waited for this shit to end. They'll

probably transfer him to my brigade – that'll be fun for him!'
Armin said, derisively.

His words struck fear into me. If that happened, Mesha would
be engaged at the front line, with only a rifle on his shoulder
and a handful of bullets. Overnight, my brother and our friends
who until recently had played pool and soccer at weekends had
become the only armed defenders of our city. I wished now
that Mesha had stayed away.

The two of us walked in silence, smoking.

'Do you reckon we'll live long enough to die of lung cancer?'
Armin said.

'Yeah, if we're lucky,' I replied. The heavily falling snow
dulled the sound of our rather desperate laughter.

By the end of that week, Mum's persistence paid off and
Mesha was transferred to Armin's brigade. He had to report
straight away.

Not long after Mesha came home, Mirza, Merima and Haris
were unexpectedly offered sponsorship to go to America and
we were all surprised to hear that the UN agreed to evacuate
them. They didn't have much information about their sponsor
but Merima decided to leave the city for the sake of Mirza
and return as soon as the war was over. We said our goodbyes
to them at Mayka's house one crispy, sunny afternoon, not
knowing if we would ever see one another again. We embraced
quietly for a long time.

'They're going to a better life,' Mayka said after they left the
house. 'America's doctors are excellent and their technology is
so advanced. They'll fit Mirza with a modern artificial leg and
he'll be able to have a normal life. I'll keep his bicycle in the
shed. One day, when he comes back, he might be able to ride
it again.' Her voice was shaking but her spirit was strong. She

cried but kept saying that she was happy because at least some of her loved ones were leaving and going to safety.

Since Mesha's return, time in our house revolved around his army duties. There were no days in the week any more, just 'stand-by', 'front line' and 'days off'. Mesha was stationed near the bombed-out Olympic Ice Hall for his two days on stand-by. It was just a twenty-minute walk from our house and it was strange to think that in 1984, only nine years ago, parts of the XIV Winter Olympics had been held there. Now, this area was a no-go zone. Mesha spent his front line days in the trenches, which were less than a kilometre from the Ice Hall. On his days off he came home shattered and covered in mud. We made sure we saved enough water so that he could wash himself and that there was always something for him to eat before he collapsed into bed. Grandma cautioned the children to be quiet while he slept.

Mesha came down to see me at work whenever he could. Late one morning, on one of his days off, he turned up at Studio 99. He and Hamo were reminiscing about the good times at the Sloga nightclub, where Mesha had been a barman and Hamo a DJ. I was preparing tapes for recording.

'Mate, nothing's as it was before,' Hamo said. 'You idiot, while everyone else is trying to get out, you come back.'

Mesha crossed his arms and leaned against the wall. 'You don't know what it's like to be alone and have no contact with your family. I'd rather be here, even if I do have to go to the trenches. At least I'm there with Fudo and Bruno, people I grew up with,' he said, with firm conviction in his voice. Hamo was silent.

'Did you get into any trouble while you were in the JNA?' another of my colleagues asked.

'Only a couple of times,' Mesha laughed, scratching the back of his head. 'Once I was reprimanded for not wearing my army cap. My sergeant asked me where it was and I couldn't resist replying, "What does it matter, sir? The whole country's falling apart and you're concerned about a cap."' He told the story so well everyone laughed.

'Were you punished?' I asked.

'No, the sergeant saw the joke, he was a good guy.'

'Was that it?' Hamo was nervously chewing on a toothpick. He'd run out of cigarettes a long time ago.

'There was another time. It was shortly after Mum became involved with the "Mothers for Peace" movement,' Mesha said, a shadow clouding his face. 'They resented the fact that she had protested with the mothers in Belgrade and the Military Police took me in for an "informative interview". They beat me and said that it was because I'd "resisted" during questioning.'

'Bastards!' I was furious. I stared at him, feeling sorry and angry at the same time. He hadn't told me anything about that before.

'It wasn't too bad, just a couple of punches. Atka, don't say a word to Mum, she'll be upset.' Mesha looked at me, putting his finger to his lips.

After a moment of awkward silence, Hamo tapped Mesha on the shoulder and said light-heartedly, 'Nothing that a tough Bosnian head can't handle, isn't that right?'

Mesha nodded.

Shortly after, he went home and I was left feeling sad and upset for my brother. I went to the other room and tried to focus on my job. I wished my friend Amna were here to take over. She usually worked with me but today she was late. There was nothing unusual about that, given that she lived in the new part of town and she had to walk or hitch a ride to the studio every day. I'd nearly finished editing by the time she appeared.

With a petrified look on her face, she walked straight past me and sat down. She was trembling. A couple of my friends came running over to us.

'Are you all right?' I said. Alarmed, I crouched down in front of her.

It was a moment before she realised I was talking to her.

'I got hit,' she said, rubbing the side of her head.

'You're kidding?' I was stunned. Amna took my hand and moved it to her right ear. I felt what seemed like a sharp pebble under her skin. I stood up and looked closely. Moving her long black hair out of the way I could see a fine, short cut on her scalp.

'I think you have a piece of shrapnel in your head,' I said, taking a step back. The others came closer to have a look.

'I thought so too, I can't believe I'm still alive.' Amna rose abruptly from her seat.

'Does it hurt?' one of our friends asked.

'No, it doesn't and I didn't feel a thing at the time,' Amna looked at us. 'I was standing near the main bakery trying to catch a ride into town when this massive bang shook the ground. I was terrified and glued to the spot. If it weren't for someone who pushed me into a car I think I'd still be standing there.'

'Didn't you know you'd been hit?' I asked.

'No, I only felt something after I got out of the car.'

We all stared at each other for a moment and then started laughing hysterically.

'Is this really happening to us?' I said.

'It's not funny,' Amna tried to stifle her chuckle but couldn't and neither could we.

'I think we've all gone crazy,' one of the girls exclaimed.

'Aren't you sharp?' I blurted out. 'You've obviously had some food today!'

'Yeah, a piece of bread. I'm full of energy,' she joked.

The four of us were laughing loudly when Hamo's head appeared around the door.

'Keep it down you lot, we're on air,' he told us angrily and closed the door.

We clasped our hands against our mouths, trying to be quiet. Once we'd managed to calm down, Amna rubbed her head with an absent look on her face. I suggested that we go to the hospital.

'No chance,' she replied. 'I want to show Mum and Dad first.'

Several weeks passed and not a single day went by without casualties. Sometime towards the end of March I interviewed an AP photographer called Peter for Studio 99. He was one of the photographers who'd made the recent journey to Gorazde. I'd seen him before his trip and was shocked at the sudden change in his appearance; he looked gaunt and his lips were dried and cracked from the cold. He told me that a small group of foreign photographers and journalists, led by local food smugglers, had traversed the steep snowy mountains, crossing front lines in their effort to get to the besieged town. They walked for over forty kilometres. Dodging rounds fired at random and hiding from flares, they struggled through the night. The bitterly cold weather took its toll and seven people froze to death on the way. The reporters arrived in Gorazde just in time to witness and document the plight of the desperately hungry people there and their reaction to the American airdrops. This was the first time that American aid had been parachuted into Europe since the Second World War.

After the interview Peter invited me to his farewell party at the new AP base at the Hotel Belvedere, which was just a five-minute walk from Studio 99. I made my way quickly in the dark and soon I heard the noise of the generator and saw the twinkling lights of the hotel. I walked through the hallway into the warm, smoky bar, which was full of people. I recognised a U2 song playing in the background. By the number of helmets and flak jackets piled in the corner, it was obvious that a large part of the foreign press corps was here tonight. I hesitated at the entrance until I caught sight of some people I knew. Aida, David and a tall Norwegian photographer whom I'd recently met were standing with a big group at the other end of the bar and I joined them.

'Peter was totally shattered when he got back, he slept for two days,' Aida was saying to a woman next to her.

'He still looks like shit, just as well he's leaving tomorrow. He needs some decent food and lots of rest,' the Norwegian remarked.

I saw Peter coming towards me. With him was a man in his late twenties with deep blue eyes. He wore a brown leather jacket and the black cap on his head was similar to the one that I was wearing.

'Atka, I'd like you to meet Andrew, a very good friend of mine. He's just come back from Gorazde too,' Peter introduced us. I sensed a feeling of unspoken camaraderie between these two men. Andrew and I smiled at each other in acknowledgement.

'So, are you leaving with Peter tomorrow?' I asked him.

'Oh no, I've just got back from Paris,' he replied.

I looked at him, confused. 'I thought you'd just come from Gorazde?'

'Yes I have, but as soon as I got back to Sarajevo I had to deliver all my film to my agency in Paris. I was on assignment for *Newsweek* and had a deadline to meet,' he explained, taking a sip of his Scotch.

'And did you make it?' I asked, trying to recognise his accent. It wasn't American or English.

'Only just.' With a faint smile, he inclined his head to one side. 'My editor was very pleased.'

Somebody called Peter's name from across the room and he turned to walk away saying, 'Excuse me, guys, I'll be back in a minute.'

Longing to hear something about the outside world, I looked at Andrew and asked, 'So how was Paris?'

'I couldn't really tell you,' he replied. He looked worn out and his eyes were red. 'I just slept for a day at my flat then came straight back here.'

We talked for some time. He was a photojournalist who had been covering the conflict in Yugoslavia since the very beginning. His knowledge of our history was impressive, as was the ease with which he pronounced the names of our towns and villages. These were usually a mouthful for foreigners.

'Do you need an interpreter?' I asked after a while.

'No, I usually work alone,' he answered, lowering his head to rub his eyelids. I was disappointed by his response but tried not to show it.

'Oh, OK,' I said. 'If you know someone who does, could you let me know?'

He raised his head and, after taking another sip from his glass, said, 'I tell you what though, I could do with someone who could take care of logistics. You know, things like finding petrol, getting permits, stuff like that.'

'Oh, you mean a fixer?' I asked.

'Yes, I suppose I do. Could you do that?'

'Of course,' I bluffed. I'd never done anything like that before but I was in my own town and around here anything was possible if one knew the right people. I did. I knew that a fixer's going rate was a hundred American dollars a day, which I'd never be able to earn at the studio or translating occasionally for Aida.

'It's a deal,' he said and shook my hand firmly.

More people joined us, the music became louder and for the rest of the night I almost forgot that there was a war raging outside.

Just after eight o'clock the next morning, I ran to the back entrance of the Holiday Inn. It was only ten minutes away from my house. The ten-storey hotel had been built for the Olympic Games and stood alone in a large open area, facing one of the main roads which was endlessly targeted by snipers. It was one of the most dangerous roads in the city and many people had lost their lives on it. The foreign journalists had nicknamed it 'Snipers' Alley'. The side of the hotel facing the main road was deserted and had been partially destroyed by shell fire but the rest of the hotel seemed to function as normally as was possible under the circumstances.

I passed a TV crew sitting in the lobby of the atrium and went upstairs to the fourth floor, looking for Room 409. Nervously, I knocked on the door but there was no answer. I knocked again and waited.

He's probably forgotten, I thought. Disappointed, I started to walk away. Then I heard the door open and I turned around.

'Sorry, Atka, I was asleep,' Andrew said, standing in the doorway. 'Come in,' he walked back into the room, buttoning his shirt. 'I'll make some tea, would you like some?' he asked, turning to the portable gas stove on the shelf.

'Yes, thank you,' I said, thinking that he must be from England. His room was a complete mess. Clothes, cans of food and cartons of Camel cigarettes were scattered around the floor, his bed and the couch. Countless rolls of film and cameras covered the table. On the shelf, next to the TV, I noticed a CD player with a couple of small speakers. Through the thick clear plastic cover fitted into the large window frame across the room, I saw outlines of the high-rise buildings in the new part of town.

'Grab a seat,' he said, gesturing to the couch. I moved his flak jacket and helmet to the side and sat down.

I felt slightly awkward and to break the silence I asked, 'What do you want me to do today?'

'I don't know yet, we'll see how we go,' he replied and passed me a cup of tea. 'What I do is tell stories through my photos and each day's different. We'll go and find out what's going on today.'

'Why do you have a B+ written on your helmet?' I asked.

'Oh, that's my blood type,' he replied.

I was embarrassed for not realising something so obvious and didn't say much until we finished our tea. He got ready and shortly after that we left the room. As he was locking the door I reminded him that he'd forgotten his helmet and flak jacket.

'Well, you haven't got any gear so I'm not going to wear mine either,' he said.

This unexpected response left me tongue-tied and I walked beside him feeling awkward. On the way to the underground car park, Andrew dropped into the restaurant on the first floor and picked up some bread rolls for both of us. We hopped into his scratched and dented silver saloon car, which had a large 'Press' sign painted on the bonnet. He turned the volume up on the stereo and to the deafening sound of music we drove straight out, with great speed, on to the empty main road. There were no traffic lights and broken power lines and tram cables dangled all around. We raced past abandoned cars and trams, towards the new part of town. We had to drive fast in an attempt to avoid being shot at. An ambulance, with a car following it, sped past in the opposite direction. Andrew pulled on the handbrake and after swiftly turning the car around, followed the two vehicles. I was flung to the side of the car, fearing that we'd either crash or be shot at. I clung tightly to the hand grip on the door, trying to make myself as small as possible.

As we drove back past the Holiday Inn, I caught a glimpse of its shattered and charred facade facing the road. It wasn't long before we passed Studio 99 and I realised that we were heading to the main hospital complex. We stopped outside the trauma centre and Andrew got out quickly, carrying his cameras. I followed. An older man and a woman in her early twenties rushed out of the car behind the ambulance. There was a look of panic on their faces.

The back door of the ambulance opened and two men jumped out. They turned around and pulled out a stretcher. A teenage boy was lying on it. His eyes were wide open and the bandages around his swollen face were soaked with blood. The men carried the stretcher inside and we followed. Andrew moved around them, taking photos. The medical staff took over and rushed the boy to surgery. The young woman screamed, 'Alen, Alen,' and tried to go after them but the older man held her back. She wept. Andrew continued taking photos and I wished that he'd stop. I felt as though we were intruding.

Minutes later, a doctor came out, shaking his head. The boy was dead. The young woman collapsed into the arms of the man. It was so terrible for them and I just wanted to disappear. I went back to the car and buried my face in my hands.

I heard the driver's door open.

'Are you OK?' Andrew asked.

'Fuck! He was just a young boy,' I muttered.

Andrew offered me a cigarette but I was shaking so much

I couldn't light it. He lit it for me. We were sitting in the car, swearing, when the young woman appeared in front of us. She was supported by the older man and was looking at us. Andrew and I glanced at each other and quickly got out of the car.

'Do you speak English?' she asked Andrew.

'Yes, I do.'

'That boy was my brother, please give me the photos you took.' Her voice trembled.

He shook his head and said hesitantly, 'Oh, I don't know if you'd really want to see them.'

'Please, please,' the woman begged. 'I need to. He was only seventeen . . . Please, mister . . .' She was desperate.

Andrew put his hand on her shoulder. 'OK, I'll bring them to you as soon as I get them developed.'

'You promise?' She looked at Andrew.

'I give you my word,' he assured her.

The old man, who I guessed was the woman's father, asked me for a pen and paper and wrote down their address for us. Bent with grief, the two of them walked away. I held the piece of paper in my hand and cried.

Later, we went back inside and found one of the doctors. He was unshaven and looked exhausted.

'What killed the boy?' Andrew asked him and I translated.

'Shrapnel. There was nothing we could do, he was dead on arrival,' the doctor said, with an air of sad resignation. The boy had been taken to the morgue. There were so many bodies. They had to be moved quickly and were usually buried within the day. Andrew asked the doctor how long he had been on duty.

'I practically live here. My wife and children are in Italy. They left the city months ago and I can't bring myself to go back to our empty apartment.' The doctor kept rubbing his neck. The hospital was often targeted by snipers and artillery fire, especially around noon during visiting hours. More often than not, there was no electricity or running water. Without those basic necessities they were able to provide only urgent treatment. Medication and food were scarce as well. Our conversation was cut short when more wounded people were brought in.

Andrew seemed to know his way around and I walked behind him to the single-storey building at the back of the hospital, towards the morgue. As we approached I was repelled by the overwhelming stench of rotting flesh. Andrew told me to wait outside. There were dead bodies covered in black plastic lined up along the outside wall. I could see their feet sticking out from under the crude covering. I felt sick and vomited behind a pile of bloody sheets on the ground. Afraid that Andrew might think I wasn't up to the job, I quickly wiped my mouth and pretended that nothing had happened.

For the next few hours he worked, taking photos of the pain and suffering of the desperate people who were crammed into the crowded rooms and corridors of the hospital complex. I'd seen wounded people before, some with missing limbs and disfigured faces, but I'd never looked at them closely. But now that we were pausing and taking in every detail, the horror of it all became infinitely more apparent to me. I mentioned to Andrew what I was thinking and he said to me, 'I can't even begin to imagine what this feels like. These are your countrymen. Before you worked with me you were a participant and now you're an observer.'

It was heartbreaking and I was relieved when we finally left the hospital in the late afternoon and drove to the relative sanity of the Bosnian Army HQ. We needed a permit to go to one of the front lines the next day. The permit needed to be approved, typed and sealed and the officials weren't in a hurry to issue it.

'It's amazing how quickly fucking bureaucracy grows, even in a war,' Andrew shouted angrily, tugging at his scarf.

'Andrew, if you keep on shouting, we'll never get it.' I tried to calm him down, conscious of the people in the busy hallway staring at us.

'What a fucking waste of time.' He shot a look at the official's closed door, and leaned against the wall next to me.

'I didn't even know you needed a permit,' I said.

'We didn't, until recently. In the early months of the war I went anywhere I liked.' He offered me a cigarette. It was our third packet that day.

While we were waiting I asked Andrew where he was from. 'I can't work it out. You sound like an Englishman but you live and work in France.'

Andrew laughed. 'I'm actually from New Zealand.'

'Oh, I've never met anyone from New Zealand before,' I replied, and asked him to tell me more about it. His description of long beaches stretching for miles on end with the high mountains rising close to the sea made New Zealand sound like an exotic and mysterious country.

'So, how did you become a photojournalist?'

'I got my first camera when I was twelve. I did a few courses through school and kept taking photos all through university. When I came to Paris three years ago, I enrolled at a photography course but when I realised that I couldn't learn anything new I started knocking on doors. Gamma is one of the biggest agencies in Paris. One of the editors there liked me and my photos, so he decided to give me a chance. They sent me to Sudan to see how I'd cope and when they saw my photos from there they took me on board.'

'So were you a professional photographer before you went to Paris?'

'No, I was a helicopter pilot,' he smiled.

I made a face at him, assuming that he was joking.

'I'm not kidding. Honestly, I got my licence when I was eighteen, and at first it was a bit of a hobby, but then I got hooked on it.'

He was interesting and I liked talking to him. I hardly noticed that more than an hour had passed, when a tall dark man with a moustache called us in to his office. He wanted to know who Andrew was working for and why we wanted to go to the front line but then he looked at the press card attached to my jacket and recognised my last name. He knew my mother.

'If I'd known whose daughter you were, I wouldn't have left you waiting for so long,' he said, apologetically and within minutes we were issued a permit. 'This will allow you unlimited movement and if you need anything else, come and see me.' He walked us to the door.

Instead of going straight home, Andrew took me to an underground club for a drink. I hadn't been to a nightclub for a long time and wasn't aware that any of them were still operating. There were lots of other journalists and locals there. Andrew wasn't concerned about the curfew and it was well after midnight when he drove me home. I didn't want to ask him if he wanted me to continue working with him but he said, 'I'll see you tomorrow morning, Atka. Well done, that was a tough day.'

Even though I was exhausted, I couldn't sleep that night.

The next day we went to one of the front lines near a residential area in the new part of town. We were led through a long narrow trench, which wound its way amongst partially destroyed houses. A dozen or so worn-out soldiers stationed there were glad to see a foreign reporter and were keen to talk to us. Most of them were poorly equipped and dressed only in tracksuits and sneakers, looking as though they were part of a sports team rather than the last line of our city's defence.

'So, *this* is the front line?' I said to one of the men slumped against the trench wall.

'Yes, the Serbs are in that big white house just ahead,' he said, gesturing towards it.

I peered out and spotted the house from which I could hear the sound of folk music. It was barely one hundred metres away.

'They're driving us mad with that, they always play the same song,' the man said. We chatted for a while. He told us that he was a gravedigger by trade.

'It's easy for me to dig trenches, that's what I've always done. I'm happy with a shovel but not so happy with this,' he said, tapping his rifle.

As Andrew walked around the trench taking photos I heard guns firing. Bullets started whistling close by and all of a sudden there was a barrage of gunfire. The guys in the trench started swearing and shooting back. Andrew ran to me.

'Keep your head down,' he shouted, pulling me down into the mud.

The noise around was deafening. I knew how close the Serbs were and I'd never felt so scared. *Keep it together, keep it together*, I kept thinking to myself, as I gripped the sleeve of Andrew's jacket. We stayed there kneeling for some time. I couldn't stop trembling. Then, just as suddenly as it had started, the shooting stopped. I waited for a while before I stood up and let out a huge sigh of relief. Andrew lit a cigarette and gave me a puff. It tasted of walnuts.

'Is everyone OK?' someone shouted. No one was hurt.

Andrew threw a packet of cigarettes down the line for the guys to share.

'Don't worry Atka, you do get used to it,' he said and put his arm around me.

Later, when we were driving back to the city I told Andrew how scared I'd been. He looked at me and said, 'I know. It is terrifying, but it's good that you didn't panic. I think you and I will make a great team.'

The Kindness of Strangers

Hana

We'd just finished watching the evening news. Recently, fighting had broken out between the Croats and the Muslims in central and southern Bosnia and reports of the latest atrocities dominated the news.

Andrea's grandmother stood up and in silence left the room. Danica started clearing the table. 'Look at what the Muslims are doing to the Croats in Bosnia,' she said, furiously. I felt as though I were to blame and was worried that they would be cross with me. Out of the corner of my eye, I glanced across at Andrea's dad. He didn't seem to be angry and just reached for his crossword. Danica turned to me and said, 'I know this has nothing to do with you, it's just that I'm so angry that while Croatia is helping Bosnian Muslims here, the Muslims are now fighting against the Croats in Bosnia.'

It was hard not to feel responsible and I wanted to point out that the Croats were attacking the Muslims too but I was scared to say anything. At least Danica knew that there was no fighting between the Croats and the Muslims in Sarajevo and that gave me some comfort.

The next morning on the way to school I worried about my classmates' reactions to last night's news and wondered if they'd blame me for any of it. Much to my surprise, no one mentioned anything. Everything was as normal. Some of my friends were chasing each other around the classroom and others sat at their desks, laughing loudly. *I wonder if they've seen the news?* I thought to myself and sat down, hoping I wouldn't be noticed. Klaudia, who shared the double desk with me, plonked herself down beside me, took a card out of the pocket of her brown coat and showed it to me. These cards came with her favourite chocolate bar series, 'The Animal Kingdom' and she'd been collecting them for a long time.

'Look, I've got the whole set now,' she exclaimed.

'Oh, I'd love to see them,' I said. Relieved, I moved closer and admired her collection.

Since the beginning of winter, Klaudia and I had been sharing desks and we'd become fast friends. For some reason, we seemed to understand each other. Perhaps it was because she was from a large family or because she'd had to change schools, like me. Her family had moved into the neighbourhood two years ago and they owned one of the local clothing shops. They were devout Catholics and Klaudia always wore a small gold cross on a chain around her neck. Every time we passed the local church on the way home from school, she made the sign of the cross. We talked about our families and confided in each other. In the afternoons after school, she helped her father in their busy shop and looked after her younger siblings. She didn't have much time to do her homework and often I helped her with it. Once, by way of thanks, she gave me some grey tights, a pair of woollen gloves and a hat from their shop.

The day passed without anyone making any remarks about the fighting in Bosnia, but the next day in history class I spoke to the teacher and used a Bosnian word instead of a Croatian one. Although everyone understood me, the teacher made a point of correcting me. 'Hana, please use the Croatian word from now on,' she insisted.

'I will,' I said. Embarrassed, and fearing that she might mention the fighting in Bosnia, I immediately corrected myself. I didn't want to be different; it would be easier for me if I just learnt to speak the way the Croatians did. Apart from the accent and a few different words, our language was essentially the same. I paid more attention to the Croatian vocabulary and learnt to shorten my vowels when I spoke instead of stretching them out. It was awkward at first but soon I began to sound like my classmates. I knew I could talk to anybody now and no one would notice that I wasn't a local.

The house was in darkness. Everyone had gone to bed. As usual, still awake, Andrea and I lay in bed, chatting. Chinks of light showed through the gaps in the heavy slatted blinds. Then the lights next door flicked on. 'Oh, my sisters are home. I haven't seen them for days,' I said to Andrea and, turning on the desk lamp, grabbed my slippers and jacket. 'I'll just go and see them for a minute.' Throwing my jacket over my pyjamas, I tiptoed through the darkness of the hallway and out of the house. Careful not to scare the girls, I tapped gently on their bedroom window. When Nadia saw me, she smiled and let me in.

'What are you doing here? It's so late,' she asked, puzzled. 'Is everything all right?'

'Everything's fine. It's just that I haven't seen either of you for a while. When I saw your lights on, I thought I'd come and see you.'

'I'm at home by myself. Lela's still at work.'

I followed Nadia back to their bedroom. The heater underneath the window was on and I leaned against it, warming my hands.

'I got a letter from Nevena in Primosten,' I told Nadia. 'Can you believe it? Most of the refugees from Sarajevo are still at the hotel.'

'Really? What else did she say?' Nadia asked, as she folded a small pile of washing.

'She wrote quite a long letter. The hotel's still full because new refugees keep coming in from central Bosnia. It's been really cold; there's no heating in the hotel. The refugees from Vukovar have left and moved elsewhere. Marko and his family have gone to Germany.'

'Yeah, I knew about Marko, he's written to me. What's Nevena doing?'

'She's at school in Primosten but she doesn't write much about it. She's missing her parents and wishes she were in Sarajevo with them.'

Nadia and I exchanged news of school and work. I mentioned to her that I had noticed recently that their lights were hardly ever on when I went to bed, and asked her what time they usually finished work.

'It depends,' Nadia answered, 'Often we go out afterwards . . .'

'Oh? Who with?'

'Some locals we've met. I go to that café, you know, the one by the tram station . . .' She blushed.

I thought that she might have a boyfriend and was hoping she'd tell me more. I waited for a while and when she didn't say anything, I asked how Lela was.

'I don't know really. I don't see her that much . . .'

'What do you mean? Don't you go out together any more?' I was surprised.

'Sometimes we do,' Nadia shrugged her shoulders. 'But we have our own friends and don't really see or talk to each other that much . . . We're not as close as we used to be.'

She said that they hadn't fought; they'd just drifted apart.

It was late and both of us wanted to go to bed. Before I left, Nadia told me she'd been to see Damir. We decided to go and visit him in the coming weekend.

Andrea was asleep when I returned and I got into bed quietly. I still prayed for my family when I was in bed at night, holding on to the piece of paper that Grandma had given me. It was lonely to be away from them and often I cried to myself. But I thought if I started feeling sorry for myself, God would think I was taking things for granted and that something bad would happen to my family. The only way to show my gratitude was to do well at school.

After the bell rang one afternoon, my Croatian language teacher, Dubravka, asked me to stay behind. She was a tall woman and her porcelain skin and blond hair made her look as though she'd stepped out from one of the paintings that hung in the art room. She taught us literature and spoke about books with such passion and knowledge that I always looked forward to her class. We regularly reviewed the books we'd read, which inevitably led to many discussions of wider topics. She was very learned and inspirational.

Feeling shy, I approached her desk, unsure why she wanted to see me.

'That essay you wrote was excellent. I gave you an A,' she said.

The week before, we had been given an essay topic in which we had to describe our lives and experiences in comparison with those of the young seagull in Richard Bach's *Jonathan Livingstone Seagull*. After tearing up a few drafts, I finally decided to write about the war and what it was like to be separated from my family. I compared the struggle of the Bosnian people to Jonathan's attempts to overcome some obstacles of his own. It was the first time I'd expressed my thoughts on paper that way.

I thanked her, pleased that she liked it.

She looked at me. 'If you don't mind, I'd like to read it to the class tomorrow.'

'Sure . . .' I replied, a little nervous but proud that she thought it was worth reading to them.

In class the next day I was glad that it was she who had read it and not me. I would have cried.

Soon, she started to recommend more books to me and a whole new world opened up. I read Hemingway's *The Old Man and the Sea*, *The Little Prince* by Saint-Exupéry and Tolstoy's *Anna Karenina*. She introduced me to art and philosophy and, with her encouragement, I began to write more. There were so many thoughts running through my head and putting them all on paper somehow helped me to look at things more clearly. I wrote an essay about the meaning of home and sent it to one of the radio stations in town, which ran a popular children's programme every weekend. My story was read out one Sunday afternoon.

Several weeks later, I found Lela and Nadia at Danica's. Their animated voices greeted me when I closed the front door.

'It's only five o'clock. How come you aren't at work?' I asked as I put down my schoolbag. 'And why are you all in such a good mood?' Nadia and Lela glanced at Danica in silence, then Nadia, trying to contain her excitement, said, 'Guess who's in Zagreb?'

'Who? Tell me!' I pleaded.

'Merima, Mirza and Haris!' the girls exclaimed in unison and rose from their chairs. 'Come on, let's go.'

I stood there, utterly confused. The last time we'd heard from our family, Merima and the boys were still in Sarajevo, waiting to be evacuated.

'Your aunt called this afternoon,' Danica said. 'They're waiting for you at the Hotel Esplanade. They'll explain everything to you. Off you go,' she said and we hurried away. We couldn't wait to see them.

The Hotel Esplanade was a grand old building near the main city square. Once inside the opulent lobby, I saw stylishly dressed people wearing elegant suits and winter coats. A musician was playing the piano in the far corner. I felt very out of place in my bright green fluorescent jacket.

The woman at reception dialled Merima's room for us and then pointed us towards the lift. We rode up to the fourth floor.

They were waiting for us outside their room and for a while, we just stood there hugging one another. Overcome with joy to see them, we kept repeating that we couldn't believe that they were really here. Eventually, we all calmed down.

'Children,' Merima said, warmly, 'come in and sit down.'

Wiping their tears, Nadia and Lela moved towards Haris' bed. I sat next to Mirza on his bed. It was a shock to see him without his leg but I didn't want to say anything because I didn't know how he'd react.

Merima's hair was pulled back from her face and she was a lot thinner than when I'd seen her last. The three of them looked exhausted and worn out. They were very pale. I knew that they'd been through so much but I didn't have the courage to ask about any of it.

'I still can't believe you're here,' Nadia kept on saying. 'How did you manage to get out?'

'We saw you being interviewed on TV!' I interrupted, nudging Mirza.

'We can't believe it either,' Merima said. She told us that after the interview an American family from Florida had somehow managed to contact the producer of the programme, offering to help Mirza by sending him food and warm clothes. The producer explained to the Americans that they could try to assist but there was no guarantee that any of their help would reach Mirza. The Americans kept on trying through various aid organisations but the result was always the same.

'In the end, they decided to take matters into their own hands and sponsor the three of us,' Merima continued. 'They said they'd do whatever it took to get us out but I think it was far from easy.' To overcome the mountain of paperwork and the immense difficulties involved in getting anyone out of a besieged city, the Americans engaged a lawyer who, for weeks, worked tirelessly with the US Embassy and the UNHCR. Ultimately, their persistence paid off and Merima and the boys were evacuated from Sarajevo on a UN plane. The kindness of these strangers was overwhelming.

Mirza looked at us, beaming. 'We were taken to the airport in a UN armoured car and when we got on to the Hercules, the pilots let me sit up with them in the cockpit.'

Lela asked Mirza why he had been interviewed in the first place. Leaning against the headrest on his bed, he explained, 'A few foreign journalists came to the hospital where I'd been treated wanting to do a story on wounded children. One of the doctors remembered that I spoke English and told the journalists where we lived. By then, we were all staying in our uncle's basement, so they came to see me there.'

'How long will you be in Zagreb?' I looked at Merima.

'Only for the night. We're here to get our visas for America.'

She explained that since there was no US Embassy in Bosnia, their visas had to be issued in Zagreb.

'Do you plan to go back when things settle down?'

'Of course, my children. The only reason we're going now is to see if we can arrange a prosthetic leg for Mirza. The doctors in Sarajevo aren't able to do anything more for him.' She spoke with sadness. 'But we'll go back . . . Sarajevo's our home, our entire family's there, my parents, sister and brother. The Serbs have destroyed everything and killed so many people. But slowly Sarajevans will rebuild the city . . .'

I kept thinking about Zoran but I couldn't bear to ask about him. It was Nadia who mentioned that we'd found out about his death from a newspaper.

Merima told us that that Sunday Zoran was waiting in line to buy some bread from the back of a truck which occasionally came to their neighbourhood. A shell landed nearby and he was hit by a tiny piece of shrapnel. It went straight into his heart, killing him on the spot.

'And then,' she sighed, 'three weeks later Mirza was wounded.'

None of us moved as Mirza told us about the day he was hit and the two months he had spent in hospital.

'I had to have three operations. I woke up during one of them because they couldn't give me enough anaesthetic. I thought I'd fallen off a horse and it was stomping on me. And then it seemed that a whole pack of them fell on top of me . . .' My sisters and I cried silently as he spoke.

'It was lucky that we had some foreign currency left,' Merima said, 'because I had to buy any painkillers I could find on the black market. The hospitals are so short of medicine that even an asprin is hard to come by.'

'The first night that I remember being in the hospital was the worst,' Mirza continued. 'The room was pitch black at night and people were crying out in pain. The day I found out that my leg had been amputated, I was really angry. It was my leg and they didn't even ask me if they could do it!'

'After Mirza was wounded, we stopped playing outside,' Haris said from his bed.

'Yeah, we used to play with the other kids,' Mirza said. 'We didn't think the Serbs would shoot at us but after I was wounded, Haris and I were really scared. Even the sound of shelling was terrifying.'

I tried to comprehend the horrors they had been through. It was as though they'd just arrived from a distant and unreal world.

There was a knock on the door and Haris jumped up. It was room service; he'd ordered a burger. 'I can't wait to eat this,' he exclaimed.

'It's been ages since we've had any meat,' Merima said. She warned him not to eat it too quickly because his stomach wasn't used to so much food but he gobbled it down anyway. Then he lay down on his bed, rubbing his stomach. 'Mum, it was so delicious. I don't even care if I get a tummy ache.'

We were so grateful to see the three of them and stayed there talking until it was time to catch the last tram. We kissed each other goodbye and wished them all the best.

'We'll be thinking of you and hope that soon we'll all see each other again in our Sarajevo,' Merima said with a faint smile as we left their room.

Empty trams rattled through the deserted street. Arm in arm, we crossed the road and hurried through the dark shadowy park towards our tram stop. The lights from the hotel rooms and apartments along the main street looked soft and inviting.

'Hey, look at that!' I exclaimed. The name of the hotel on the other side of the road was lit up in the dark. Lela and Nadia looked towards it.

'The Hotel Palace!' Nadia said in surprise. 'That's where we stayed with Dad when he took us on one of his business trips.'

As we walked Lela reminded us of the havoc we had caused in the hotel bathroom that time. I was seven; the three of us were in the bath together and we'd filled it right to the top. Dad brought a bowl of vanilla and strawberry ice cream for each of us. Accidentally, I'd dropped mine into the bath which turned the water pink. The girls, thinking it was hilarious, tipped their ice creams in as well. We were so happy then.

'Look at us now,' Nadia said. 'That life seems like a distant dream.'

The Fixer

Atka

It was April. Almost overnight, the chill of winter left the air and only a few patches of snow remained high in the hilltops.

'Maybe you should drive today,' Andrew suggested, handing me the keys to his car.

'Oh, no, I can't drive.' I backed away, raising my hand.

He paused for a moment, and unlocked the door. 'Well, you'll just have to learn,' he said and got in behind the wheel.

'You must be kidding, I don't think this is a very good idea,' I said, opening the passenger door. I hadn't been expecting a driving lesson today or any other day during the war.

Andrew looked seriously at me. 'Why not? Who'll drive the car if I get shot?' he asked, bluntly.

I looked at him, stunned. For some reason, it hadn't occurred to me that something like that could actually happen but then I thought of the day before when the car had been hit by a few stray bullets.

'All right, you'd better teach me,' I said, 'but I'm warning you, I've never driven before.'

'Come on, it's not that hard, I was fifteen when I learnt,' he said, trying to encourage me.

He pointed to the ignition and the pedals and showed me how to change gear. I asked him to repeat everything a few more times. It seemed easy and we swapped seats.

'Take your boots off,' he said, 'you'll get a better feel for the clutch.'

'What's a clutch? I don't know that word in English,' I said and he pointed at it.

I threw my boots into the back, adjusted my seat and started to drive. I tried to manoeuvre around the underground car park, repeatedly stalling the car. The security guard, who was patrolling the car park for the hotel, laughed derisively.

'This is too hard,' I shouted, angry and frustrated.

'There's not enough space here,' Andrew said. 'Come on, let's get out of the car park.'

Nervously, I drove up the ramp and turned into the street at the rear of the hotel, where it was relatively protected from sniper fire. The hotel building sheltered us and I drove up and down the street to practise. It was easier here but I was confused, with Andrew constantly yelling instructions at me. Finally, I told him to shut up so that I could concentrate. After a while, I got the hang of it.

'You're a natural,' Andrew complimented me. 'That was the easy part. Now you have to drive us into town.'

I was frightened but in the excitement of it all there was a part of me that wanted to show off. I put my foot down on the accelerator and hung on to the steering wheel. I thought I was driving quite fast but Andrew shouted, 'Come on, give it some more power or you'll get us both killed. Be more aggressive.'

I was shaking. This time I pushed the pedal hard to the floor and drove a few hundred metres up the street to the centre of town. Tall buildings on either side of the street shielded us from the direct line of fire and I slowed down. As we drove past the checkpoint near the Bosnian Presidency building, a soldier signalled for me to stop. Vehicles that displayed press signs were often pulled up, mainly in an attempt to cadge cigarettes. I tried to brake slowly but got confused and instead stalled the car. I wound down the window, feeling slightly scared and embarrassed. The young soldier rested his arms on the window and leaned inside.

'Good afternoon,' I said.

'Good afternoon. May I see your documents?' the soldier asked.

I translated this to Andrew and he handed me a piece of paper from the glove box. I passed it to the soldier.

'This is not enough,' he said, looking at it. 'I need your driver's licence and the car registration.'

At that moment, he noticed that I was only in my socks and he asked, 'Where are your shoes?'

'I took them off . . . he's teaching me to drive,' I gestured towards Andrew.

Pushing his automatic rifle aside, the soldier leaned down and poked his head through the open window.

'Are you having me on?' he asked.

I shook my head, trying to keep a straight face.

'Tell that foreigner that I don't know who's the bigger fool, you or him.' The soldier started laughing. I translated this to Andrew and he, laughing too, leaned over and in very basic Bosnian offered the soldier some cigarettes.

'Thanks,' he said, grinning. He took the cigarettes, banged the roof of the car and shouted, 'Go on, go easy on the clutch.'

I drove for a little while but then handed the wheel back to Andrew. I'd had enough of driving for one day.

A small blue gumboot lay on the pavement, left behind after a vicious attack that had taken place earlier. We walked through the debris looking at the reddish-brown bloodstains on the asphalt. A few children had been playing around some of the burnt-out cars lying on the street, when the mortar had struck.

A scrawny man yelled at us from the graffiti-covered entrance of one of the buildings nearby. 'Are you two journalists?' He was standing with a small group of people who were watching Andrew and me.

'He's a foreign journalist. I work for him,' I called back. 'We've come to see what's happened.' We walked towards them.

The man told us angrily that there had been a lull in the shooting and the children had gone out to play.

'Come, come with me, you have to see this.' He led us up the stairs to the third floor. The front door of one of the apartments was open and we heard sobs coming from inside. A strong smell of burning frankincense, indicating a death in the family, drifted through the hallway. We walked into a very crowded living room.

'Here,' the man looked at me. 'Tell this journalist to photograph these two destroyed souls. One of their sons has been killed and the other one is fighting for his life,' he said bitterly, pointing towards a man and a woman in their late thirties, who were sitting on the couch. The man was staring at the floor, smoking and the woman's face was twisted with pain. Tears flowed from her bloodshot eyes. Andrew and I approached them to express our condolences. The woman was too distressed to notice us but her husband stood up and shook our hands. Andrew asked him if he could take some photographs and he replied, 'Take as many as you like, my house is your house.'

He sat back down on the couch and someone offered us a glass of very weak raspberry cordial. Knowing our customs, Andrew accepted the drink. He took a sip then handed the glass back to me and started taking photos. I moved to the side of the room and in the glass window of a cabinet, saw a couple of school photos of the two young boys. They were no older than Janna and Selma. The older one was slightly chubby, a happy smile on his face. The younger one had his lips firmly pressed together, as if trying to hide his missing front teeth. Sadly, I wondered which one of them was dead and which one was still alive.

A woman wearing a dark green jersey, said loudly, 'Go on, my son, take as many photos as you can. Let the world see what these poor, innocent people have to endure.' A murmur of approval and agreement spread through the group.

'Who does he work for?' a man with thick glasses asked me.

'Gamma, a photo agency in Paris,' I said.

'Will they publish these photos in France?' the man continued.

'Probably all over the world,' I replied.

'Good,' he exclaimed with a nod of his head.

After Andrew had finished taking photos, we chatted to everyone for a while and just as we were getting ready to leave, the father of the boys approached me.

'Have you got a car?' he asked.

'Yes,' I nodded.

The man rubbed his forehead and said, 'Would you be able to drive us to our son's funeral tomorrow?' He was struggling to talk. 'It's in the cemetery in the old part of town and we have no way of getting there.'

'Of course we will,' I replied without hesitation. Although I'd known Andrew for only a short time I knew he'd do anything to help. I promised the man we'd come and collect them the next morning.

Night had fallen by the time we drove back to the sanctuary of the Holiday Inn. The stark contrast between life in the hotel and life in the city became even more apparent in the evenings. The lights from the large chandelier illuminated the atrium, music was playing quietly in the bar and the hotel restaurant was bustling with journalists who were sitting down to continue their heated discussions over dinner.

We went up to Andrew's room. Even though the foyer was lit most of the time, often the rooms had no power. He lit some candles and poured each of us a glass of Irish whiskey. I'd never been much of a drinker but since I'd started working with Andrew, a strong drink and the endless repetition of Pink Floyd seemed to be the best way to end the day.

There was water in the hotel that night and Andrew offered me a shower. The thought of standing under running water was too tempting to resist. I went into the bathroom. The shower felt incredible even though the water was lukewarm and the pressure low. I washed quickly, conscious that the water could stop flowing at any moment, but to my delight it kept on running. I lathered myself again and, closing my eyes, lifted my face and let the water trickle down over me.

When I returned to the room, a couple of Andrew's friends were sitting there. I'd met them before. Ariane, a dark, feisty-looking woman who worked for a French radio station and Gary, a tall, gentle, English photojournalist, were chatting in a mixture of English and French. Although Gary and Andrew worked for different agencies, they were good friends and their friendship was further cemented after their time in Gorazde. In the candlelight, the four of us shared a can of couscous, heated on the portable gas stove. I listened to them talking passionately about their work. They swore in frustration at the unwillingness of the outside world to intervene and stop the killing. I was glad that at least these guys understood us. We talked long into the night.

The next morning, as we had promised, Andrew and I drove the dead boy's parents to the old Turkish cemetery. No one spoke as we drove. A handful of family and friends gathered around the small dirt mound and prayed. The funeral was short, as all funerals had to be now. The small group dispersed quickly, but the little boy's parents, their heads bowed, stayed kneeling beside their son's grave. Andrew and I waited in the car and later, took them to the hospital to see the son who had survived, the younger of the two brothers. The shrapnel wounds to his leg and the back of his arm weren't as bad as was first thought and mercifully he was out of danger. His parents insisted we stay in his room and the boy managed a tiny smile while Andrew took photos. At the end of visiting hours, we took his mother and father home.

'Thank you, we'll never forget what you did,' the father said to us as we said goodbye outside their building. He shook our hands and his wife embraced us before they walked away, hand in hand.

That night, over a glass of whiskey in Andrew's room we talked about the day.

'That poor couple . . . I don't know how you guys cope. I admire your strength and stoicism,' he said.

'That's all we have left now. If it happened to you, you'd be the same.'

'Perhaps. I hope I never have to find out.' He got up to put on some music.

We talked long into the night about life, politics, war and ourselves. Even though we came from such different worlds, we shared the same views on so many things. It was as though we were old friends. We sat on the couch, talking and smoking till dawn. A line of pink sky appeared on the horizon and Andrew opened the window to let in some fresh air.

'Come and check out the sky,' he said, turning to me. 'There's still some beauty left in this blighted land.'

★   ★   ★

A couple of days later, on a wet, grey day, Gary, Andrew and I ventured out together. We parked the car in the centre of town and walked through the partly destroyed buildings. To my eye, they were just a pile of ruins and rubble but Andrew and Gary seemed to see pictures all around. I watched them as they moved about, their cameras clicking continuously. I walked up to a glass door, which was riddled with bullet holes and peeked through one of the holes. Gary was on the other side of the door and he took a few photos of me. I smiled.

'Do you think we could get into the Parliament Building?' he asked me. 'It would be interesting to take photos from one of the top storeys.'

'Well, we can try,' I said.

The twenty-storey white building had been battered by mortar fire and was now derelict. It stood directly across the road from the Holiday Inn and only a block away from the front line in this part of town. We drove as close as we could to the Parliament Building and parked. Bullets whistled past us as we ran across the road, up the concrete steps and across a large plaza, until we reached the relative safety of the entrance. We were breathless.

'Is everyone OK?' Andrew asked.

An armed soldier who was guarding the building ordered us to keep away. 'No one's allowed to enter,' he said.

Gutted, I looked at Gary and Andrew.

'Why not?' Andrew demanded. 'Do we need another fucking piece of paper?' he shouted impatiently.

Gary was calm. He put his hand on Andrew's shoulder and said, 'Take it easy, Andrew. Leave it to Atka, I'm sure she'll sort it out.'

'OK. Try one of these,' Andrew said, and handed me a packet of cigarettes. I walked towards the soldier, who didn't look much older than me.

'Is there any chance you could make an exception for these two men?' I pleaded. 'They're photojournalists and just want to take some photos from the upper floors.'

'No, I'm under strict orders.' His hands were deep in his pockets. He shook his head and stamped his feet. He looked cold.

I offered him a cigarette, hoping that this small gesture might change his mind, but he refused. He wasn't a smoker. I knew that if I could somehow find a common link between us, he might relent. I lit a cigarette and started talking. 'If it weren't for this crazy war, we wouldn't be standing here in the cold, like penguins. We'd be sitting in a café somewhere in town, drinking coffee and having a good time with our friends.'

He agreed and we started to chat. Within a minute or so we'd established that we had a couple of mutual friends, one of whom had been wounded recently.

'Come on then, call your two journalists, I'll take you up.' He smiled at me with an amused look on his face.

We started climbing the stairs. Rainwater ran down the scarred and blackened concrete walls. Bits of smashed furniture and charred heaps of rubble lay scattered all over the ground. We were near the top floor when the soldier said, 'Don't go any higher, if the Serbs notice any movement in the building they'll start firing at us straight away.'

Keeping close to the wall, I walked towards a large gap that used to be a window and looked down at the city. The streets were empty and lifeless. Nervously, I poked my head out to look at Mt Trebevic on my right and to the part of town held by the Serbs. I expected to catch a glimpse of the evil lurking there but all I could see were familiar houses and buildings. I moved back inside and talked to the soldier, while Gary and Andrew took photos.

'Do you think this war will drag on much longer?' I asked him.

'I'm afraid so,' he replied. 'If I were a woman, I'd hook up with one of those journalists and get the fuck out of here,' he joked.

'You think so? You'd miss Sarajevo and all your friends in a second. I miss it even after a week at the seaside.'

'Tell me about it. I used to be the same but what is there to miss now?' He kicked a broken telephone lying on the floor. 'I'd leave in a second if I could.'

Gary and Andrew walked back towards us.

'*Dobro?*' The soldier asked, looking at them. I didn't need to translate, both Gary and Andrew knew that the word meant *All right*.

'Totally *dobro*,' Gary replied, giving him the thumbs up.

Andrew pointed to a large, framed black-and-white photo of Tito lying on the ground.

'I wonder if I could take this with me?' He asked me to check with the soldier.

'Take it, Tito deserves a better place than this anyway,' the soldier replied. Andrew picked up the photo and we made our way down to the ground floor.

Back at the Holiday Inn, I was surprised and glad to see Mesha waiting for me in the lobby. We hadn't seen each other for a few days. He'd been at the front line and I'd been busy working. I introduced him to Gary and Andrew, before he took me aside.

'Atka, there's no food left in the house,' Mesha frowned with worry. 'I feel bad for the kids. They've got nothing. At least I get a meal when I'm on duty.'

'Well, I haven't received my pay yet but I'll ask Andrew about it,' I said, uneasy. I didn't like talking about money, it made me feel uncomfortable. I looked away. Gary was talking to a couple of English journalists and Andrew, catching my eye, walked towards me.

'Are you guys all right?' he asked.

I looked down, ashamed, and wanted to avoid saying anything but then I thought of my little brothers and sisters and I knew I had to ask.

'Yes, we're fine,' I looked at him. 'I was wondering, would it be possible for me to be paid today?'

'Of course,' he replied. 'I'm glad it's nothing serious. By the look on your faces I thought something awful must've happened.'

Mesha looked at Andrew and in his broken English, started explaining why he was here. Embarrassed, I tried to stop him talking but Andrew looked at me and said, 'Atka, we've got to get food for your little brothers and sisters.'

Mesha thanked him and I was grateful that Andrew understood the difficulty of my family's predicament. He offered to buy supplies from the UN depot at the airport, probably realising that the money I earned wouldn't go far on the black market. I'd never heard of this depot, but Andrew told us that he could buy cigarettes, cooking gas and other essentials for himself because he'd befriended one of the French legionnaires who worked there.

Trips to the airport were risky because the road was controlled by the Serbs. They often stopped or fired at anyone driving along, including UN armoured vehicles transporting diplomats, foreign journalists and aid workers to and from the airport. Earlier in the year, the Serbs had stopped one of the UN vehicles and shot to death the Bosnian Deputy Prime Minister who was on his way to the airport to welcome an aid cargo from Turkey. The UN soldiers stood by and watched as the

Serbs fired rounds of shots at him. I told Andrew I didn't want him to put himself in any danger, just because of my family and me.

'Look, I have to go to the airport anyway,' he said. 'I need to find someone who's flying out today who can take my films to my agency in Paris.'

We walked up to his room. The small table was covered with notes and rolls of film and Andrew hurriedly put them into a white postage bag.

'I shouldn't be too long, you two can wait for me here,' he said as he wrote his agency's address on the bag. I felt we'd intruded long enough and told him that we would wait in the lobby until he got back but he disappeared into the bathroom and we heard a tap running. Amazed, Mesha looked at me and before I could explain that sometimes the hotel had running water, Andrew came out and said, 'Hey, man, how about a shower?'

Mesha didn't need to be asked twice and headed to the bathroom straight away.

'Oh, I feel terrible. You don't have to do all this,' I said to Andrew.

'Atka, it's not a big deal. The man's been at the front line and I happen to have water.' He put his hand on my shoulder. 'Just chill, I'll be back soon. Help yourselves to anything.' He grabbed his bag and left. The more I knew him, the more I liked him.

'I feel like a new person,' Mesha said, stretching his arms high when he came out of the bathroom.

I made coffee and we chatted while we waited.

'How is it at the front line?' I asked him.

'Pretty awful. We never know what's coming. Last night, the Serbs rolled a barrel full of petrol down at us but luckily the lit fuse fizzled out by the time it reached us.'

I asked him to tell me more about what went on at the front

line but he didn't want to talk about it. We were both relieved when Andrew returned two hours later. We drove to my house with the supplies he'd bought and I couldn't believe how much food there was. The boot was full of perishables, along with cans, cigarettes, torches and batteries. My brothers and sisters rushed out to help and started to carry the food back inside; their faces glowed with happiness. In all the commotion, Grandma walked out carrying some empty jerry cans. She handed them to Andrew. 'Son, you have a car. Can you please fill these for us?' Unaware that he was a foreigner, she spoke to him in Bosnian.

I rolled my eyes in embarrassment.

'*Nema problema*, no problem,' Andrew replied and we both laughed. Grandma disappeared back into the house and within seconds she returned with more empty jerry cans. Soon, half the neighbourhood descended on us, asking if we could collect water for them too. We filled the car with as many jerry cans as we could and drove away to the brewery. When we returned, I introduced Andrew to my family.

The hotel restaurant was full of journalists eating breakfast. Food was plentiful here but after a year of going hungry I was only able to eat a little bit at a time. Andrew stopped at the door to talk to John, a tall man with a beard and wild, curly hair. He was a writer for the *New York Times* and had just been told that he had won a Pulitzer Prize for his reporting from Bosnia. He was thanking Andrew for introducing him to the cellist. 'You certainly started something by telling me about Vedran and getting me to go out to talk to him even though I wasn't keen to do so at the time.' John smiled and invited us to a small celebration that he was organising for that night. The head waiter came over to congratulate John, telling him that his chef would be delighted to prepare a small cake to celebrate.

'How do you know Vedran?' I asked Andrew as we moved away.

Vedran was the cellist who played in memory of the twenty-two people who were killed while waiting to buy bread in the first big massacre last May. He played on that street for twenty-two consecutive days in spite of the danger and everyone in town knew of him and admired him. He had become a potent symbol of our city's defiant spirit.

'I met him a couple of days after that horrible massacre,' Andrew said. 'It was so strange to see a man dressed in tails playing the cello on that deserted street. I took photos of him and we spent a couple of days together in the basement of a restaurant, which belonged to one of his friends. We drank a lot and every now and then we went out on to the street where Vedran played Albinoni's *Adagio in G Minor.*' Andrew lit a cigarette and continued, 'I know that piece of music well, it really struck a chord with me. It's the piece they played in the movie *Gallipoli* which told the story of the infamous First World War battle in which so many New Zealanders and Australians died. As you can imagine, I was completely blown away by this man. I did a photo story on him and managed to convince John to go and meet him also. John wrote a story about him which his paper liked so much that they decided to assign John to Sarajevo permanently.'

'That's very interesting,' I remarked, and was about to say something more but John called out to Andrew and he turned around to talk to him.

I glanced around the room, looking for a place to sit. I'd met most of the people here. They were either part of the press corps or UN officials.

Susan, a woman in her late fifties, was sitting on her own, dressed in black. She had long jet-black hair with a startling grey chunk at the front. We'd spoken before; she was a famous writer from New York. In an attempt to draw the world's attention to our plight, she had come to Sarajevo to direct the play *Waiting for Godot*. She noticed me and pointed to a couple of empty seats next to hers.

'You remind me of Gavroche,' she said as I sat down.

'Gavroche?' I said, confused.

'Yes, you know, that character from *Les Misérables*,' she explained.

'Oh, yes,' I said. 'But he was a boy, wasn't he?'

'He was.' She smiled and told me it was my cap, scarf and black dungarees, combined with my perceptive manner that reminded her of him. We were still talking when Andrew and Gary joined us.

'You're not going to believe this,' Gary said, leaning over the table. 'I just met a couple of photography students from Germany who flew in this morning. They've asked me to take them for a bit of a ride around town but it seems to me that they have no idea what's happening here.'

'What? I can't believe the UN gave them passes to come in.'

It made me angry to think how easy it was for these foreign students to fly in with the UN while there were so many wounded in the city who couldn't be evacuated.

'I know, it's insane,' Gary remarked. 'Anyway I'm going to show them around. I'll see you later.' He turned and left.

'We'd better go too,' Andrew said to me.

'Where are you going?' Susan asked, settling back in her chair.

'To the Lion Cemetery. One of Atka's uncles is buried there and she hasn't been to his grave yet,' Andrew said.

'That's very sad. Would you mind if I came with you?' She looked at me.

'Of course not,' I replied.

The cemetery lay on the side of a gentle rise, overlooking the Olympic Hall. The ground was wet and the ochre clay stuck to our shoes.

'I don't know exactly where my uncle's grave is,' I said, looking at the large statue of the white lion in the middle of the cemetery. To the left were the pre-war black marble tombstones. Amongst those tombstones, and to the right of the statue, were hundreds of makeshift wooden crosses for the Christians and temporary headstones for the Muslims.

'We'll just have to look among the headstones,' I said to Susan and Andrew. I wrote my uncle's name on the palm of their hands and the three of us separated.

I walked past the graves, looking at the names and dates. There were so many people of my age and younger buried here. After much searching, I found my uncle's grave at the bottom corner of the cemetery, not far from the road. Seeing his name inscribed there brought home to me the finality of it all. I crumpled to the ground and cried. Ever since the beginning, I'd assumed that when the war finished we'd all return to life as it used to be. But Zoran, and so many others, had gone for ever and nothing in our lives would ever be the same.

On the way back to the hotel, Susan asked me about my uncle. I told her how he died and what had happened to Mirza. I went on to explain about the kind American family who'd helped my aunt and her two boys. The news had reached us recently that the three of them were now in Florida. We talked about them all the way to the hotel lobby. Susan gave me her phone number. 'I'm going back to the States in a couple of days. If you ever happen to come to New York, you'll have to give me a call.'

'Thanks Susan,' I replied, looking at the piece of paper. I was certain that I'd never see New York but, touched by her gesture, I put the note in my pocket.

'I'll see you two later,' she said with a smile and went upstairs.

I turned around and looked at Andrew. 'Thank you for taking me to the cemetery,' I said.

He put his arm around me, 'Atka, don't even mention it.'

We sat down at the bar and ordered a Bosnian coffee. I asked Andrew about his family back in New Zealand. He was one of four boys and his parents had been married for thirty years.

'My father's very sick,' Andrew said, frowning. 'He has cancer.'

'Oh, I'm sorry. I hope he gets better,' I said. Death had become such an ordinary part of life, that it hadn't occurred to me that people elsewhere were facing it too.

'Me too. He looked all right when I saw him at Christmas time, although he was quite a bit thinner because of his chemotherapy treatment.'

Gary saw us sitting at the bar. He came over to us and laughingly told us how he'd taken the German students out for a short ride around the city. Fearing for their lives, they'd wanted to leave as soon as possible but to their horror found that all flights were now suspended because of the intensified fighting. These two naïve people were now trapped, just like the rest of us.

'So, what have you done with them?' Andrew asked.

'They found a correspondent from Germany here and ran immediately to his room for shelter. I don't think we'll see them until the airport reopens.' Gary was amused.

'Didn't they realise how dangerous it is here?' I shook my head.

'It's one thing to see it on the news but another to understand the reality of it,' Andrew said, shrugging his shoulders.

I took the last sip of my coffee and pushed the cup aside.

'Where are you two going?' Gary asked.

'We're going to try and find petrol,' I replied.

'Well, good luck,' he said as Andrew and I left.

We headed towards the old Marshal Tito Barracks where the Ukrainian UN soldiers were stationed. We'd heard rumours that they were selling petrol and charging much lower prices than on the black market. Andrew parked the car on the pavement outside the long, square building which ran for an entire block. Through the guarded iron-gated entrance we could see through an alley into the large courtyard, where many UN armoured vehicles were parked.

'Wait for me in the car and I'll go and check it out,' I said as I got out.

I noticed a large double door to the right of the iron gate. It was unguarded. Assuming that there might be an easier way in, I opened the door and walked straight into the canteen, which was full of Bosnian soldiers eating their lunch.

'Can anyone help me? I want to buy petrol from the Ukrainians,' I announced loudly and all heads in the room turned to me. Two serious-looking men with Military Police signs on their sleeves left the food queue they had been standing in and slowly walked towards me.

'Don't you know the Military Police arrests people like you for selling petrol on the black market?' the taller of the two asked me in a harsh voice. He looked intimidating with a large scar across his cheek and a furious look in his eyes. I feared that he might be one of many small-time criminals who, in all the confusion of the war, had climbed up the ranks of the army.

'Yeah, we'll have to take you in for questioning,' the shorter man said. He turned around telling everyone in the canteen that they had the situation under control.

Petrified and angry at my stupidity, I tried to explain to them that I didn't intend to sell the petrol on the black market, but they weren't listening.

'Are you hungry?' the shorter man asked me.

'What?' I was confused.

'We're going to have our lunch first, before we take you in for questioning.'

They took me to one of the tables and bought me a plate of beans. The man with the scar leaned towards me and whispered, 'Listen, young lady, I'm not going to arrest you but you have to be more discreet about these things. You might get yourself into big trouble.'

I nodded, relieved.

'Now,' he smiled at me. 'I can get you petrol. How much do you need?'

Unsure and suspicious, I was reluctant to say anything but he nudged me as though to assure me that he wasn't playing tricks.

'I need about forty litres,' I said in a low voice.

'Is that all?' he laughed, taking a spoonful of his lunch.

'Yes,' I replied, explaining that I worked for a foreign photojournalist and we needed it for his car.

'No problem. I'll take you to see someone who can help as soon as we've had our lunch,' he said, urging me to eat my meal.

When we'd finished, the man with the scar took me to the back of the barracks to talk to a Ukrainian UN soldier. In a strange mixture of Bosnian, Russian and English, we agreed that I could have the forty litres of petrol in exchange for forty American dollars and a few rolls of film. I was told to come back alone after dark to collect it. On the black market, they charged ten dollars a litre, so it was a really good deal.

The man with the scar walked me back to the car and, assuming that he might want to get paid for doing me a favour, I asked him what I owed him.

'For forty litres?' he raised his eyebrows. 'Don't worry about it,' he waved his hand in dismissal. 'When you come back tonight, report at our checkpoint.' He pointed at the iron-gated entrance. 'I'll tell our guard to keep an eye out for you, just in case.'

I thanked him and handed him a packet of Camels. I always carried a few packets in my bag as sweeteners. Pleased, I got back into the car.

'I was worried about you,' Andrew said, turning the key. 'I was about to come and look for you.'

'You're not going to believe what happened,' I exclaimed, shaking my head. I told him what had gone on inside the barracks.

We worked for the rest of the day and, as agreed, went to collect the petrol that night. I reported to the guard at the gate and walked through the dark alley towards the barbed wire. The Ukrainian was waiting for me behind the wire and heaved two cans over to me. I was scared but everything went smoothly. We agreed to meet again in a week's time and I staggered out carrying the heavy cans.

Back at Andrew's hotel room, sharing our usual glass of Irish whiskey, we laughed at the absurdity of the UN. I looked at the large photo of Tito, which Andrew had taken from the ruins of the Parliament Building, and said, 'I wonder what Tito would have said if he could see the UN now, selling petrol from the barracks that still carries his name.'

'Tito was an opportunist, he'd understand,' Andrew said, lighting a cigarette.

'I have to tell you a funny story,' I said. 'My grandma is very religious and back in 1975 she went to Mecca to do the Hajj.'

'Oh, yes,' Andrew nodded his head.

'Anyway, one day she became separated from her group and,

not knowing a word of Arabic, couldn't ask anyone for help. She didn't know the name of her hotel so she just stood in the middle of the city and started yelling, "Tito, Tito".'

Andrew started laughing. 'I can just imagine your little grandma . . .'

'A local passerby came to her rescue and after a short search, found the hotel where the pilgrims from Yugoslavia were staying.'

'That's a great story.'

For some time, we drank and smoked our cigarettes without saying a word, as we listened to the endless sounds of gunfire.

'Atka,' Andrew broke the silence between us. 'I have to tell you something.'

'What is it?' I asked.

He looked at me. 'I'm in love with you,' he said, quietly.

'I'm in love with you too,' I whispered.

We'd only known each other for a couple of weeks but it seemed like a lifetime. We held hands and I felt an overwhelming sense of freedom. At that moment, it didn't matter that everything around us was so sad, tragic and futile.

No matter how gruesome and heartbreaking the stories reported from Bosnia were, the UN remained unmoved and the arms embargo continued. Judging by the number of reporters in the Holiday Inn, it was clear that Sarajevo was the centre of media attention, yet every Sarajevan I talked to felt alone and abandoned.

Every day was busy but whenever we had a spare moment, Andrew and I took water and supplies to my family. I missed seeing the children and never stopped worrying about them. On days when the shelling was particularly heavy, Andrew drove me home to check that everyone was safe. Lately I had started interpreting for other journalists whenever I could. I was the only one earning money in my family and they relied on me for food and other essentials. Now that I was Andrew's girlfriend and practically lived in his room, I wouldn't accept money for the work I did for him any more.

Andrew met all my friends and Mesha came to see us in the evenings on his days off. We often sat in Andrew's room with Gary and Ariane, listening to music and talking. Mesha's English was pretty basic but he always tried to make conversation.

'Life is a beach, my friends,' Mesha said one night.

'You mean a *bitch*?' I said to him, trying not to laugh.

'Yes, beach, beach,' he repeated. He sounded so funny.

'What did I say?' Mesha was confused and I explained, hardly able to contain my laughter.

Mesha chuckled, embarrassed, 'Oh, no, they'll think I'm an idiot.'

'Don't worry, man, we understand,' Gary smiled, turning the music up.

One relatively quiet afternoon, I invited Andrew to meet Mayka. I'd told him so much about her. She was a mere shadow of the woman she used to be but her face lit up when she saw us at the door.

'My girl, I'm so glad you've come.' She hugged me. 'Since you started working for those journalists, I don't see you much.'

I gave her a bag of food and a couple of apples.

'I know, Mayka, but if I weren't working I wouldn't be able to buy you these,' I replied, feeling sad and slightly guilty.

Mayka introduced herself to Andrew and, before we sat down, she directed a flurry of questions at him. She was obviously slightly suspicious of this foreigner and wanted to know everything about him. Thankfully, it didn't take long for Andrew to put her at ease with his frank and direct manner.

We spent the afternoon with her, looking through her family albums. Mayka commented on each photo while slowly eating the apple I'd cut for her and I was happy to see her smiling and joking again.

'I worry about the girls in Zagreb,' Mayka said to me, when we were leaving.

'You don't need to worry about them, they're fine. There's a satellite phone at the TV building and whenever Andrew calls his agency, I'm able to call and check on them,' I explained as we walked out to the courtyard.

'Thank God. At least they're all right. If you hear any more news from Merima, come and tell me,' she sighed and hugged me. A couple of shells crashed nearby and we urged her to go back inside.

That night at the hotel, Andrew found out that some of the journalists were heading out of Sarajevo the next morning. Their attention was directed to the mounting reports of bloodshed in central Bosnia as well as the possibility of the UN evacuation of hundreds of wounded from the smaller besieged towns in the eastern areas.

'I'll go with them. I can get a ride with one of the guys with an armoured car.' Andrew hurriedly packed his cameras and a couple of shirts and left at dawn.

While he was away, I was very busy interpreting, working at Studio 99 and helping at home. Grandma, Mum and I dug a vegetable plot in our garden and planted all the seeds donated to us by the UNHCR. Tarik helped with the planting and Selma, finding a little plastic bucket amongst the old toys, volunteered to water the plot.

Andrew had left me the keys to his car and to his room. I rented out the car on a daily basis to other journalists. One evening, on the spur of the moment, my girlfriends and I drove from the studio to the hotel. The car was unusually slow and smoke billowed out of it as I drove into the underground car park. Fearing that I'd damaged the car in some way, I asked the security guard to look at it.

'Who's the idiot who left the handbrake on?' he asked, laughing.

'Oh, well, me, I suppose,' I stumbled, embarrassed. 'I've been driving like that all day. How stupid of me.' Turning to the girls I said, 'Let's go upstairs and have a drink.'

Up in Andrew's room we finished the bottle of whiskey, laughing and partying till the early hours of the morning. It was the first time we'd stayed out all night since the war had started.

Andrew had been away for a week now and it was awful. We had no means of communication and I was so worried about him. When he returned, he told me that he'd been worried about me too. We made a pact never to be apart from each other for more than a few days at a time.

Two weeks into May, Andrew and Gary talked about going to Mostar, a town in the southern part of the country. The Croats, supported by the Croatian Military Defence Force, had recently taken over the western side of the city and were expelling all the Muslims from there. The fighting between them was particularly vicious.

'I think we should go there as soon as possible,' Andrew said, Gary agreed. 'Let's go in the next day or two.'

'Our best option is to fly to Split and from there, drive to Mostar through Croatian-held territory,' Andrew said. 'It's only a couple of hours' drive.'

'What about Atka? I'm not sure that she should go to Mostar at all. It's too dangerous,' Gary said.

'You're right, Gary. I wouldn't dare to go there, not with my Muslim name,' I said.

'We'll try to get you to Split with us and then we can make a decision,' Andrew suggested, and I agreed. It was hard enough to know if we were going to make it to the end of this day, let alone tomorrow. To plan that far ahead seemed as though we were tempting fate.

The Visit

Hana

*P*rofessor Devide. I looked at the name on the door and
pressed the bell. Professor Devide was one of the names
on the list my father had given me when we left Sarajevo.
The sound of footsteps behind the door grew louder and
a few seconds later a short Asian woman with silky black
hair appeared at the door. I was taken aback. The only time
I'd seen an Asian person before was in magazines or in the
movies. She looked delicate and pretty. She opened the door
wider and said in a light, singsong voice, 'Do come in.' I
followed her into the long hallway, noticing the fine paintings
of exotic birds, which hung on one side of the wall above the
bookcase.

'Come in, come in!' a friendly voice called from behind the
glass door at the end of the hallway. A slender man with white
hair was sitting in an armchair. The walls were lined with shelves,
crowded with books.

'You must be Hana,' he said as he stood up. 'I'm Vladimir
Devide. This is my wife, Yasuyo.' She bowed her head and
smiled and he extended his hand to me. We sat down and
Yasuyo excused herself.

'I'm glad you called us,' Vladimir said. 'Tell me, how is your
father and the rest of the family?'

'The last time we heard from them, everyone was alive. But
that was ten days ago. My sister Atka's able to call us occasionally

from a satellite phone, because she's now working for a foreign journalist.'

'I'm glad that you have some contact with them. It must be so hard for you all. I follow the news every day but I've noticed that as the war drags on reports of Sarajevo are becoming briefer. It's tragic, Sarajevo is such a beautiful city and very dear to my heart. I used to spend a lot of time there,' Vladimir said.

While we were talking, Yasuyo came back into the room carrying a tray with a teapot and some small cups on it. As she passed one of them to me, Vladimir said something to her in a language I'd never heard before.

Curious, I asked, 'What language are you speaking?'

'Japanese,' he said. 'Yasuyo and I met through work when I was in Japan. We alternate between English and Japanese because she's still learning Croatian.'

'Yes, my Croatian not so good,' she said with a grin.

'Japan must be so interesting!' I said, intrigued. 'When I was little, I saw a picture book on Japan and dreamt about being a mountaineer there.' Then, realising how silly I must have sounded, I stopped, feeling awkward.

They both laughed and Vladimir remarked, 'Well, the scenery is spectacular.'

Happily, I took a sip of the aromatic tea and asked, 'Do you mind if I have a look at your books?'

'Not at all,' he said, and we moved towards the towering bookshelves. Stories from all over the world were patiently sitting on these shelves, waiting for their turn to be read. There were book titles in Croatian, English, Russian, German and a script I didn't recognise. One of the books caught my eye. *Haiku* was written on the spine, with Vladimir's name below it. We'd studied haiku poetry in our literature class. I looked at Vladimir for approval before I pulled it from the shelf.

'Is this one of yours?' I asked, opening the book. There were beautiful illustrations of cherry blossoms and birds on the inside covers.

'It's a collection of haiku with my translations and commentary.' He smiled and glanced at the book in my hand. 'You can have that one.'

'Oh, no, I couldn't . . .' I said, handing the book back to him.

'Take it, it's a gift,' he insisted.

We spent the rest of the afternoon in their living room, chatting. Vladimir told me that while he had been a guest lecturer at a university in Sarajevo, he and my father had become good friends. Later on, they worked together when Vladimir edited Dad's mathematics books for him. Hearing about my father made me feel happy.

We drank more tea and I listened to Vladimir and Yasuyo talking about their work and travels abroad. Their lives sounded so adventurous and fascinating. Listening to them, I wondered if my family would still be together, had we been born in one of those foreign and faraway lands.

Spring had arrived and the first flowers blossomed. The streets were crowded with people and Zagreb seemed to have woken from its long winter sleep. My sisters were earning enough money for rent and food, so these days the only reason we went to the Red Cross was to check for mail.

Nadia still worked long hours but one Saturday she found time to come along with me to see Damir. He took us to a small grill across the road from his studio for a quick lunch. The smell of cooking meat and freshly baked bread greeted us on arrival. A stocky man behind the counter was busy grilling meat patties and taking orders from the customers while another young man was delivering food to the tables. As we were ordering at the counter, a table against the side wall became available and we moved quickly to take it.

'I'm glad to hear that Atka called you this morning,' Damir said, pulling out a chair. 'I'm so pleased that they're all in one piece,' he put his glass of lemonade on the table and sat down.

'It's so much easier for us now that Atka can call us every few weeks,' Nadia said. 'Before, we'd be living in fear for months, never knowing what was happening to them.'

'Have you girls seen on the news that the UN has proclaimed Sarajevo, Srebrenica and a few other towns in Bosnia, "UN safe zones"?' he asked.

'Yes, we've heard. But what does it mean?' I looked at him for an explanation.

'Well, supposedly it means that all civilians in these designated areas are under UN protection. But as we all know, it's not stopping the Serbs from attacking. Things are getting worse everywhere.'

The food arrived and our conversation changed direction. Damir was just starting to tell us about his latest paintings but was disrupted midway through his sentence by a man's rowdy voice. The man became more boisterous and soon the sound of swearing and cursing dominated the little room. Conversation died. I turned around and saw an unshaven man swaying between the tables and chairs on his way to the counter.

'Look at you all, sitting so comfortably here! It's lucky that some of us are fighting at the front, defending our homeland,' he shouted, knocking over a chair.

The man behind the counter tried to calm him but he only became more aggravated and boorish. A couple of people stood up and left. We remained where we were and avoided looking in his direction. Soon, the man was given some food and was told it was on the house. He took the parcel and staggered out, swearing again.

When the door closed, I asked Damir, 'Was he drunk?'

'You bet,' Damir replied. 'Girls,' he said, gravely, leaning towards Nadia and me, 'do take care of yourselves and be careful where you go. There are a lot of men who come back from the front very angry.'

'But he wasn't wearing a uniform. I didn't think he was a solider,' I said.

'He's probably on leave. All able-bodied men have to go to the front. But a lot of those called up avoid being drafted. He's probably pissed off about that and thinks we're all draft dodgers.'

'Does everyone have to go? Even people who are working?' I asked.

'Yes. I've been to the front too, many times.'

'You?' I said with surprise. 'But you're an artist!'

He said that didn't matter. Everyone had to go.

'It's not a pretty place,' he remarked. 'It's no wonder that a lot of men return tense and angry. And no one understands. Some of these guys can become pretty disturbed and they find solace in the bottle. Who knows what they're capable of in their drunken state.' He drummed his fingers on the table.

'We see a few of them at work sometimes but my boss normally handles them,' Nadia said.

'At least I have my art to keep me sane,' Damir sighed.

After his warning, I avoided walking past bars and bistros, scared of who might be inside.

It was a warm Monday in May and nearly the end of the school day. A girl from my class and I were playing chase in the hallway. Just as I turned the corner at the far end of the corridor,

I bumped into Klaudia and a few of my other classmates. They were huddled together, as though they were trying to hide something.

'There you are!' Klaudia said and her face lit up. 'We've been looking for you. We've got a surprise. Close your eyes,' she ordered, grabbing me by the hand.

'Surprise?' I laughed excitedly, shutting my eyes.

Klaudia led me in the direction of the classroom. 'Keep them closed,' she warned me.

We walked slowly and I could hear my classmates whispering around me. I wondered if they had put some sweets on my desk, or written a joke on the blackboard.

'All right, we're here,' Klaudia said. 'Open your eyes.'

I was expecting to have reached the classroom by now, but found that we were still in the hallway. I was confused and unsure where to look.

'Where's the surprise?' I asked.

'Over there,' Klaudia said, pointing towards the classroom door. Somebody was hiding in the corner behind it. I knew it was a woman by the shape of her body but I couldn't tell who it was. Her face was hidden beneath a black cap. It was only when I got closer to her that she took off her cap.

'Hana,' she said, with a big grin on her face.

'Atka?!' My jaw dropped and immediately I rushed towards her. We squeezed each other in a tight hug. Something inside me collapsed and I started to cry.

Atka held me, crying too. After a few minutes she said, 'Look at us, our tears are like the Niagara Falls.' We laughed. I wanted to see her face, but didn't want to let her go.

'Was that a good surprise?' Atka took a few steps backwards. She was still holding on to my arms. She was smiling now.

'Atka, I can't believe this,' I said, amazed that she was

standing in front of me. My hands were shaking. 'Let me see you,' I said and looked at her properly. Her dark brown hair reached down to the collar of her blue denim jacket and she was wearing her jeans. Her face looked pinched and she was very thin but her eyes sparkled despite the big, dark shadows underneath them.

She squeezed my hand tighter and laughed. 'Look how much you've grown! And you sound just like a Croatian.'

It was only then that I noticed my classmates standing in a circle around us. Some of them had tears in their eyes. Klaudia disappeared behind the classroom door and moments later returned with my schoolbag. 'You go,' she said. 'We'll explain to the teacher.'

Arm in arm, Atka and I left the school building and as we walked to Danica's questions tumbled from our mouths. Atka wanted to know how we were getting on and about my school. I wanted to hear about our family, Sarajevo, and how she had managed to get here. We talked all the way and with Atka next to me, everything around me came to life. Trees along the street looked greener and even the sky was a more vivid blue. For a few minutes, I forgot where we were.

Nadia and Lela, who'd seen Atka already, were waiting for us at Danica's house and she made coffee when we arrived.

'I'm dying to find out how you got out,' Nadia said.

'I came with a foreign journalist,' Atka replied. 'But I can tell you all about that later.'

'Is it any better in Sarajevo now?' Lela asked.

'No, it's terrible and only getting worse,' Atka said and paused. 'It's so quiet here, I'm used to constant gunfire. Even when I walk down these streets I expect to be shot at.'

'We're lucky here that we didn't end up like Sarajevo . . .' Danica remarked.

'How is everyone?' Nadia asked.

'They're surviving. There's not much food and everyone is malnourished. The children are really thin but they don't complain. And Grandma, you know what she's like. If it hadn't been for her, I don't think I could have carried on. She's so strong.'

Danica poured more coffee for everyone. Atka reached for the bowl and put three teaspoons of sugar into her cup.

'Have you got enough?' Nadia teased her.

'Let me enjoy it. I haven't had sugar in ages.'

'How are Mum and Dad?' I asked.

'Mum's busy looking after the children. Occasionally, she helps out at aid agencies. But Dad . . . he's in a world of his own. He sends hundreds of letters all over the world, appealing for help for Sarajevo. I don't know whether to pity him or to be angry with him. He spends a lot of time looking after poor Mayka too. She's just holding on.' Atka lit a cigarette. 'I feel so sorry for Mesha. He has to go to the front line armed only with a rifle and a handful of bullets.'

On hearing all of this, I felt as though I had let my family down by being here, even though we had had no choice when we were put on the bus from Sarajevo. No matter how difficult it was for the three of us, we were safe and we were not starving.

'Anyway,' Atka continued, 'at least when it comes to food, things are much better now that I'm working as an interpreter.'

'I'm so glad. If it hadn't been for your English, you wouldn't have a job. Remember how I used to help you practise your vocabulary before your exams?' I said.

'Of course I do,' she nodded.

'Atka,' Lela said, 'you know how you wrote in one of your letters that Tarik has sworn allegiance to the Bosnian Army Brigade. What was all that about?' she asked.

'Oh, you should've seen him. He knows all the words to the

Bosnian Army songs. He told the guys in the neighbourhood he wanted to join them and they took him to a swearing-in ceremony at the school hall. He was proud to be told that he is officially the youngest "soldier" in town.'

It was hard to imagine Tarik at the ceremony. He was so small, the rifle would have been bigger than him. We sat in the kitchen for another hour or so, then strolled down to the local park. We spread our jackets on the ground. The grass was covered in daisies and Nadia made a daisy chain while Lela weaved little plaits in my hair.

Atka turned over and lay on her stomach, picking at the grass. 'It's been such a long time,' she said, thoughtfully, 'everyone's so tired, just trying to survive. We live like caged animals. No one's safe anywhere. You can try to hide from bullets but there's no escape from shells and grenades. People are killed in their houses, on the streets and even in the shelters. You never know where death will strike. It's impossible to describe . . .' She sat up and lit a cigarette. As she smoked, she explained how she had got out of Sarajevo. Everything had happened quickly. She told us that Andrew, the foreign journalist who she worked with, wanted to cover the fighting in Mostar. They'd flown to Split on a UN flight.

'How did you manage to get on a UN plane?' I asked.

'When I started working for Andrew he and his agency managed to organise a UN press card for me but because I'm a Bosnian, the UN officials were reluctant to let me on the flight. They thought I was trying to escape but Andrew guaranteed that we'd return.'

Atka showed us a UN stamp in her new passport. It read 'Maybe Airlines'.

'I've never seen a Bosnian passport before. I'm used to the Yugoslavian ones we used to have . . .' Nadia said, flicking through it.

'I have Dad to thank for that,' Atka replied. 'Typical him. Early on in the war, he organised it for me as a symbol of our country's recent independence. At the time I couldn't see the point of having a passport. After all, all we were doing was trying to survive and anyway where was I going to go in the middle of a war? But it was lucky he insisted. If I hadn't had it, the UN wouldn't have let me on the plane.'

Atka had arrived in Split with Andrew yesterday, and had gone straight to the Hotel Split which had become one of the bases for foreign journalists covering the war.

'We talked to a few of the journalists who'd just come back from Mostar. The fighting between the Croats and the Muslims there is ferocious; it would've been foolhardy for me to go there.' With an amused look on her face she said, 'You'll never believe what happened next! We went to the reception so that Andrew could call his agency and when the receptionist saw me, she asked me if I were Nadia's sister. "You're so alike," she said.'

'Oh, that must be Mladena!' Nadia exclaimed. 'She was so kind to us when we first arrived.'

'Yes, I heard. She told me about the day you two turned up at the hotel and how Hana was on her tiptoes, trying to see over the desk. What a coincidence!'

'So did you stay the night at the hotel?' Lela asked,

Atka shook her head. 'No, no, we drove to Pisak to see Seyo.'

Seyo was one of our neighbours back home and he and his wife had left Sarajevo with their children at the very beginning of the war. We all knew that they had a holiday house in Pisak, near Split.

'He and his family left Sarajevo in such a hurry, they didn't take anything with them; not even their birth certificates, just like you,' Atka said. 'When one of our neighbours heard that I was going to Split, he asked me to take Seyo's personal documents to him.'

Atka and Andrew stayed the night at Seyo's.

'Early this morning Andrew suggested that I might as well spend a couple of days with you in Zagreb while he was working in Mostar, I had no idea that I would be coming to see you. He took me to the airport in Split and before I knew it, I was on the plane.'

'You can only stay for two days then?' I asked, disappointed.

'Yes, I have to go back to work. I'm meeting Andrew in Pisak in two days, and then we've got to go back to Sarajevo.'

'Does Andrew have any UN protection when he crosses the front line?' I asked Atka. I found his foreign name difficult to pronounce.

She shook her head. 'No, there's no protection. Journalists go in by themselves. It's a really dangerous job and they risk their lives, taking photos and getting stories. A few of them have been shot and killed. I really worry about Andrew.'

We'd been sitting in silence for a few minutes, each of us lost in our thoughts, when Nadia remarked that today was the 17th of May, exactly a year since we'd left Sarajevo.

'And we thought you were only going away for a few days,' Atka said. 'We were so blind. None of us knew what was coming.' Then she stood up and said, 'Come on, let's go and take some photos and celebrate the fact that we're together.' She pulled out a small camera from her bag. 'Andrew gave this to me. I have a whole roll of film.'

We raced to the large birch tree in the middle of the park. 'Wait for me!' we heard Nadia shouting.

'Hurry up, you snail!' I shouted. She had a stomach ache and was left running behind us.

Lela gave Atka a leg-up into the tree and we followed. We

settled into a fork between two large branches and Nadia took photos. Afterwards, we ran through the park doing cartwheels and dancing. I wished it could be like this for ever.

It was past midnight and the four of us were lying close to each other in bed, wide-awake. We were in the girls' house, telling Atka about all that had happened to us in the last year.

'That's enough about us,' Nadia said. 'Tell us some more stories from home.'

'OK, I have a funny one for you,' Atka said.

'Last year,' she began, 'before Mum came back, we'd received our humanitarian aid, which Grandma and I always divided into small portions so that they would last us for a week or two. We always stored the supplies in the cupboard. Anyway, after collecting water one day, I came home to find the cupboard was completely empty and the children unusually cheerful and happy. I asked Janna and Selma where all the food had gone. "Oh, we had a picnic," Selma told me excitedly and explained that Tarik, Asko and Emir wouldn't stop crying, so to cheer them up, the girls had pretended to take them on a picnic. They ate all the food,' Atka said, 'but I didn't have the heart to tell them what they'd done.'

It was a funny story but at the same time the thought of how hungry they must have been was crushing.

In the morning, Lela made coffee and the girls sat up in bed, chatting. I dressed for school. Atka was telling us about the day Mesha had come home.

'He made his way through the deserted streets from the airport to our house carrying a heavy backpack full of food. You know how far that is . . . Anyway, Mesha stopped to light a cigarette when a man appeared out of a building nearby and asked him if he could have one. Mesha gave him two. The man took the cigarettes and insisted on taking Mesha's heavy backpack and carrying it for him. Mesha was suspicious and asked the man if he was going to run away with it. "No," the man replied. "You gave me not one, but two cigarettes. For that, I'd carry your bag to Mt Everest."'

We laughed and as we did, Nadia reached for her suitcase to get something from it. She leaned into it and the bottom of her baggy T-shirt flopped forward.

'Nadia, your stomach's so big!' Atka remarked.

Nadia laughed and waved her hand, 'I know, all my weight goes on to my stomach, but my legs stay skinny, like chicken legs.'

Atka stared at her for a few moments longer. I was halfway out the door and blew a kiss to the girls. 'See you soon. Don't go anywhere without me.'

I was so happy that day and couldn't wait to get back to my sisters. I raced home straight after my geography test.

'Hello, I'm back,' I yelled as I opened the door. I could hear the girls' voices in the bedroom so I hurried in.

Atka was standing by the window, with a grave expression on her face. 'How could you let this happen?' She was looking at Nadia, who was sitting on the mattress, staring at the floor.

Lela was leaning against the wall and looked furious. She said she couldn't believe how irresponsible Nadia had been.

'What's happened?' I asked, not having any idea what they were talking about.

'I took Nadia to see a doctor,' Atka explained, leaning her head against the window frame. 'She's five months pregnant!'

'What?' I said. 'How could you be pregnant?' I was shocked.

'That's what I want to know too.' Atka was biting her lip. 'You're only a child yourself,' she said, turning to Nadia. 'What were you thinking?! How do you think you're going to look after a baby?'

Lela kept repeating how disappointed she was with Nadia for letting this happen.

I couldn't believe what she'd done.

'I'll cope. I'll find a way,' Nadia said. She was unbelievably calm.

'What about the father? Does he know?'

'I'll talk to him,' she said. 'I'll figure it out . . .'

'I don't know how you're going to do this on your own. I haven't even got any money to give you. I spent it all at the doctor's this morning.' Atka raised her arms in despair.

For the rest of the afternoon we sat trying to work out what we could do. Undoubtedly, this couldn't have happened at a worse time. The shock of the situation was starting to sink in but that didn't make it any easier to accept. We knew we had to tell Danica and so, late in the afternoon, we went to see her.

She was stunned but, to my surprise, wasn't angry. She talked to Nadia for a while and told us she had a friend who worked for a Catholic charity, who might be able to help. I overheard Atka thanking Danica for all her help, when they were alone together in the living room. I had a knot in my stomach. Nadia was so young. Having a baby wasn't only going to be difficult financially, it was also shameful. The only boy I knew whose mother was unmarried was always picked on and called names. All the neighbours looked down on his mother. Overnight, Nadia's life had changed for ever.

We cried and talked more and by evening managed to calm down a bit. Nadia started making dinner for all of us and Atka and I went for a walk to the school, talking along the way. It was good to get out of the house.

'Hana, it makes me so proud to see how well you're doing at school,' she said. 'I know I don't have to worry about you. Keep on studying hard.'

'I will, Atka. I definitely will.' In all this madness that was the only thing I thought I could do.

We were nearing the school gate when Atka asked, 'Do you remember the promise we made to each other?'

I nodded. I thought about it every day.

'I want you to keep it, stay brave,' she said and pressed my arm. It meant so much to me that she remembered. We made our way back to the girls' house. Dinner was ready and we ate it on our laps.

It was mid-morning the next day. Outside, the taxi honked its horn but the three of us kept hugging Atka, reluctant to release her. Finally, she said, 'I have to go or he'll drive off.' She wiped her tears away. It was hard to believe that she would soon be back in Sarajevo. I wished she could stay.

'I have your letters,' she said, pressing her hand against the handbag hanging from her shoulder. She walked over to Nadia. 'Please, look after yourself,' she tucked Nadia's hair behind her ear. 'Everything will be fine.'

Tears were rolling down Nadia's face. We watched the taxi drive off. Once it turned the corner, I ran upstairs into the bedroom and buried my face under my pillow. I started sobbing and didn't even care any more if anyone heard me. I felt so angry and powerless.

Some time later, Andrea came over and put her arm on my shoulder. 'Hana, don't cry, you'll see Atka again,' she said, 'and Nadia will be fine too. I'm sure Mum will be able to help.' I felt so alone, but Andrea kept on talking to me. Eventually, I managed to lift my head from under the pillow. The room looked hazy.

'I have a good idea,' Andrea said, sitting next to me on the bed. 'When the war is over, I'll come and visit you in Sarajevo and meet all your brothers and sisters.'

I sat up and smiled at her suggestion. 'That would be wonderful,' I said, and took a deep breath.

Coming and Going

Atka

Pisak was a quiet village spread across a steep, rocky bay. It was hard to comprehend that war was raging just a couple of hours' drive from this idyllic and peaceful place. For two days I'd been staying with Seyo, waiting anxiously for Andrew and Gary to return from Mostar, so that we could go back to Sarajevo. I hated not knowing what was happening with my family.

Seyo's house sat perched above the village, overlooking the sea and the lovely white stone houses. The turquoise hue of the Adriatic reminded me of long summer holidays, when all of us, smeared in Coppertone sunscreen, spent entire days jumping off the jetty and swimming in the warm water. But now the sea held no attraction for me. I didn't even want to swim.

'You look as though all your ships have been sunk,' Seyo looked at me. He was well into his forties but with his athletic build and sun-bleached hair, he looked much younger.

'That's just how I feel.' I broke a small branch from a rosemary bush in the courtyard and started tearing off its tiny leaves. We heard the sound of cars and the two of us walked out into the little lane, which ran alongside an old olive grove.

'Here they come,' he said. My heart leapt when I saw Andrew and Gary arriving in their ancient, dusty Range Rover. I was so relieved to see them back safely. Following behind was a large white armoured car, which looked ridiculously out of place in the narrow lane. The cars stopped in front of us and the doors were flung open. Andrew and Gary scrambled out of their car and Patrick, a French photojournalist, jumped out of the armoured vehicle. With him was a somewhat dishevelled-looking man, dressed in a crumpled white shirt. I hadn't seen him before.

'Fucking brilliant!' the man exclaimed in a strong English accent, raising Patrick's arm triumphantly. He shook hands with Andrew and Gary, with a jubilant look on his face. They were all laughing and congratulating each other, while Seyo and I looked at them, eager to find out what had happened.

Andrew came towards me and hugged me, before introducing me to the man. His name was Laurie. He had a trimmed grey goatee and wrinkles around his eyes. I noticed a large tattoo of a dragon on his forearm and the words *Love* and *Hate* on the knuckles of his hands.

We sat down in the courtyard and Seyo's wife offered everyone a shot of grape brandy.

'Fuck, Mostar was intense,' Gary looked at us shaking his head. 'There's so much street fighting; the front line changes from street to street. We didn't know where to run or where to look for cover. Just as well we stumbled across this man,' he said, toasting Laurie.

Andrew told us that Laurie was an English mercenary. Originally, he had come to Croatia to train the Croatian Army but when the war in Bosnia broke out, he was sent to Mostar to train the Croats there. Recently, when the Croats turned against the Muslims, throwing them out of their houses and attacking them, Laurie had an unexpected crisis of conscience and switched his support to the Muslims' side.

'In fury, the Croats put a price on his head. He was trapped in Mostar and, fearing for his life, pleaded with us to smuggle him out,' Andrew said.

'What?' I was aghast. 'So, he's wanted by the Croats everywhere and you brought him here?'

'Well, we couldn't just leave him. They'd have killed him.'

'They'll kill him if they find him here.' I was alarmed.

'How did you get past the roadblocks?' Seyo asked, amazed.

'It was pretty tense. We had a couple of narrow escapes at one or two of the checkpoints. Luckily, the Croats only searched our car, not Patrick's. Come on, I'll show you where we hid him.' Andrew walked to the armoured car. At the back of the vehicle, between the rear lights, was a small locker.

'This is where the spare fuel tank was,' Andrew said, pulling open the door of the locker and pointing to the empty space. The area wasn't much bigger than a suitcase.

'We took the tank out and Laurie squeezed in there for the whole trip. We got him out just before we reached Pisak.'

Leaning down to examine the space, Seyo said, 'Fuck, you would've been arrested if the Croats had caught you. I'd hate to think what they would've done to you if they'd discovered what you were doing. You're all crazy.'

That evening we tried to think of ways to get Laurie safely away. Italy was close and Andrew suggested that Laurie could sail across the Adriatic by night but Laurie was no sailor and his chances of being intercepted and arrested by the coastguard were high. Not knowing what else to do, we accepted Seyo's offer to hide Laurie at his house but none of us wanted to endanger Seyo and his family for longer than necessary. The next day we noticed a 'Wanted' sign matching Laurie's description plastered on one of the lampposts in the area, so we kept a very low profile. Two days later, a colleague of Andrew and Gary's came to Pisak and offered to drive Laurie to the British Embassy in Zagreb. We were all relieved when he left.

Andrew and Gary were on assignment in Mostar. They had

to leave every day at the crack of dawn and returned to Pisak at night, filthy and exhausted, never quite knowing if they'd find anyone to take their films out in time to meet their deadlines. I knew I had to wait for Andrew to finish his assignment but the anguish of waiting for him and being away from home was driving me out of my mind. Now I began to understand how difficult it was for people who had had to leave their homes and had no contact with their loved ones. I couldn't eat or sleep and was glad when we flew back to Sarajevo at the end of the week. We took two large bags of food for my family with us.

Enticed by the sun, my pale, skinny siblings were playing outside and they jumped up and down when they saw Andrew and me arrive. They helped us to unload the bags from the car and we all went inside. I couldn't stop hugging and kissing them and was grateful that they were all still alive. With the money I'd given them before I'd left, they'd been able to buy firewood for cooking and there was still some left. We sat down in the living room while Grandma made coffee and I told them about my trip.

'I took lots of photos of the girls in Zagreb. Have a look.' I passed the black and white photos around, which triggered an outbreak of tears. Grandma stared at each photo for a long time before passing them on, one by one, to the others.

Nadia's pregnancy wasn't obvious from the photographs and I didn't mention anything in front of the children. I knew that Grandma would be mortified and expected my parents to be angry too. I decided to tell Mum and Dad in private. Later, as we were about to leave, I signalled to Andrew to wait for me in the car.

'I could be a while,' I warned him.

'It's fine, take your time.' He said goodbye to everyone and then wished me luck. Janna, Tarik and the twins walked him out but Selma sat on the couch, frowning and squeezing her hands between her knees.

I went over to her and whispered, 'Selma, what's wrong?'

'You're always with that foreign journalist.'

I looked at her sad brown eyes. 'But he helped me to go and see our sisters. Look, they've sent you a letter.' I handed her the envelope and ruffled her hair. She tore it open and started reading.

I asked Mum and Dad to come to Grandma's room and I closed the door behind us.

'You need to read this,' I said, handing them the letter from Nadia. I waited for their frantic and angry reaction. Mum looked furious when she'd finished reading and buried her head in her hands.

Dad put his arm around her and said, 'Congratulations, you're going to be a grandmother.'

I looked at him in disbelief. His reaction surprised me.

'Dad, aren't you worried? She's only sixteen and a refugee. The father of the child's not interested. What's going to happen to her?' I demanded.

'I'm just trying to make light of the situation. What do you expect me to do?' Dad raised his voice. 'What can I do from here?' He pressed his hands against his chest. 'Look at all the people dying around us. Nadia's baby is a new life.' His eyes filled with tears.

Mum was crying. Every now and then one of the children peeped through the door and asked what was happening.

'Psst . . . we're talking.' I put my finger to my mouth. Trying to console Mum, I told them a friend of Danica's worked for a charity organisation and might be able to help Nadia.

We sat in the room for some time. No one said anything.

Dad was just breathing heavily. I stared at them and then sighed, looking down at the floor. It was obvious they were not going to discuss it any further and, after a while, not knowing what else to do, I said I had to go to work.

I cried in the car.

'I hate what's happening to us,' I said bitterly to Andrew. 'If it weren't for all this, Nadia would be at school and my uncles would still be alive. I'm so angry . . .'

'This fucking war,' Andrew said and banged his fist against the steering wheel. We drove away.

All I could do to help my family was keep working and earning money. The next day, I worked for an American journalist who interviewed a Bosnian civilian man who had been captured by the Serbs and recently released through a prisoner exchange. He recounted his horrific experiences at the hands of the Serbs in one of their concentration camps in northern Bosnia. He showed us burn marks and scars of the wounds that had been inflicted on him. He didn't know where his wife and family were and fought back the tears while he talked about them. 'I live in hope, because I've got nothing else left,' he said at the end of the interview.

I admired his strength – after everything he'd been through he still had hope. In the face of his horrors, my family's situation didn't seem so grim.

Within a week the shock of Nadia's pregnancy had eased. Even Grandma, who was initially angry and ashamed, said it was, after all, God's will.

Andrew and I were working in town one afternoon, when we heard someone calling from across the road. A man with a droopy moustache waved and ran towards us. It was Vedran, the cellist.

'Hello, Andrew, my friend,' he said.

'Hi, Vedran,' Andrew shook his hand before introducing me to him.

'You've been here for too long,' Vedran said to Andrew with a wry grin.

'Yes, you're right,' Andrew replied, 'I almost feel at home here.'

Vedran told us that he'd been invited to play at a concert abroad and that the UN had agreed to help him get out of the city.

'I don't need a visa and the UN can take me, the biggest problem's getting a new passport,' Vedran laughed and, amused, pointed to the documents he was carrying.

'It's probably the most worthless passport in the world at the moment, yet it's so difficult to get one,' I said.

'Why? It's just a passport,' Andrew remarked.

'Well . . .' I started to explain, 'first, you need to get proof of address verified by the Ministry of Internal Affairs, which is in that part of town,' I said, pointing down the main street. 'That can take at least a week in peace time, so you can imagine how long it takes now . . . And then you need to get a birth certificate which must be less than six months old. You get that from this place here,' I said, indicating the building behind us, 'which is often closed now because of the war. And that's only the start of it . . .'

'What's with this country's obsession with paperwork?' Andrew asked. 'Can't they speed it up for you, Vedran? You're famous!' he said.

Vedran shook his head, with a resigned look on his face.

'Do you want to see my passport photo?' he asked, showing us a very revealing Polaroid photo of himself. It was very funny.

We chatted with Vedran for a while. A passerby recognised

him and stopped to talk. Andrew and I wished him luck with
his passport then headed back to the hotel.

I'd heard about the existence of an ammunition factory in
the city and I organised a permit for Andrew to do a story about
it. Due to the secretive nature of the factory, we were told to
wait at the back of the Holiday Inn, where someone from the
Bosnian Army would pick us up.

While we waited we discussed how, as the war progressed, small
criminals had risen quickly through the ranks of the Bosnian
Army. Some of them were now running and orchestrating their
own military operations, completely disobeying and ignoring
government orders.

'What do you know about Caco?' Andrew asked me.

'He's a scary man with a shady past,' I replied. Caco was
now a commander in the Bosnian Army. In the last few weeks,
soldiers under his command had started patrolling the town,
picking up civilians and draft dodgers and forcing them to dig
trenches at the front line.

'But, if it weren't for individuals like him, I don't know what
would've happened to us. They were our only means of defence
when the Serbs first attacked.'

'This place is like the Wild West,' Andrew commented.

'No, it's worse. You've heard my friends say that the Wild
West is Disneyland compared to this.'

A maroon VW Golf drove towards us. An unshaven soldier
with a ponytail and Ray-Ban sunglasses jumped out of the car.

'Are you Atka?' he asked.

'Yes.' I replied. 'And this is Andrew. He's the photojournalist
who'll do the story.'

The man greeted Andrew and asked us to get into the back
of the car.

'You'll need to be blindfolded,' the driver said.

'Why? Are you joking?' I asked.

'No, it's for security.' The driver reached into the glove box for a couple of pieces of black fabric and the soldier asked us to lean forward. Andrew and I giggled and the soldier apologised, saying that he agreed it was ridiculous to blindfold us, but he was just following orders. He tied the fabric tightly around Andrew's eyes and then around mine. I heard the engine starting.

'This is hilarious,' Andrew said, and I felt his hand reaching for mine.

They drove us around for some time and I tried to work out where they could possibly be taking us. I heard shots in the distance and ducked down, gripping Andrew's hand.

'What's happening?' I shouted. One of them told me not to worry and that we were seconds from our destination. We stopped and they led us out of the car. When they removed our blindfolds I recognised the courtyard of the building to which we had been brought. We were literally three hundred metres down the road from the Holiday Inn. Andrew and I exchanged looks but didn't say anything. The solider led us into what seemed to be a workshop, about the size of a classroom. It was not the large factory that we'd expected. The strong smell, which reminded me of nail polish remover, was overwhelming. A bald man in a blue coat welcomed us and introduced us to three other men, all qualified bomb technicians.

'Where do you get the gunpowder to build your ammunition?' I translated Andrew's question.

'We make all the bullets, grenades and mortars from the Serbs' unexploded weapons. Because of the arms embargo we have no supplies of our own,' one of the men explained.

'My cousin works in one of your factories. He lost three fingers while defusing a hand grenade a few months ago,' I said. The bald man nodded. He'd heard about the accident.

'Yes, we did have a few mishaps at the beginning, but with experience we're improving,' he remarked, wiping the sweat from his forehead.

'It's a dangerous job, I take my hat off to you,' Andrew said.

'It's not easy, my friend. One has to have nerves of steel.'

The man tapped Andrew on the back and showed us the small wooden boxes packed with ammunition that they had manufactured. It was a pitiful amount but it was all they could produce. There were a few other ammunition factories in the city but we were told that this one was the largest. I understood now why my brother was equipped with only three bullets each time he left for the front line. We stayed for half an hour longer while Andrew took some more photos.

'Did you see what they've got to work with? There's nothing there,' Andrew said when we were dropped back to the hotel. 'Given the few arms and weapons you guys have, it's a miracle the city is still holding out.'

Later that afternoon Andrew and I drove down the main road to the new part of town. The road was under frequent and indiscriminate sniper fire and every time we drove this way I was frozen with fear, expecting to be shot at at any moment. We spent a couple of hours with a man who worked for one of the daily newspapers. I dreaded the drive back. As always, Andrew put his foot flat to the floor, in the hope that the faster we drove the harder it would be for the Serbs to hit us. My palms were sweating and I felt my heart thumping as we sped along. Suddenly, the car came to a halt.

I looked at Andrew, terrified that he'd been shot.

He turned to me. 'Will you marry me?' he asked.

That was the last thing that I'd expected to hear. 'What?' I yelled. 'Yes, I will! Just get us the hell out of here before we get shot.'

He grinned and, grabbing the steering wheel, drove us back to the hotel.

As soon as he stopped the car, I shoved him on the shoulder and shouted, 'What the fuck were you thinking, you idiot?!' I was furious and shaking with fear. 'You stopped the car in the middle of Snipers' Alley! You could have got us both killed!'

'I know, but it was worth it.' Smiling, he looked at me. I couldn't resist his grin and we both started laughing.

I loved Andrew and I wanted to be with him. But then the sobering reality hit me. 'Andrew,' I said, 'do you have any idea what you're getting yourself into? I'm a Bosnian and Bosnia's future is looking pretty grim . . .'

'Yes, I know all that, but none of it matters,' he replied. 'All I want is you and for us to be together for the rest of our lives, however long they may be.' He looked at my hand and took off the ring that Grandma had given me.

'We can't waste any time, I'm marrying you now.' He put the ring back on my finger and we promised to love each other for ever.

The main Bosnian TV station was a long, multi-storey concrete building. Its walls were now wrecked and full of large deep holes. Andrew and I walked through the security entrance into the foreign press satellite communications centre. The place was teeming with journalists, all speaking in different languages. We waited for a while, until one of the satellite phones became available. Andrew talked to his agency in Paris and then to his parents in New Zealand. I made a quick call to my sisters.

'How are they?' Andrew asked after I hung up.

'I talked to Lela. She's taking good care of Nadia and I reassured them that the family has accepted Nadia's situation. What about your parents?'

'They're all right.' Andrew lit a cigarette. 'My father has finished his chemotherapy.'

'Does that mean he's cured?' I was glad for him.

'Not really,' he replied. 'His illness is terminal but he's feeling stronger now and is able to travel. I'm going to meet them in Hawaii next month.'

'Are you leaving?' I was surprised. It was the first time I'd heard about it and my heart sank.

'Yes I am, but only for a short time,' he said. 'My father has organised for my brother and me to sail in the Transpac. That's a yacht race from Los Angeles to Hawaii and my parents will meet me at the finish.'

I didn't know what to say. A couple of journalists were waiting to use the phone and so Andrew and I moved away from the desk.

'If we can organise it, I'd love you to come with me,' Andrew said.

'What? All the way to America?' I was taken aback.

'Yes, I'd like you to meet my parents. I don't know how much time my father has left.'

'It would be nice to meet them but you know how difficult it is for Bosnians to go anywhere . . . I'll never get a visa and I can't afford a ticket anyway.'

'We can only try and don't worry about the ticket,' he replied.

'I'm still not sure. My family will have no money without me.'

'Don't worry, we'll only be gone for three weeks and we'll make sure they've got enough food and money to last them while we're away.'

As we were leaving the centre, Andrew pointed to a large white wall where foreign journalists had written numerous messages. Although I'd seen the wall before, I'd never stopped to read what was written there. Some messages were cynical and others were messages of hope. He pointed to a particularly banal one *It's been real, it's been fun, let's have peace for everyone.*

'Where is yours?' I asked.

'Here,' he said and showed me. He'd written *No war, no work.* 'That's much closer to the truth, don't you think?'

I thought his message blunt, but I admired his honesty.

Afterwards, we drove to see my family to tell them about the phone conversation with the girls in Zagreb. When we arrived at the house I was alarmed to see a crowd gathered in our courtyard. Mesha was there, furiously kicking the front wall. Fearing the worst, I rushed towards him.

'What's happened?!' I shouted.

'Fudo and Feris were killed by a sniper early this morning,' one of the neighbours said, enraged.

'What!' I couldn't believe it. I didn't know Feris well but Fudo was one of Mesha's good friends. The two of them had been in the trenches together.

'Oh, Mesha . . .' I tried to hug him but he didn't want to look at me.

'Fuck this life,' Mesha said, furious. 'Atka, I watched them die.' He kept kicking the wall. Grandma brought him a glass of sugared water to calm him down. He was shaking his head. 'His poor wife and their little daughter. She's only three.' Mesha stared at the ground and it took a while before he was able to speak again. 'We were on duty this morning,' he said, 'when we noticed a light in an abandoned house, you know, in no-man's-land . . .'

I listened, stunned.

'The house was only a few metres away from our trench and Fudo crawled there to have a look. He shouted back to us that he'd found an extension cord and was crawling back with it, so that we could plug our radio in, when a sniper shot him.' Mesha was distractedly pacing up and down.

'And then Feris jumped out to help him but the fuckers shot him in the head.' Mesha was crying. 'I tried to follow but the others held me back. They were only a few metres away from us but we couldn't get to them. There was nothing we could do . . .'

It wasn't until a few hours later, in the cold light of the morning, that Mesha and the others found some hooked steel rods and were able to drag their dead friends back into the trenches.

'Fudo always said, "Fuck this war. You fight only to end up under a goal post,"' Mesha said. 'It's as though he knew what was going to happen.'

The next day they buried Fudo in the soccer stadium, which had now become a cemetery.

The increasingly warm June weather and the reopening of a few cafés in town lifted our spirits. Despite the risk, more and more people were out on the streets strolling in the sun, or sitting in the cafés enjoying their weak coffees, cordials and watered-down beers which were the only drinks available. Just sitting at the tables made life seem more normal. Some of the cafés stayed open in the evenings and sometimes Andrew and I caught up with my friends there. We sat and talked in the candle-lit gardens, which were heady with the scent of flowering blossoms. Occasionally it was so tranquil that sometimes it was hard to grasp the fact that we were still trapped in a siege. My friends liked Andrew, not only because he was my boyfriend but because he knew the history of our country and understood us so well. I'd only told Samra that we were engaged.

For the next two weeks I worked for various journalists who

covered different stories. Some of them interviewed doctors, firemen, soldiers and army officials while others just wanted to record the lives of ordinary people. There were always one or two journalists who came to Sarajevo briefly and they were more interested in showing that they'd been in the midst of the war rather than reporting on it. When I worked with these people, I felt more like a tour guide than an interpreter. But because they paid me well, I didn't mind.

Most of the time when Andrew was on assignment for magazines, he worked with the magazine writers and I translated for them. While Andrew was covering a story for *Time* magazine one day we met a Palestinian doctor. He'd been married to a Sarajevan for many years and when the war started, he had refused to leave. While we were talking to him, a wounded man was brought in. The doctor rushed to his aid. We stood there watching him remove a bullet from the man's back without the help of anaesthetics or painkillers. Andrew took photos. The man's screams were unbearable and I had to leave the room.

We also met a man whose baby boy had died of meningitis. He lived on the other side of the runway, under the slopes of Mt Igman. When the baby became sick, he endeavoured to carry him across the runway and into the city to the hospital. Three nights in a row he tried but every night he was turned back by the UN forces patrolling the airport. On the fourth night he managed to cross but by the time he got to the hospital it was too late. The baby had died.

On Andrew's assignment for the *Sunday Times*, we interviewed a young boy from my neighbourhood who had joined the Bosnian Army. He was only thirteen but because he was unusually tall, no one had checked his age when he enlisted. His demeanour was more akin to that of an older man. Before the war I used to see him playing marbles with the other children in the schoolyard and it was horrifying to find him in a trench.

'You're so young, why did you decide to join the army?' the writer asked.

'I wanted to fight,' the boy replied.

'What about your parents? Why did they allow it? Aren't they worried about you?'

'My father's dead and my mother's very sick. Of course she worries but she knows that I'm in danger anyway, wherever I am. At least on duty, I get a meal every day and when I go home I take some of my food to her.' He scratched his chin.

Encouraged by the other soldiers around us, the boy showed us the ease with which he handled his rifle.

'Have you ever shot anyone?' we asked.

'I don't know for sure,' the boy shrugged his shoulders, 'but I've seen plenty of people being shot.'

We found his commanding officer and the writer questioned the morality of this unusual situation but the officer cleverly avoided giving any straight answers and in the end we gave up. As I walked towards the door he said to me in Bosnian, 'These foreigners are questioning my morality? What about the morality of the world, sitting by, watching us being slaughtered?'

I shrugged my shoulders and raised my eyebrows. I didn't know what to say.

'Imagine the long-term effects this war will have on everyone, especially the children. Quite aside from all the damage caused by malnutrition,' Andrew said afterwards, as we drove back to the Holiday Inn.

'Everyone has lost someone or something. There's so much hurt and hatred now,' I said with sorrow, staring blankly out of the window. 'I don't know how we can ever forget what's been done to us.'

'It'll probably take a generation or two,' the writer remarked, matter-of-factly.

Her words upset me. I wasn't angry with her but it was frightening to think that, even if we did survive, it could take more than a lifetime to recover.

One morning, Gary came to Andrew's room.

'Dudes, I don't think I can go anywhere today,' he said, with a hint of panic in his voice.

'Why, what's happened?' we asked.

'I've lost my lucky charm. It's a silver bracelet and I've been wearing it since Cambodia. I can't find it anywhere,' he frowned, looking somewhat lost.

I understood his angst. I always carried the piece of paper that Grandma had prayed over in my pocket. Many of my friends and family carried their own charms too, and some, who'd never been religious, even started going to mosques or attending church.

'Oh, come on Gary, don't worry about it too much,' Andrew tried to reassure him. But Gary couldn't keep still and decided to go back to his room to look for it again.

'My mother always prays to St Anthony when she loses things, try him.' Andrew followed Gary to the door.

'I hope he finds it,' I said, showing Andrew what Grandma had given me.

'I don't believe in all that superstitious stuff,' he said, turning on the portable gas stove.

'Really?' I looked at him. 'Then why do you start every day by saying, "Today is not a good day to die"? Isn't that for good luck?'

'Hmm, I suppose it is. I'd never thought of it that way,' he replied.

'I don't think it's a matter of superstition. We all need something to believe in. Look, I'll show you. Come and have a look at this.'

I opened the window. A sniper was shooting at a tall apartment building nearby.

'Despite the shooting, every day that same woman pegs nappies on the line outside her window. It doesn't make sense to continue to do it but she obviously believes in something.'

'I see your point,' Andrew said, lighting a cigarette.

A few minutes later, Gary came back smiling. He'd found his lucky charm. 'I'm never taking it off again,' he said, turning the bracelet on his wrist.

We'd just sat down to drink the tea that Andrew had made, when there was a firm knock on the door. Our friend Ariane was leaving for Paris and had come to say goodbye.

'Atka, you can have this.' She handed me a bag full of face creams and toiletries. I thanked her and hugged her.

'I'll miss you and your crazy Arab French music,' I said. Although she had been quite reserved when we'd first met, the two of us had become friends.

Ariane embraced Gary and Andrew. She looked so little next to the two of them.

'Take care, you guys, and if I don't see you in Paris, I'll see you back here on my next assignment.' Holding back her tears, she left the room.

'I love her fiery spirit. The Holiday Inn won't be the same without her,' Gary remarked.

That night, just before curfew, Andrew and I made our usual trip to collect petrol from the Ukrainian soldier. Up until now, we'd been trading in films and in American dollars, but this evening the Ukrainian demanded that from now on we were to bring him porn magazines.

'Where are we going to find those?' I said to Andrew, while he was loading the jerry cans into the boot.

'I have no idea,' he was bemused, 'but I'm sure we'll think of something.'

The next morning we searched through the trashed and empty rooms on the southern side of the hotel, hoping to find some magazines. All the rooms on that side were facing Mt Trebevic, and the two of us, fearing that the Serb snipers might spot us, ducked down while looking through the debris.

'This is stupid. We could get shot and we probably won't find anything here anyway,' I said.

'Perhaps not, but we really need the petrol, so let's look for a bit longer,' Andrew replied.

We climbed the stairs to another floor and noticed a small storage room, full of dusty brushes and buckets. I looked into the dingy room and in the corner of one of the bottom shelves, saw a stack of magazines. I carried them out to the daylight.

'Hey, Andrew, look at this,' I laughed, showing him a picture of a semi-naked woman on one of the covers. I glanced through the pile. 'These are *START* magazines from the seventies.'

We dusted them down.

'I can't believe these photographs,' Andrew said, flicking through the pages. 'They're graphic even by today's Western standards. I think our Ukrainian friend will be a very happy man.'

It was now mid-June. Andrew had had to go to Paris the day before to deliver his films to the agency. He'd arranged with Chris, a UN liaison officer, to put me on a flight out of the city the next day and we hoped to meet in Zagreb in a couple of days. But only hours after Andrew left, the Serbs closed the road to the airport as they often did, reducing my chances of leaving.

I didn't want to waste any time, so I went to Studio 99 to do some work.

'Have you seen this?' Hamo said, pointing angrily to a piece of paper on the desk.

He'd never been short with me before and I wondered what was wrong. I picked up the paper. It was an official report on the number of casualties in Sarajevo and I read it slowly.

'Oh my God,' I gasped. 'Look at this, thousands have been killed and wounded . . . and so many children . . . I dropped the piece of paper and looked across the room at Hamo. He was shaking his head.

'They're systematically killing us all,' he said, winding a cassette tape with his pen. 'It's only a matter of time before it's our turn.'

I sat on the edge of the desk for a few minutes, thinking about the many hospitals and graveyards in the city.

Hamo put the cassette down. 'Mesha told us that you might be going to America. When are you leaving?' He tried to sound indifferent.

'I don't know. Maybe tomorrow if the Serbs open the road,' I replied, feeling like a deserter.

'Don't forget to send us a postcard then,' Hamo remarked, sarcastically.

I snapped back at him, 'Well, what would you do if you were in my place? I want to see my sisters.' I glared at him. 'And as far as America goes, you know I'll never get a visa anyway.'

Hamo sat down. 'Don't take any notice of me, I'm just pissed off with this fucked-up life,' he said. He wished me luck and asked me to bring back some music cassettes for the studio if I could. There was not much to edit and shortly afterwards, sad and uneasy, I went to see Mayka to tell her that I might be going away.

'Why didn't you bring your boyfriend?' she asked.

'He had to go Paris to deliver his films and if I'm able to leave, I'll meet him in Zagreb.'

'It seems to me that he's your destiny, don't be surprised that you two have fallen in love in the middle of a war,' Mayka said. 'It happened to your grandfather and me during the last war,' she said with a tender look on her face.

'I know, Mayka, but it seems silly to talk about it when so many people around us are getting killed.'

'I understand. This war is hell,' she said, patting my hand. 'Don't forget to tell your boyfriend that I like him, but that you're my girl as well, and he's not allowed to steal you away.'

'Don't worry, Mayka, he won't.' I kissed her and hugged her tight. Her hair and clothes still had that faint smell of citrus and I closed my eyes for a moment.

'I'll come and see you as soon as I get back,' I promised as we made our way to the front door. There was no point mentioning anything about America to Mayka. It would only upset her. Besides, I was convinced that I'd never get a visa and even if I made it to Zagreb, I was sure I'd be back in two or three days.

'Be sensible,' Mayka advised.

'I will,' I assured her and walked down the street. I turned around and looked back at her. She was standing in the doorway, waving to me. I waved back.

The next morning, before I left home, a few friends came to see me off. It was hard to leave them. They followed me outside and Grandma splashed a glass of water behind me for good luck. She always did this before we had anything important to do, believing that water washed away all the difficulties and troubles along the way.

Having said goodbye to everyone, I kissed my little brothers and sisters and said, 'If you're good, I'll bring you back some treats.'

I was almost at the bottom of the street when I heard Tarik's shrill voice shouting after me, 'Atkaaaa, I'll be good if you'll bring me back a big chocolate.'

By the time I reached Chris's office in the Holiday Inn, I was nervous and sweaty. He told me that the road was still closed.

'Why don't you wait in the foyer for a couple of hours. The Serbs may change their minds,' he suggested.

I waited all morning but nothing happened. A tall, brash, French journalist I knew approached me and said, 'Atka, I hate seeing you sitting here like this. Come with me, I'll teach you how to abseil.' Casually blowing the smoke from his Cuban cigar, he took me by the hand. I'd seen him abseiling many times before on days when it was too dangerous to venture outside and his offer came as no surprise. He dragged a few other journalists with us and we abseiled inside from the top floor down to the atrium, four or five times. It was hilarious but I felt sick afterwards.

The road was still closed that evening and, reluctantly, I returned home. I was angry and frustrated that I had wasted an entire day of work and didn't want to say all my goodbyes again.

But the children were happy.

'Great, maybe you won't go at all,' Selma said.

Her endearing little face cheered me up. For the moment, the guns were quiet and we all sat outside in the courtyard chatting and enjoying the beautiful balmy evening, just as we used to do.

The next morning, as I was leaving for the Holiday Inn, I told Mum that if I couldn't leave straight away, I'd carry on working as usual.

The Serbs hadn't changed their minds and Gary, knowing that I was looking for work, introduced me to an American journalist who needed an interpreter for the day. We were in the atrium talking when I saw Chris running along the corridor towards me. With him was Andrew's friend David, a writer from New York.

'The road's open, you can go,' they shouted. 'Come on, we'll take you.' Before I could explain anything to the American, Chris and David had hurried me to their car.

'We'll go to the UNHCR Headquarters first. I'll try to put you in an armoured transporter there, let's hope they'll be able to take you to the airport,' Chris spoke hurriedly.

David handed me a note with his address. 'If you do make it to New York go and stay at my place.'

We drove down the back street, speeding past a few people. I saw an old woman struggling with a wheelbarrow full of jerry cans. I stared at her until we turned the corner and then she disappeared from view.

Andrew

Hana

It was a warm summer evening and I was lying down reading a book. From underneath the open bedroom window, I could hear Nadia and Danica talking quietly. Nadia had stopped working and was at home most of the time now. I laid the book on my chest and listened to them.

'I don't know how to thank you,' I heard Nadia say.

'Don't worry. The main thing is that you and your baby will have a safe place to stay.'

It sounded as though Danica's friend had found a place for Nadia and her baby at a house run by Catholic nuns. They provided accommodation and food for women refugees and young girls in situations similar to Nadia's.

'They'll take you at the end of July,' Danica said.

'Why so soon?' Nadia asked. 'The baby isn't due until September.'

'They'll want you to settle in in plenty of time. I don't know all the details but I think you can stay there for a month or two after the baby's born. My friend will talk to you about it.'

She invited Nadia to come upstairs and moments later their footsteps echoed down the passage. I ran to the bathroom and turned on the tap, not sure whether I was supposed to have overheard their conversation or not. But later Nadia told me about it as we sat at the table in the kitchen. Although she could manage at the girls' flat with the baby, she thought that being with other mothers and babies would be a valuable help to her.

It would also take some of the pressure off Lela who was the only one supporting them.

'How is Lela?' I asked.

'She's been working crazy hours and is looking after me so well. I don't know what I'd do without her.'

'Yes, she's never behind in the rent,' Danica said with approval.

I wished I could do something to contribute but the only way I could help was by being a good student so that Lela wouldn't have to worry about me as well.

'Come and feel this.' Nadia took my hand and placed it on her stomach, which was the size of a large, inflated balloon.

'I can feel a little kick,' I said, intrigued, and kept my hand pressed against her, waiting for the baby to move again.

'I think I'm having a basketball player!' Nadia joked.

'What about the baby's father? What did he say when you told him?' I asked.

Nadia lowered her eyes and Danica looked at me, shaking her head. I bit my lip and for a few seconds stared at the clock on the wall. It was ticking loudly.

'Not much,' Nadia said finally, without lifting her eyes from the table. 'Let's just say, I'll be better off without him.'

'You have us anyway,' I said, nudging her with my elbow, but I felt so sorry for her.

'Exactly!' Danica agreed, as she reached for the sugar and a mixing bowl from one of the cupboards.

It was obvious that Nadia didn't feel like talking about it and, not wanting to upset her, I turned to Danica and asked what sort of cake she was making.

'It's my roulade. Can you separate a couple of eggs for me?'

'Oh, I love your roulade,' Nadia said, 'but I have a real craving for cherry cake.' Nadia's eyes widened. 'Remember, Hana? The one that Mayka used to bake for us?'

'Of course I do.' The last time we'd been at Mayka's, she had given us a slice of her cherry cake with a glass of homemade rosewater cordial. 'It's so sad, we didn't even have a chance to say goodbye to her,' I said, wondering when we were going to see her again.

'If I'd known that we were going away for such a long time, I'd never have boarded that bus,' Nadia said with conviction, folding a table napkin over and over. Soon, she stood up, saying she was tired and hot and went to the girls' house to lie down.

After we'd made the roulade, I sat on my bed, thinking how kind and understanding Danica had been with Nadia. It was strange because she was always very strict with Andrea and me. Even the message that Atka had passed on from Mum and Dad surprised me. I'd expected harsh words and scorn from everyone but they didn't seem in the least bit angry.

At the start of the summer holidays, Andrea's grandmother went to the countryside to see her cousins and Andrea went to Germany to visit family friends. I was invited to go with her but because Germany had already taken in tens of thousands of refugees from my country, its visa requirements for Bosnians were very strict. Besides, the only documents we had were our refugee cards and we needed more than that in order to travel.

The day after Andrea left, I went to the market with Danica to help her with the shopping. The rows of market stalls were piled high with heaps of fresh fruit and vegetables. Vendors shouted to the shoppers, inviting them to their stalls. Danica and I pushed our way through the crowd, carrying our bags. She headed for the tomato stall but I was stopped by a woman selling strawberries.

'Try this,' she said, giving me one. 'They're the sweetest strawberries you'll find.'

I tasted it. 'Oh, it's delicious,' I said as I took a bite.

'Tell your mother to come and buy some,' the woman urged.

The word *mother* struck me and I felt my face going red. I wanted to tell her that Danica wasn't my mother. *My* mother was in Sarajevo. But I was too embarrassed to say anything. Instead, I ran off looking for Danica. She was at one of the stands haggling over the price of some potatoes. We continued shopping and I didn't mention anything about the strawberries or what the woman had said.

On our way home, we bumped into one of Danica's colleagues from work. We stopped to talk and Danica introduced me.

'So, this is your refugee from Bosnia,' the woman said, patting my head. 'There are so many of you in Zagreb now, I'm afraid that soon you'll outnumber us,' her tone was sarcastic.

'It's not the children's fault,' Danica replied and, complaining that her bags were heavy, cut short the conversation. The two of us continued on towards home. It was sunny outside; some of my friends were playing in the street and asked me to join them. But I didn't want to play. I shut myself in the bedroom, drew the curtains and cried.

With Andrea away, I spent most of my time in our room, reading and listening to classical music. Now that there was no schoolwork or study to do, I couldn't stop thinking about my Sarajevo. I wished that I could just close my eyes and be there. That's where I was born. That's where I belonged. Everything and everyone I loved was there. I knew I had a family but I felt like an orphan.

Sometime ago, Lela had brought me several newspapers and magazines from work. In them were special sections dedicated to stories and poems written by Bosnian refugees. Everybody's experiences were different but all shared the same thoughts. All of them felt as though they were a burden to the countries which had taken them in and longed to go home. Had they known their exile would be so lengthy and harsh they would never have left. I cut and glued some of these stories into my diary and re-read them every night.

I was glad when Andrea came home.

My Croatian teacher had given me a reading list at the end of the school year and one hot afternoon, I headed to the local library with Klaudia who wanted to come along. We met on the main street and her brothers, four-year-old twins, were with her.

'Sorry, I had to bring them. Mum and Dad are busy in the shop,' Klaudia said and rolled her eyes.

'Don't worry,' I said. I took one boy by the hand, which felt tiny in mine. I teased him that his black hair made him look like a chimney sweep. As we walked, the boys tried to break away from us but we managed to keep them under control.

'Behave, you two, or there'll be no ice cream,' Klaudia threatened.

'I used to get annoyed when I had to mind my brothers,' I said to her. 'Now I wish I could look after them every day.'

'I don't know what I'd do without my family. I'd be completely lost,' Klaudia said, pulling her little brothers closer to her.

I wanted to hear about her family's upcoming holiday to the seaside but before I could say anything she asked if we'd spoken to Atka recently.

'She called a few days ago,' I replied. 'Touch wood, my family's fine and she might be able to come and see us again soon.'

'Really?' Klaudia said.

'Yes, if she's able to get on a UN flight. But nothing's certain. I hope she can,' I said, crossing my fingers. 'Do you know what's really sad though? When Atka returned home after she saw us she took some oranges to my little brothers and they didn't even know what they were.'

'That's sad,' Klaudia said. 'I'll never complain about having to eat fruit and vegetables again. Do you have any family in other parts of Bosnia? You know, where those concentration camps are?'

'No, thank God,' I replied. The images of gaunt faces behind barbed-wire fences, filmed by foreign journalists, sent shivers down my spine. The Serbs had imprisoned, starved and tortured civilian men, both old and young, proving that they were capable of much greater evil than anyone had ever imagined.

'All those poor people . . . I can't forget the picture of one of the men. He had no shirt on and his ribs and bones were sticking out. He looked like a skeleton.' Klaudia spoke quietly, so that her brothers wouldn't hear.

'It's dreadful,' I said. 'I often wonder which of my friends' parents have joined the Serbs in the hills. I can't understand how the Serbs can do this to us.'

'I can't either. They are supposed to be Christians,' Klaudia said. 'Aren't they afraid of God's punishment?'

'They believe God is on their side.'

'He wouldn't permit such evil,' she said, 'at least not the God I believe in.'

I asked her about her faith. She told me about her love of Jesus and the importance of forgiveness.

'Is your family religious?' she asked, interested.

'No, not really,' I replied, 'but we always celebrate all the Muslim holidays because it's our tradition and culture. Grandma is our only strong believer. But since I've been away from home I've started praying every day . . .'

'The main thing's to be a good person, even if you're not religious,' Klaudia said.

We stopped to buy ice cream and afterwards talked about our school friends and holidays. When I returned home later that afternoon, I thought about our conversation and wrote in my diary.

Sooner or later, life teaches us to forgive. In my case, life taught me that fairly early on, but that doesn't matter. I'm prepared to forgive the enemy, I'm prepared to forgive everyone, just so that I can return to my own home. I hope that this will happen one day and that the enemy will understand my desire for all of us to live in peace, happiness, friendship and love, because that is the essence of human life.

'Are they here yet?' Andrea said as I looked once again through the kitchen window.

'I can't see them,' I replied.

Atka had called us unexpectedly from Split last night. She had managed to fly out of Sarajevo and was meeting Andrew at Zagreb airport this morning. They were coming to see us. I couldn't sit still and ran to the window every time I heard a car drive past. Around midday, a taxi pulled up in front of the house and a tall man got out from the front seat. He had short brown hair and was dressed in black jeans and a green shirt. Seeing this stranger I hesitated, but within seconds Atka got out of the car and I rushed out yelling, 'They're here, they're here.' Nadia and Lela raced out after me.

Atka opened her arms wide when she saw us and we all squeezed together in a tight hug. The taxi started pulling away and we moved aside to let him pass. Atka looked pale and worn out but she was bubbly.

'This is Andrew,' she introduced us.

'Great to finally meet you,' Andrew said, and hugged us as though we were his little sisters.

'Sorry, my English is not good,' I said.

Nadia looked at Atka after shyly introducing herself. 'You'll have to translate everything for me, Atka. You know I only studied Russian at school . . .'

'Don't worry, I will,' Atka laughed. 'Look how much your stomach's grown in a month! I still can't believe you're going to be a mother.'

'I'm becoming used to the idea,' Nadia said. 'What did everyone say when you told them about it?' she asked timidly.

'They were shocked at first but they told me to tell you not to worry. All they want is for you and your baby to be safe.'

We went into the girls' house, arm in arm.

'I'm so glad to see you again,' Atka said, squeezing my arm firmly. I squeezed hers back.

Once inside, Lela apologised to Andrew about the place being so small. We had very little furniture and were embarrassed that we couldn't even offer him a seat.

'Don't worry about Andrew. He doesn't mind about things like that,' Atka assured us.

'I've heard so much about you girls.' Atka translated as Andrew spoke. 'I think you're very brave.'

We smiled shyly, unsure how to answer.

'Thank you,' Nadia said, making a face. 'No one's called us brave before . . .' She cleared the mattress and asked him to sit down. But he sat on the floor to leave room for us.

We talked for hours and every so often we apologised to Andrew for not including him in the conversation, but he was quite happy just to sit and listen. Later, he offered to take us out for a drink.

The city centre came alive in summer and it was lovely to be there on this warm evening. Couples with children were strolling along the streets, licking their ice creams. The outside tables of the cafés were packed with people, chatting, smoking and sipping their drinks. The cathedral bells chimed the hour as we sat down in the garden of one of the side-street cafés.

'How long will you stay this time?' I asked.

'A day or two, I think. Andrew's parents are in America and he wants me to go with him to meet them.'

'America!' we chorused.

'Are you kidding?' Nadia asked, her jaw dropping.

'No, I'm not. I know I won't be given a visa but try telling that to Andrew,' Atka replied with a smile. 'He insists that we should go to the American Embassy tomorrow anyway.'

'Good luck,' Nadia said sarcastically.

'I doubt that they'll give you one. Everyone's sick of Bosnians,' Lela agreed.

'I know,' Atka said, tilting her head. 'But Andrew wants us to try. His father is very sick and he really wants to see him. But if I don't get a visa, we'll go back to Sarajevo and work. At least I've seen the three of you.'

A short while later, Andrew went to buy a newspaper. The moment he left, the three of us teased Atka about her handsome boyfriend.

'I'm so glad you girls like him, he's smart, honest and completely different from anyone else I've ever met before,' Atka said.

'I think someone's in love here,' Lela smiled, then started singing the chorus of a popular Bosnian love song. The four of us giggled.

'Enough about me,' Atka said, turning to Nadia. 'It's a huge weight of my shoulders to know that you can stay with the Catholic nuns. I'll help you as much as I can.'

'Has anything improved now that Sarajevo is a UN safe zone?' Nadia asked.

Atka dismissed the suggestion. 'A UN Safe zone? What a

joke. The shelling's even heavier now. The Serbs love to spite the West.'

Atka told us that more of our friends and neighbours had been killed. Although we knew that the Serbs were killing many people, hearing about the deaths of people we knew was chilling. We could easily picture their faces and imagine their families' grief.

Andrew returned with an English newspaper and spread it on the table. I knew just enough English to understand that the headline was about the failure of the latest peace plan for Bosnia.

Andrew summarised the article and Atka translated. 'Essentially, what they tried to do was divide Bosnia among the Serbs, Croats and Muslims. The Serbs were offered almost half of the territory and the remainder was to be divided between the Muslims and Croats. But the Serbs wanted more, so they rejected the plan, which is now officially dead. The fighting continues . . .'

The idea of a divided Bosnia, even after a year of war, didn't make sense. We'd always lived side by side and, for some reason, I'd imagined that when the war was over everything would be the same.

'How long has Andrew been working in Bosnia?' Lela asked, looking at Atka.

'He covered the war in Croatia, he's been to Vukovar, Dubrovnik, Knin . . .' Atka explained, 'and while it was still peaceful in Bosnia, he used to come to Sarajevo for a break.'

'I'd seen the JNA tanks amassing in the mountains surrounding Sarajevo and it was obvious to me that they were preparing to attack. But when I told people in the city about it, they laughed at me and told me that the war would never spread to Bosnia. I couldn't believe their naivety,' Andrew said and Atka translated. 'The Muslims and the Croats are victims of a well-planned aggression and without arms to defend themselves, they simply don't stand a chance.'

I'd never heard a foreigner's opinion about the war and was glad that his sympathies were with us. He was friendly and we asked him more about his work. He told us that one of the difficulties the media faced was keeping the world interested after an entire year of fighting. It seemed that only very shocking reports were making the news these days. Not long ago, his agency had asked him to provide them with some inspirational stories. The Miss Sarajevo pageant had been held recently and they wanted a story on the girl who'd won, so Atka had tracked her down. After spending a few hours with her and her family, Andrew took many photos of her in the city, even around landmarks exposed to snipers.

'She's young but very brave,' Andrew said.

It was the first time we'd heard about anything remotely normal happening in Sarajevo. Atka commented that people had accepted the fact that the war was now an everyday reality and everyone tried to get on with their lives as best they could.

It was sometime after midnight when we parted. Atka and Andrew were staying in town at the apartment of a photographer whom they'd met in Sarajevo and I went home with the girls.

The next morning, I woke up with the same feeling of anticipation I used to have before going to the seaside for our summer holidays. I jumped out of bed, threw on my clothes and rushed to the kitchen. Danica was heating some milk. A plate full of biscuits sat in the middle of the table.

'I thought you'd be up early! I'm just making some cocoa.'

All morning, we stayed at the house, waiting for Atka to come. There was no sign of her and we kept calling the number she'd given us but no one answered.

'You've seen the queues outside the embassies,' Danica

reminded us. 'They'll be there for hours,' she said, urging us to eat some lunch.

After eating, Nadia and I sat at the kitchen table, playing a game of Jacks and Lela went to work. It was just after three o'clock when Atka and Andrew finally arrived.

'We were starting to think that you'd forgotten us,' Nadia joked when they came inside.

As Danica had suspected, the two of them had spent the entire morning waiting in the queue at the embassy. When Atka's turn had come, the woman in charge of visas demanded, in a patronising and unpleasant manner, to see Atka's latest bank statement and show her some proof that she was not intending to seek refugee asylum in America.

'Andrew tried to explain to her that we'd just come out of a war zone, where there were no banks operating, and that he'll be paying for my trip, but was told rudely not to interfere and to step aside. You should've seen the way the woman treated me. It was so humiliating and, of course, she rejected my application without even looking at it,' Atka said.

'From what I've heard, most people queue for hours and have to return the next day,' Danica said. 'I'm surprised you even managed to talk to anyone.'

'So, you're not going?'

'Well,' Atka said, 'Andrew wasn't going to give up, so when we returned to the apartment, he called our friend Susan in New York to ask her for help. She told us to give her half an hour and then go back to the embassy. I have no idea what she did or what she told them, but the same woman at the embassy who had refused me the first time, stamped a visa on my passport without any questions and, smiling, told me to enjoy my trip.' Atka looked bemused. 'I had no idea that Susan was a woman of such influence and I'm still shocked that I'm actually able to go.'

'I can't believe this. First, you couldn't even get out of Sarajevo and now you're going all the way to America,' Nadia remarked.

'I know. I was absolutely sure I'd be going straight back to Sarajevo. I can't even think straight,' Atka said.

But Andrew was delighted.

'So, Atka, what's the plan?' Nadia asked.

'I don't know exactly,' Atka said, turning to Andrew. She asked him something in English.

'Andrew's booked flights for us,' she explained nervously. 'We have to fly to Split tomorrow and then catch a flight to New York via Rome the day after.'

'But I thought Andrew's parents were in Hawaii. Why are you going to New York?' I asked.

'Andrew has to meet some of the editors of the magazines he's working for.'

'Lucky you! And then?'

'Andrew's taking part in a yacht race from Los Angeles to Hawaii which takes about ten days . . . So, he'll fly to Los Angeles and while he's racing, I guess I'll go and see Merima and the boys in Florida. But I honestly didn't think I'd be going. I don't even have their address. I'll need to track them down somehow . . .'

'Atka, we've got their address and phone number,' Nadia exclaimed. 'I'll get them for you.'

'Oh,' Atka looked confused.

'They'll be so surprised to see you,' I said happily. 'Give them hugs from us.'

'So, when will you be back?' I wanted to know.

Atka checked with Andrew, then said, 'We should be back in three weeks and I'll definitely come and see you before I go back to Sarajevo.'

I'd often dreamt about going to America. I loved their music and movies and it seemed that everything there was brightly coloured and prosperous. I asked Atka if she could bring back some notebooks and pens.

We went to the movies that night. Afterwards, as we walked to the main square Atka and Andrew started singing, '*Start spreading the news, I'm leaving today, I want to be a part of it, New York, New York . . .*'

'I've never heard that song, who sings it?' I asked.

'Frank Sinatra,' Andrew replied. 'Come on, I'll teach you the words.'

We were all in a good mood and very cheerful. Feeling more comfortable with Andrew, I asked him why he had become a photojournalist.

'I always wanted to be in places where history is being made,' Andrew replied. 'For me, photojournalism is the best way to tell a story.'

'You must be good if your photos are published in *Time* magazine,' I said, with admiration.

'I love my job,' he said, 'but, to be honest, it's a horrible industry to be in. It's very cut-throat and competitive. And, though you're bringing stories to the world from places that are dangerous, essentially you're making a living out of people's misery. I'm not sure that I like what I'm becoming.'

He seemed very successful and I wasn't quite sure what he meant.

Andrew looked at Atka and winked at her. They were so happy and it was comforting to be with them. I wished they could stay.

'Take photos when you're in Florida, so we can see what Merima, Mirza and Haris look like now,' I said to Atka when we said goodbye that night.

She bit her lip. 'If it weren't for Andrew I wouldn't be going.

It's hard to leave you and I worry about our family. They have no means of buying food without me and I just want to get back as soon as possible.'

They left early the next morning and Nadia said she was sure that the three weeks would soon fly by.

Far Away

Atka

I woke up in the middle of the night, frightened and in a cold sweat. It took a moment before I realised that I was in Split. Andrew was asleep beside me and through the open door I could hear the waves lapping on the beach. I went outside to the terrace for a cigarette. It made me feel sick.

'Are you all right?' I heard Andrew call from the room.

'I don't think so . . .'

He came out to the terrace. 'What's the matter?'

'Oh, I don't know where to start . . . I'm so worried about my sisters who have so much on their plate. I didn't even tell them that you asked me to marry you. It didn't seem fair. And then I feel dreadful for leaving everyone in Sarajevo. I feel as though I've walked out on everyone. I'd never expected that I'd actually be going to America with you. I don't know what to do . . .' I looked at him, hoping for an answer.

'Your sisters are very sensible, they're managing just fine. And as far as your family goes, even if we were in Sarajevo, we couldn't stop them from being shot . . . nobody can.' He hugged me.

'At least when I'm there I know exactly what's happening. Now I have no way of knowing . . .'

'Atka, I know three weeks seems like ages, but they've survived all this time . . .'

We stayed up a bit longer on the terrace, talking. In the

morning, I felt no better and was sick on the way to the airport.
We had to stop the car.

'I've been feeling like this for a few days,' I said. Concerned,
I looked at Andrew. 'I don't think it's just my kidney . . . I'm
worried that I might be pregnant.'

He gripped my hand. 'Well, there's only one way to find out.
As soon as we get to Rome we'll get a pregnancy test kit from
a pharmacy,' he said calmly.

A journalist I had worked for in Sarajevo lived in Rome and
we stayed the night at her place. When at last we had a minute
alone, we raced to the bathroom to do the test. Nervously, we
stared at it until two pink lines appeared in the tiny square
window.

'What does that mean?' I asked Andrew who was reading the
instruction leaflet.

'Two lines? That's positive.'

'Positive!?' Taken aback, I slumped on to the edge of the bath.
Shit! How are we going to have a baby in a war? I thought. *I'm so
stupid.* I was furious with myself. But before I could voice my
worries, Andrew came and sat next to me, wrapping his arms
around me. I lay my head on his shoulder.

'As if things weren't complicated enough already,' I said,
unsure of what to do.

'You have to stop worrying. You and I are in this together and
we'll just make it work,' he tried to calm me down.

'I don't know how . . . this is so unplanned. The war's
still going, with no sign of it ending and I need to work . . .
I want to finish my degree,' I said, angrily. 'I'm so stupid . . .
and such a hypocrite at that. I was lecturing Nadia and now
look at me!'

'But we love each other. That's all that matters,' he said.

'I know, I love you too. But it's nothing to do with that.

You don't know what it's like to be a Bosnian. Things always go from bad to worse for us. I warned you that it would be complicated,' I said, shaking my head.

'Only if we make it so,' Andrew replied. 'Maybe we could rent a house in Pisak, which we could use as a base and your sisters could live there too.'

'Hmm . . . maybe that could be an option. But you know I need to be in Sarajevo to work and support the family.'

'Well,' Andrew looked at me, 'we can't really plan anything now. You know how quickly things can change. Let's see what the situation is when we get back from America.'

The next morning we flew to New York. Stuck in a seat between a plump woman and Andrew, who was completely engrossed in his book, I tried to concentrate on a crossword. The scent of the woman's flowery perfume was overwhelming and I felt nauseous. I tried to breathe but soon I felt the sharp, familiar pain in my back. I groaned and closed my eyes, hoping for everything to go away.

What am I doing here? My whole life's in Sarajevo, I thought in panic. Agitated, I shook Andrew's arm. 'I want to get off the plane,' I said.

'What do you mean?' he frowned. 'We're in mid-air over the Atlantic.'

'I don't care!' I raised my voice. 'I want to get off, I want to go home.'

'It's not a bus, you know,' he replied. His brusque tone made me furious.

'How dare you say something like that! You're not sick, you're not pregnant and you haven't had to leave your family behind. You have no idea how I feel! So, fuck you.' I snapped and, grabbing a white paper bag from the seat pocket in front of me, I vomited.

'Oh, shit, what have I done to you?' I heard him say. He handed me a tissue and rubbed my back, 'I'm sorry, Atka . . .' He passed me another sick bag, then called for the stewardess to bring me a wet cloth.

'I'm sorry too,' I whispered, after wiping my face. 'I just can't stop thinking about my family. I feel so torn and my kidney's killing me . . .'

He placed a small cushion behind my head then held my hand. 'Atka, it might sound awful but right now there's nothing we can do about your family. Just try to get some rest if you can.'

Eventually, I drifted off to sleep.

We arrived in New York in the evening and I couldn't wait to get to our friend David's place to call Merima. She was flabbergasted when I told her where I was and that I'd be coming to see them soon.

The next day, after Andrew's meetings with his magazine editors, we went to see our friend Susan. She was thrilled when we appeared on her doorstep.

'We wouldn't be here without your help. Thank you,' I said. 'Who would've thought that we'd see each other in New York . . .'

We spent the entire afternoon with her, looking through the recent photos that Andrew had taken of the war. Later, she took us to the rooftop of her building. Spellbound, I looked around at the thousands of lights illuminating the city. They looked magical. I took a deep breath, thinking of my besieged city forgotten in the darkness and I clenched my teeth in an effort not to cry.

With only a couple of days in New York, Andrew was keen to show me around. We walked downtown. Tall buildings towered above us on either side of the streets. Streams of people rushed past as if caught in a rapid current at the bottom of a deep canyon. Neon lights flashed from the shop windows. Drivers noisily beeped their horns. The chaotic beat of the city mirrored the turmoil in my head. I wished I could get excited about being in the Big Apple but my heart wasn't in it. I wanted to run back home but, knowing how important it was for Andrew to see his parents, I fought the urge. Just before he flew to Los Angeles the next morning, Andrew gave me a T-shirt with *Vendetta* written across it. That was the name of the yacht he was racing on.

'I'll see you in ten days but don't panic if I'm not at the airport in Hawaii to greet you. Just wear this T-shirt and go to the hotel where my parents are staying. That way they'll recognise you and please don't worry if my father seems distant, he can be a bit shy.'

'Won't you be there to meet me?' I was startled.

'I'll try but you never know with sailing. I might get held up on the race,' he hugged me again before hurrying through the departure gate. I'd never been abroad by myself before and too intimidated to wander around such a large airport, I went straight to my gate. Two hours later, I boarded the plane to Miami.

Merima, the boys and I were so thrilled to see each other that for the first few nights we hardly slept. The three of them lived in a modestly furnished two-bedroom condominium, which was part of a large apartment block, surrounded by lush tropical plants. There were only three beds in the apartment so Merima and I shared hers.

The look of melancholy hadn't left Merima's face but she seemed to be managing. Mirza and Haris spoke English with an American accent and, dressed in brightly coloured T-shirts, shorts and caps, they looked as though they'd always lived in

Florida. They'd started school when they arrived and were now on their summer vacation.

One evening, we sat in their small back patio watching Mirza on his bike, balancing and peddling with one leg.

'Mayka would be proud of you,' I shouted to him. Encouraged, Mirza continued to show us what he could do. Merima smiled.

I turned to her. 'What do you think you'll do while you're here?' I asked, fanning myself with a magazine.

'I don't know yet. My English is improving and hopefully I'll find some work soon,' she replied, wiping the sweat from her face with her handkerchief.

'What do you think you could do?' I asked.

'I doubt that I'll able to work as a project manager as I did at home, but I'll do anything, I'm not in a position to choose. Hopefully, the war will be over soon. The thought of returning home some day is what keeps me going. My main priority at the moment is my children's education and well-being.'

'When's Mirza going to get his artificial leg fitted?'

'Our sponsors are working on it,' she sighed, blowing the smoke from her cigarette. 'Healthcare's very expensive here, it'll all take some time . . .'

As the evening grew longer, I plucked up the courage to ask her how she was surviving without Zoran.

Her eyes filled with tears, 'I miss him every second . . . but what can I do?'

We sat in silence in the sultry air. After a while I told her that I'd just found out that I was pregnant and was wondering what to do.

'I'm sure that whatever you two do, you'll make the right decision. Zoran and I always thought of you as mature and smart and, from everything you've told me about Andrew, he sounds like a good man.' Her words were reassuring.

It rained heavily every afternoon. Flashes of lightning ignited the sky and crashing blasts of thunder sent Haris scurrying under his bed with his hands clasped to his ears.

'We've told him that the noise is not from shelling, but he's still very afraid,' Mirza explained.

Merima didn't have a car and walking anywhere in the suffocating heat was gruelling. One day, the boys and I walked to the mall, some distance from the apartment, so I could buy them a stereo with the money I had left. By the time we returned I almost fainted from the overwhelming heat and the persistent pain in my kidney. Most of the time we stayed inside their air-conditioned apartment or went for a quick swim in the swimming pool at the complex. Mirza had become a strong swimmer and enthusiastically showed me how many laps he could do without taking a break. I took photos of them all, so I could show everyone back home.

Over the following days my kidney pain became worse. Merima made soups for me but I couldn't keep anything down. At night, I tried not to toss around in bed too much, so that I wouldn't wake her.

A week after I'd arrived, Merima invited Philip and Sandi, the couple who had sponsored them, to come for dinner. She prepared *musaka* and *baklava*, traditional Bosnian dishes. Philip was a tall man with a broad frame and dark, short hair. His wife, Sandi, was attractive and lively. They were a gregarious and talkative couple. Every time Sandi moved her arm a row of gold bracelets clinked on her wrist. During dinner I asked them what had prompted them to help a family from Sarajevo.

'It was Christmas last year, we were on holiday in Virginia,' Philip said. 'One evening, after a great day's skiing, we were sitting in our lodge when Sandi saw this young man on TV,' he smiled, turning to Mirza.

'We were having such a grand time, with Christmas and everything . . .' Sandi continued. 'Seeing a young boy like that, we just knew we had to do something to help . . . we have children of our own. It was only after we'd managed to track down the producers of the report that we found out how devastating the situation in Sarajevo really was. We couldn't believe how difficult it was just to try to send food to you,' she shook her head, looking at Merima.

Philip rested his elbows on the chair. 'I called all the aid agencies I could find but none of them were sure if our help would ever reach the family. So, that's when we decided if we can't get help to them, we'll have to get them out. We're glad that we did because now we have Merima and these two fine young men with us.' His voice was loud and strong.

The night before I left Florida, Merima's brother called from Sarajevo. Because he was the chief of the fire service, he was able to use a satellite phone. As far as he knew, my family was fine.

'Please go and see them,' I cried. 'Tell them that I'm with Merima and that I miss them enormously.'

It was hard to part from Merima and the boys.

Andrew wasn't at the airport when I landed in Honolulu. Wearing the *Vendetta* T-shirt, I took a taxi to the hotel where his parents were staying. The traffic was moving very slowly. The taxi driver turned towards me saying, 'Ma'am, there are a lot of cars out today, Bill Clinton's visiting Pearl Harbor.' Stuck in the traffic I gazed out of the window. A few limousines sped past us flanked by security men.

'I think that's our president,' the taxi driver said.

Maybe I should throw myself in front of his car and beg him to help Bosnia, I thought. I leaned back in my seat and closed my eyes for a bit.

It was late evening when we pulled up in front of a grand white building. Tall columns surrounded by palm trees marked the entrance of the hotel. Tired and nervous, I walked through the foyer towards reception when someone tapped me on the shoulder. I turned around. A man with greyish hair smiled at me. The enthusiastic look on his face reminded me of Andrew.

'You must be Atka. I'm Bill, Andrew's father.' He greeted me with a hug. He was wearing sandy-coloured trousers and a red T-shirt. Taking my rucksack from my shoulder he led me on to the terrace outside. 'Come and meet Rose, we've been waiting for you all day. We're having a drink.'

Although I couldn't see the ocean I could hear the surf from the beach. Thick branches spread themselves out from the large tree in the middle of the garden. At a table under its enormous canopy was a graceful-looking woman dressed in white. Her blond hair was pulled back in a ponytail. She looked tanned and relaxed.

'Hi, darling, I'm Rose,' she said, getting up from her chair. 'You must be exhausted,' she said, smiling. She embraced and kissed me. Bill pulled up a chair for me and we sat down.

'Andrew's told me so much about you . . . How are you?' I asked them.

'Well, things have been pretty awful, but are much better now,' Rose smiled at Bill.

'Yes, I'm fine,' Bill smiled back at her. He clasped his hands, leaned on the table and gave me a quick update on the race. Because of the light winds *Vendetta* was making very slow progress. Crushed, I felt like crying.

'We'll go to the yacht club first thing in the morning to check on their position,' Bill said, clearing his throat. 'Now, more importantly, how's your family?'

'The last I heard of them, they were all alive but I can't

count on that for sure because things change by the minute in Sarajevo.'

'Oh, you poor thing, how awful. Can't you get in touch with them on that satellite phone that Andrew's been using to call us?' Rose asked, concerned.

'I wish it were that easy. Only foreigners and senior government officials have access to it.'

'Oh, darling, it's ghastly that you can't even contact them. I'll pray for all of them when I go to mass on Sunday.' She touched my hand. 'Why don't you write down all their names and teach me how to pronounce them.' She found a pen and paper in her bag and put it in front of me.

'But Rose, there are so many of them . . .'

'Oh, I don't mind,' she insisted.

I wrote their names down then read them out to her.

'Phew, they sound so foreign.' She let out a brief chuckle. 'But I'll learn how to pronounce them. So many children – you must be Catholics,' she joked.

'No, we're not,' I replied, laughing.

'Do people in your country have lots of children?'

'No, not at all, Rose, we're a very unusual family.'

'Join the club,' Bill said grinning. He signalled to the waiter, asking him to bring me some juice. 'I've read a lot about your part of the world. President Tito did a remarkable job to hold Yugoslavia together for all those years.'

'I know, we all cried when he died. After his death everyone feared that the country would go under, people joked that Yugoslavia should be renamed the *Titanic*.'

'That's a beauty,' Bill laughed. He and Rose wanted to hear more about my family, Andrew's work and me. Without Andrew with me, I didn't mention our engagement or the fact that I was pregnant. Despite feeling unwell, I stayed talking to them until long after midnight. When I finally went to the room they'd organised for me, I sank on to the bed in my clothes and fell asleep straight away.

The next morning, the race official at the yacht club told us that due to continuing light winds, there was hardly any improvement in *Vendetta*'s position and it could be a week before they finished. I was angry but there was nothing we could do except wait. On our way back to the hotel Bill asked if he could have my passport.

'Now that we have a few days to spare, let me organise a visa for you in case you and Andrew want to come to New Zealand,' he said.

'Oh, you don't have to worry about that. We won't be going there, we need to get back to Sarajevo,' I replied.

'It'll come in handy even if we never use it,' Bill said, jokingly and, out of politeness, I agreed.

Bill and Rose were lovely and although I wanted to spend time with them, I was too sick to leave my room. Worried about me, they took me to a medical centre to see a doctor. I told him that I was pregnant but also complained about the sharp pain in my kidney. He assured me that it was probably some kind of travel bug combined with a bit of morning sickness and advised me to rest.

'Travel bug?! Did you tell him about the pain in your back?' Rose was appalled. 'You look so sick. What did he say about the shadows under your eyes?'

I shrugged my shoulders. Being in a foreign country with people I hardly knew, I was loath to make a fuss. Without medical insurance, the cost of my short visit to the doctor was very expensive but Bill and Rose assured me that they'd taken care of it.

That afternoon I made an effort to go for a swim with them.

But mostly I was in so much pain that I couldn't get out of bed. I watched every CNN report from Sarajevo, obsessed with thoughts of my family, and worrying about how Andrew and I were going to cope with the baby. I missed Andrew terribly and on the day that *Vendetta* finally arrived I was able to gather enough strength to greet him with Bill and Rose at the finish line. They were very excited, they hadn't seen him for six months.

Andrew leapt off the deck to hug me and as though he knew what was on my mind, he whispered, 'We'll have the baby in Sarajevo . . . I'll do anything to make you happy.'

'Me too. I know we'll cope,' I whispered back. 'Your parents have been so kind to me,' I said to him before he turned around to greet them.

'Oh, Andrew, it's so good to see you again,' Rose said as she hugged him.

Andrew hugged Rose back and, shaking Bill's hand, he said, 'Good to see you guys, too. Thank you both for looking after Atka.'

I listened to them talking and looked at the happy faces of the yachties around me. *This is so strange*, I thought. *Am I really standing in the middle of a yacht club in Hawaii or have I been shot in the head by a sniper and now I'm lying in a hospital bed imagining all this?*

Andrew's younger brother and the rest of the crew joined us and while they celebrated the end of the race at the yacht club, I sat outside where the air was cooler. Later that evening on the balcony of Andrew's parents' room we told them that we were engaged and expecting a baby. Having just met them I was apprehensive about how they might react but Bill immediately ordered champagne to celebrate and Rose said, 'When I saw the way you two hugged each other this morning, it was obvious that you're very much in love. How lovely about the baby. Darling, I wish you'd told us before that you were pregnant. Then we would've known why you've been feeling so sick – although being pregnant doesn't cause pain in your kidneys,' Rose hugged us both. 'I can just imagine you two living in Paris with the baby,' she said.

'We won't be living in Paris,' Andrew replied.

'Why not?'

'Well, I'm not a resident in France and Atka wouldn't be able to live there. Besides, she wants to be near her family which is fair enough,' he explained, smiling at me.

'Do you think it's a good idea to have a baby in Sarajevo?' Bill frowned.

'I've seen plenty of babies born there, Bill,' Andrew said. 'People go on with their lives in spite of the war, you just learn to live with what you've got.'

I could tell that Bill and Rose were worried about us going back but they didn't mention it again.

The next day, Andrew had to sail *Vendetta* to the island of Maui and I wanted to go with him. Bill cautioned us against it, because of how I was feeling, but Andrew and I were so happy to be together again we didn't want to part. An hour into the trip, feeling queasy, I curled up in the small cabin down below, trapped in the stench of musty wet weather gear, cigarettes and stale beer. The sea was rough and the erratic motion of the boat was making me violently sick. I felt as though I were being spun around in a large washing machine. All I could do was clutch on to the sick bucket. Every time Andrew came down to see how I was, I moaned and said that I just wanted to die. When we arrived at the dock twelve hours later, I couldn't even make it out of the cabin. For the next three days in the hotel I drifted in and out of sleep, hardly eating anything. Andrew's parents were very concerned about me, suggesting they cut their holiday short, so that we could go to New Zealand straight away for a proper medical check. Andrew was reluctant, knowing that I wanted to return home as soon as possible. But when the pain became unbearable I gave up. 'I don't care any more where I'm going . . . I just want this pain to end.'

Andrew called his agency to let them know that he wouldn't be back at work for at least another week. Bill had already organised my visa for New Zealand so we were able to leave immediately. I thought I was already far enough away from home but, after flying a further ten hours, I felt as though I had arrived at the very end of the world. We went to see a doctor straight from the airport. It was the middle of winter in New Zealand.

My tests came back indicating multiple deficiencies. I weighed only forty-eight kilograms and, for the sake of the baby, which was due in February, the doctor advised me to rest for at least a month. He didn't think an ultrasound for my kidney was necessary and diagnosed a bad case of morning sickness. Frustrated, I tried to explain that I had had pain in my kidney before I'd become pregnant but he smilingly told me to take things easy and not to stress too much.

'Take it easy!' I said to Andrew. 'How can I?'

Being in a peaceful place with an abundance of food made me feel so guilty and in a strange way I felt that the pain I was in was some kind of connection with the rest of my family. It was summer in Europe, and most of the journalists who Andrew knew had gone on holiday, so it was impossible to find anyone who was going to Sarajevo. I often called my sisters and Merima. They had not had any news from our family either. Talking to them was comforting since they understood what it was like to be away from home.

Weak and sick I hardly ventured out, spending most of the time tucked up on the green couch in Bill and Rose's living room. They lived in the South Island, in a bushy bay, just over the hill from the city of Christchurch. The views from their house stretched out to the surrounding bays and to the small port town of Lyttelton at the head of the harbour. Their house was spacious and elegantly furnished, with an enormous fireplace in the living room. Bill and Andrew kept the fire going all the time.

'I wish I could send all this wood to Sarajevo. Each load of firewood you bring in would last us a week at home,' I couldn't help remarking.

With Andrew's brothers living away there were only the four of us in the house. Bill regularly recorded the local news reports from Sarajevo, which were brief. He also showed me every newspaper article he found on Bosnia. His cough was becoming more persistent every day but I never heard him complain about it.

After two weeks in bed, I felt able to go to town with Andrew to book our flights back to Europe. I wanted to leave straight away but he was adamant that we should remain in New Zealand for at least another month because of my ill health. Waiting until September sounded like a life sentence but I was too tired to argue. We drove up the winding road to the top of the hill. I was feeling sick again so Andrew stopped the car.

'Come on, let's get some fresh air,' he opened the car door for me. I had no winter clothes and was wearing his old grey coat, which Rose had found in a cupboard. The freezing wind chilled me to the bone, a strong gust slammed the door behind me. The fresh air reminded me of cold winter days at the open ice-skating rink.

'Not a bad view,' Andrew said.

Far in the distance, on the edge of the vast flat plains, majestic snow-covered mountains rose like a long fortress wall.

'Behind those mountains is the wild West Coast, then it's three thousand kilometres across the open ocean to Australia.' He took my hand.

'It's scary to think how far we are from the rest of the world,' I remarked.

Andrew smiled. I glanced down at the city below us. It looked so small, with a handful of tall buildings standing close together somewhere in the middle and suburbs of low-lying houses sprawling around them.

'Is that the whole city?' I asked.

'Yes. There's so much space here, we don't have to live in big apartment blocks as you do in Europe. That's the beauty of New Zealand.'

Shivering with cold, I hurried back to the car and we headed down the other side of the hill. We drove past a small stone building, resembling a castle, then down a wide street dotted with pretty gardens and large Victorian weatherboard houses on each side. Everything looked so tidy, charming and colourful, just like a picture from the pages of some children's book. The streets of the town seemed deserted, as the streets of Sarajevo used to be during an important soccer game when almost everyone was inside glued to their TV screens.

'Is it a holiday today?' I asked.

'No,' Andrew replied.

'So, where are all the people?' I was confused.

He laughed, 'I told you – there's no one here. We have more sheep than people. I'll drive you past Hagley Park, you'll love it.'

Tall oaks and chestnut trees cast long shadows on the vast empty green fields in the middle of the park. A few ducks ran away from the cyclists whizzing pass on their bicycles.

'It's such a big park, look at all those trees. If we were in Sarajevo, they'd all be cut down for firewood.'

'They're only surrounding the sports fields, where people play rugby and cricket,' Andrew said. 'There's a big botanic garden too, a golf course and a lake. The whole park's huge.'

'This place looks like movies I've seen about England,' I said, looking at a long Gothic-style building near the park and groups of schoolboys wearing striped black and white blazers and ties.

'The city was settled by the English, it's named after Christ Church College at Oxford University in England. The first four ships with settlers docked in Lyttelton. It would've been great if they had built the city on the harbour, but because there was no source of water there they trekked over the hill and, discovering two rivers, built the town here.'

'It's a pretty city,' I said. Soon we pulled up outside the travel agency. The agent was a friendly woman with dark red hair who'd known Andrew for years. When she heard that I was from Sarajevo, she was very sympathetic. 'Oh, it's horrible to see what's happening over there. We're so far away here, it's hard for us to understand what all that fighting's actually about,' she said offering us a seat.

Andrew started explaining to her the reason the war had started, but by the look on her face I could tell that she was completely confused. Still, she listened patiently. 'We're so lucky here . . .' she said, then looked at the computer screen in front of her. 'Now, how about those bookings?' We booked our flights for the middle of September.

'I have no idea how my family's going to survive that long without me,' I said to Andrew as we left the agency.

'Maybe there's a way to send money to them so that they can at least buy food,' he replied.

'Oh, I feel that I'm such a nuisance to you. It's not your responsibility, you don't have to help,' I muttered.

'Atka, they're my family too now. Of course I'm going to help. At least we don't have to worry about money.'

We drove back over the hill. 'I'm so sorry we're stuck here because of me,' I said in despair.

'Atka, this is what we have to do and you don't ever have to apologise to me for anything. My work's fine, fortunately my editor understands our situation . . .'

That week, we talked to our friend David in New York. He was returning to Sarajevo shortly and promised to go and see my parents to explain to them where we were and why we hadn't returned to Sarajevo yet. Finally, we'd made a connection! The next morning Andrew went to the bank and transferred money to David's account so that he could take it to Sarajevo and get it to my family.

Rose had learnt the names and ages of all my brothers and sisters. She wanted to know about each one of them and we spent hours talking.

'Atka's little brothers look like a bunch of Oliver Twists,' Andrew said to Rose late one afternoon as the four of us sat in the living room.

'I wonder why Sarajevo was built there?' Bill asked studying the large world atlas on the coffee table in front of him.

I turned to him from the green couch. 'Originally there was a Roman settlement at the thermal springs near Sarajevo. Centuries later, during the Ottoman period, traders travelling east and west used to stop to rest their horses at a roadhouse in our valley and the settlement grew from there.'

'That makes sense,' Bill replied, coughing sporadically. 'And what about the name Sarajevo? Has it got a meaning?'

Andrew was on the other end of the couch, reading the paper. He lowered the page. 'Someone told me it comes from a Turkish word.'

'It does. When I was little my grandfather told me a story about a Turkish grand vizier who was . . .'

'Vizier . . . that's a potentate, isn't it?' Rose said. She was sitting next to Bill with her legs curled up on the couch.

'That's right, Rose,' he said.

'Anyway,' I continued, 'hundreds of years ago, this grand vizier was travelling through our valley when suddenly a big storm hit his caravan. There was no time to pitch a tent and line it with the Persian rugs, silken cloths and other riches that the grand vizier was used to. The only shelter they could find was the humble stone roadhouse, with small stables for the horses. The servants, ashamed that they could not find anything better, kept apologising to the vizier but he replied that in a fearsome storm like this the roadhouse looked as grand as a *saray*, which in Turkish means a palace. Sarajevo is a combination of the word *saray* and *ovasi*, which in Turkish means fields, so the name literally means the fields around the palace.'

'That's a lovely story,' Rose said. 'There's so much history in your country. New Zealand's so young . . .'

'Yes, the buildings here are so new the paint on them is still wet,' Bill added, and we all laughed.

Rose went and got her notebook from the kitchen and started looking through the pages. 'I was thinking,' she said, slowly. 'Since you're staying for a bit longer, why don't you get married here?' She looked at Andrew then at me, 'What do you think, darlings?'

'As far as we're concerned we're already married, the ceremony is just a formality,' Andrew said, glancing at me.

'I understand that,' Rose said, tilting her head, 'but you're in love, why wait? And for us, it's more than just a formality, you know that, Andrew.'

'Oh, Rose, I can't imagine my wedding without any of my family or friends . . .' I explained.

'But you can have a wedding with your family when you get back to Sarajevo. It would mean a lot to us if we could see you married here and it wouldn't be anything big, just a few friends and family.'

'I think it's a good idea,' Andrew looked at me, waiting for me to say something.

'But I feel so sick . . . and to be honest I'm not in the right frame of mind to think about a wedding . . .'

'You wouldn't have to worry about a thing, little one, we'd be more than happy to organise everything,' Bill said, quickly.

Andrew and I looked at each other. 'It's up to you, Atka,' he said.

'Well,' I hesitated, 'I suppose we could but it would have to be small.'

'Of course, it will be very simple,' Rose assured us.

Later, I told Andrew how sad and strange this wedding was going to be for me without any of my family or friends there.

'Just think of it as a party and we'll have another one for everyone in Sarajevo when we get back there,' he suggested. 'Anyway, it's been a long time since I've seen any of my friends and cousins, it'll be great to see them and you'll be able to meet them all.'

A few days later, in the middle of the night, we received a call from Ariane, who was back in Sarajevo. My mum and Mesha were with her. I trembled as we spoke, nervously waiting for my own echo to end before they could reply. Everyone was alive and they'd just received the money we had sent them. A long narrow tunnel that had been dug under the runway was now open allowing for food and military supplies to be brought into the city. Being the only lifeline to the city, people accordingly named it the Tunnel of Life. Because of the tunnel the food on the black market was now cheaper to buy.

When I told them how I missed them all, they told me to think of the baby first, look after myself and to give their best wishes to Andrew and his parents. Andrew wrote down Ariane's satellite number in Sarajevo and we arranged to call them again soon. Just before we hung up Mesha said, 'Good luck for the wedding. It'll be good but I guarantee we'll have a bigger party here.' I smiled and called my sisters in Zagreb straight away to tell them I'd spoken to Mum and Mesha.

Icy winds blowing in from Antarctica dominated August, which passed in a blur of pain and sleep, punctuated by sporadic phone calls to my family. The ongoing news coverage of my home country was always uppermost in my mind. We went back to the doctor a few more times but each time he assured us that the first three months of pregnancy were often hard for healthy women, let alone for someone like me who'd just spent a year in a war zone. He was still of the opinion that a scan for my kidney was not necessary but he scheduled one for the baby two days before we were due to fly back to Europe.

My family was able to buy plenty of food with the money they'd received through David. With winter coming, people from the neighbourhood organised themselves to dig trenches through our street and gas pipes were installed in the houses that had not had gas before. Our house was one of them. Knowing that my family would not be freezing and would now have gas to cook with was the best present I could have received for my twenty-third birthday, which was coming up at the end of the month.

And then came the wedding day. Not knowing anyone, I asked Rose to be my bridesmaid and Bill gave me away. As I walked through the crowd of strangers, I feared that I would burst into tears but then I saw Andrew smiling at me and everything felt right. The ceremony was short and simple but the party after was big. Most of Andrew's friends and family were there. We celebrated it at Bill and Rose's house. A small plane towing a banner with *Bon chance de Paris* written on it flew over the house. Andrew's editor from Paris had organised it as a special surprise. Without any of my friends and family there I felt strangely removed from it all, as though it were someone else's wedding.

'Atka, I know how you feel,' one of Andrew's uncles came over to me. He was a genial man with a strong Austrian accent. 'When I came here to New Zealand all those years ago, I didn't know anyone, not a soul. Later on, when I got married I had no one at my wedding, just like you . . .' He spoke with tears in his eyes. He turned around to the other guests, and raising his glass proposed a toast to Andrew and me. Before everyone sat down for dinner, Bill toasted my family. Andrew held my hand tightly.

On Monday after the wedding we went to the hospital to have the first scan for the baby.

'That's your baby's heartbeat,' the radiologist said, explaining the sound of the muffled thudding. Holding hands, Andrew and I looked at the screen and smiled.

The radiologist moved the scanner up and down my stomach for a few minutes, then a grave look appeared on her face.

'Hmm . . .' she mumbled staring at the screen. 'Let me just have a closer look at this,' she said.

'Look at what?' Andrew and I were alarmed.

The radiologist moved her chair closer to the screen. 'It

looks like . . . looks like gastro—' She said something I couldn't understand. 'I'll go and get a doctor.' Abruptly, she left the room.

I had no idea what she meant. Terrified, I looked at Andrew. His face fell.

'What did she say? What does that word mean?' I tugged his hand.

An image of our baby with two heads raced through my mind and I felt as though I was sinking through the bed then falling deeper and deeper into the ground.

'I'm not sure. I don't understand the word either, but I suspect it's something to do with the baby's stomach,' Andrew said. 'Whatever it is, we'll deal with it.' He held my hand as we waited in the small, dark room.

The doctor came in and, after looking at the screen for what seemed an eternity, he confirmed that our baby had gastroschisis, a large hole in the abdominal wall which meant that some internal organs were developing outside the baby's stomach. 'I'm very sorry,' he said.

I felt as though I'd been knocked out.

'Is it operable?' Andrew's voice was shaky.

'It depends, we have to run more tests, you see gastroschisis is a chromosome-related problem which often has added complications, Down's syndrome and a whole lot of other things, which I don't think I should go into until we do more tests.' The doctor spoke slowly.

I gasped, it seemed as though all the air in the room had been sucked out.

'What causes it? Is it stress? Malnutrition?' I managed to ask.

'We don't really know for sure,' the doctor shrugged.

'If all the other tests are fine, can you tell us what the prognosis is?' Andrew asked.

'If it's a straight case of gastroschisis, usually a couple of operations are required straight after the birth. Babies need to be in intensive care for up to ten weeks but once they manage to start eating, their recovery is normally pretty good.'

'Can we do those tests sooner rather than later?' I asked. 'We're going back to Sarajevo in two days.'

'Are you? Isn't there a war going on in Bosnia?' he asked, concerned. 'This is a very serious condition. Do you think that the hospitals there would be able to deal with it?'

'No, not at all,' Andrew was adamant, 'they don't even have the basics any more.'

'Well, it's up to you,' the doctor said, 'but I'd strongly advise you against going.'

Devastated, Andrew and I left the hospital, and cried all the way back to his house. We cancelled our tickets and helplessly waited for the tests to be carried out. There was nothing else that we could do. Nothing. I was so distraught and powerless. The next day out of sheer anger I cut my long hair short.

A Flicker of Hope

Hana

It was the first day of the new school year and groups of students were standing in the schoolyard, waiting for the bell to ring. Pleased to see some of my classmates gathered in a circle next to the main entrance, I squeezed my way through the crowd towards them.

'Hana,' one of the girls shouted when she saw me and moved aside to create a space for me. The rest of my friends were pleased to see me too. 'I wasn't sure if you'd be coming back to school this year,' she said.

'Neither was I,' I replied, trying to sound indifferent. 'We're not sure when my sister's coming back from New Zealand or how much longer we'll be staying here.'

'Well, we're happy to see you again. The class wouldn't be the same without you,' the boy who sat at the desk behind me said, looking around the group. Everyone agreed.

'At least your life's interesting,' one of the other girls blurted out. 'You know, one day you're here, the next day you might be going somewhere else . . .' My classmates shot her a look and she covered her mouth with her hand. 'Oh, I'm so sorry. I'm so stupid, that's not what I meant.'

'It's so adventurous for us refugees,' I joked, putting my hand on her arm. 'No parents, no family, no home . . . If you want to swap places with me, we can do it any time! Then you'll see how interesting it *really* is . . .' My classmates laughed.

The main door was flung open and together we pushed our way into the entrance hall. Everyone was excited because this was our last year before going to high school and, although I still didn't know how long I'd be staying, we wanted to make the most of our time together. While some ran around the classroom, the rest of us chatted about the summer holidays, then one by one we took our seats. Klaudia and I chose the same desk by the window as last year. I remembered how terrified I'd been the first time that I had walked into this classroom by myself and how completely different I felt today.

The form teacher appeared at the door with the class book under her arm and walked swiftly to her chair. She called the roll, briefly asking everyone about their holidays. When she came to my name she told me how pleased she was to see me again, then asked about my family. The weather was warm, so she opened one of the windows, then started the class.

The teachers gave us plenty of homework each day and the first two weeks of school flew by. Every Friday after school a big group of us went for long walks to the main city park. Sometimes we carried our English textbooks with us, reciting lessons or pretending to be American tourists. We often went to each other's houses to study together.

A four-day class excursion to the coast was being planned in the second half of the school year and the form teacher needed to confirm who was going.

'I'll be here for it,' I said, when she called my name. My friends at the desk behind me gave me the thumbs up and Klaudia looked quizzically at me, without saying anything until class had finished.

'Hana, are you staying for the whole year now?' she asked as we were walking to the classroom on the first floor.

'Don't ask me.' I pulled the books in my arms closer to me.

'Has something happened?'

I told her that Atka had found out that their baby had a hole in its stomach. Fortunately, all the tests had come back clear but the baby would still need to be operated on straight after the birth. Atka wasn't sure how long they'd be staying in New Zealand.

'Oh, no. Poor Atka. First the war and now this.'

'I know. She's longing to go back to Sarajevo but it would be impossible for the hospitals there to take care of the baby properly. I mean, it's a war zone. And she said her kidney's constantly sore. She sounds very sick . . .'

We reached our classroom, placed the books on our desks and sat down.

'I'm so sorry, Hana. I know you can hardly wait for them to come back.'

'What can I do?' I said, doodling on my notebook. 'At least Atka's in a safe place and Andrew's family seems very kind. I spoke to his parents on the phone the other day. You know, with the little bit of English I know.' I looked at her and made a face.

'Don't worry then, I'm sure it'll all work out,' Klaudia tried to cheer me up.

'I'm *so* happy for Atka. She deserves the best. It's just that she's so far away now. What if she forgets us? My whole family's scattered and I have no idea what'll happen to us all. I'd never imagined that our lives would turn out this way.'

She was silent for a minute. 'Look, if you can't stay with Danica much longer, I'm sure you could stay with my family for a while. Our house is big enough and my mum always tells me what a good example you are to me.'

'Oh, thank you but don't worry about it. Danica's told me that I can stay with them for as long as I need to. It's just that this war's only becoming worse. How much longer can people carry on like this? When's it all going to end?'

Later, at home, I looked at the little piece of paper Grandma had given me and again read some of the letters from Sarajevo. After eighteen months of not seeing my family, I sometimes wondered if they were real. Selma and Janna had signed one of the letters with 'your little sisters' and, remembering my promise to Atka, I closed my eyes, thinking about the day when we would all be together again. *I believe, I believe, I believe,* I kept on repeating to myself.

The day before my fourteenth birthday, Nadia gave birth to a girl whom she named Romana. They came to visit us two weeks later on a cloudy autumn day. I had always thought of people with children as being much older and more serious but when Nadia walked in with the little wrapped bundle in her arms, wearing the jacket we had collected from the Red Cross, she didn't look much older than my school friends. I wished our parents or Grandma or someone older were here to look after her. When she saw me she smiled serenely and without saying anything, I rushed towards her.

'Here's your aunty Hana,' she said, looking at the baby before she handed her to me. 'She'll hold you for a second while I take my shoes off.'

I looked at Romana who was dressed in a tiny green baby suit and was sleeping peacefully wrapped in a soft cotton blanket. I leaned closer to kiss her and only then noticed her soft, little breaths and the sweet smell of baby shampoo.

'The baby's suit is a present from Lela,' Nadia whispered, tucking the wrap tighter. 'Here, I'll take her.'

'Does her name mean anything?' I whispered, passing her back to Nadia. It was not a common name in Bosnia.

'Romana means a small Roman empress,' Nadia said, her face lighting up. She went into the living room with Romana and after I'd made coffee for her, we sat on the couch talking. Nadia was very grateful to Danica's friend; the house in which she was staying had everything she needed. She shared a room upstairs with two other girls who'd recently had their babies and they all helped each other. All the baby clothes, nappies and food had been donated by Caritas.

Two older women from Bosnia were staying in a room downstairs with their children. One of the women's husbands had been killed recently during the fighting in central Bosnia and she was now completely lost.

'All this time, she's been living in hope that they'll be able to return home,' Nadia said. 'Now he's dead and she's left alone with two children. The day she found out, all night we listened to her weeping and crying. Awful . . .'

'I don't know how people have any strength left after something like that,' I replied. 'You build your whole life and then it just disappears, almost overnight.'

'I know,' Nadia sniffed. 'You have to start all over again. It must be hard for older people, but I guess you just find a way somehow,' she said, gently kissing Romana on the cheek. 'It's different when you have a child, Romana's my world now. Look at other people, Merima for instance. Atka said she's incredibly strong.'

'I'm so glad she saw them,' I said. Then, remembering that Nadia hadn't seen the photos that Atka had sent us from Florida, I ran to my room to collect them.

'Look how tall Mirza and Haris are,' Nadia said, pausing for a while to look at each photo. 'I'm so glad they got out when they did.'

'It's strange, you never really know what's going to happen,'

I said, thinking of Atka. She was so far away and it seemed odd that no one from our family was at her wedding. We had never imagined that all these important life events would happen without all of us being together.

Before Nadia left she asked me about school.

'My classmates elected me to be the class president,' I said proudly.

'Oh,' she said, with a cheeky smile on her face. 'You'll be good as the class representative. There's a reason Dad nicknamed you "the lawyer".'

Before I opened the front door for her, we hugged and I kissed Romana's soft little forehead.

'Look after yourself,' I heard myself saying. Nadia smiled and left. Even if she were worried, she hid her feelings very well.

As I watched her walking away with her little bundle, I thought of Grandma. When Asko and Emir were very little, she used to sing lullabies to them before their afternoon sleep, all the while rocking them gently. She liked to pat and tickle all of us. I missed that. And I missed hugging and playing with my brothers and sisters. But I knew there was no point thinking about this or saying anything to anyone about it. It seemed that whenever people complained something bad happened to them, so instead of brooding about it, I went to my desk to study.

One day, we finished school early because our English teacher was away. I raced home to drop off my bag before meeting my friends. Andrea was in tears when I opened the bedroom door. Her eyes were swollen and her face was red. No one else was at home.

'What's happened?'

She was sobbing, hardly able to speak. 'It's Mum. She's been in an accident.'

'Where? When?'

'She was coming home from the market when a car hit her. It didn't stop for her at the pedestrian crossing.'

My stomach turned. 'Where is she now?'

'At the hospital. Dad's with her but he wouldn't let me go with him . . .'

I embraced her, assuring her that everything would be all right. When Andrea's dad returned later that evening, he told us that Danica had been badly hurt but was now in a stable condition. We'd be able to go and visit her in a couple of days.

Danica had been admitted to the military hospital since it was the one closest to where we lived. It was a cold day when we went to see her. We walked through a long dark hallway to her room, a nurse came past us wheeling an old man who had a drip in his arm.

Danica's face was bruised and her arm was in plaster. The rest of her body was hidden under the sheets. She smiled when she saw us, trying to sound chirpy but it wasn't long before she closed her eyes, saying she was tired. We left the room quietly. Andrea cried on the way home. She was shocked and scared to see her mother in such a bad way. For the next few days I spent all my spare time with Andrea.

When Danica returned home after nearly two weeks, she was on crutches. Her hip had been badly injured in the accident and although she was recovering well, the chances were that it was never going to heal properly. She looked tired but she managed to joke with us.

'I won't be able to chase after you when you're misbehaving,' she laughed. 'The frustrating thing is,' she continued, 'that I was going to visit Nadia and the baby after the market that day. I'd bought fresh fruit for them.'

Putting on our pyjamas that evening, Andrea said, 'I don't

know how you've coped without your parents for so long. Until now, I hadn't realised how hard it must be for you.'

The doctors ordered Danica to have plenty of rest but it didn't surprise me to see her up early the next day, making tea for us.

'Take your umbrella with you and put your jacket on!' she called from the hallway as I was leaving for school. 'It's wet and cold out there.'

Although Atka was at the other end of the world, she was our only direct connection to Sarajevo. Every time she talked to our family via satellite phone she always called us straight away with all their news. They now had gas in the house which was a huge relief and thanks to the money that Atka and Andrew were able to send to them through foreign journalists, they were no longer starving. Atka said she had no idea how Sarajevans would survive a second winter in the siege.

'I'm worried about Mayka,' Atka said, one evening when she called. 'Mum told me she's very frail.'

'That's awful. All the papers here are writing about the cold, predicting a huge number of deaths if the Serbs continue to block the aid convoys. They're holding up trucks which are trying to bring blankets and winter clothes,' I said.

'That's on top of all the shelling and starvation. Mesha told me people have given up all hope. Sarajevans have dug a tunnel under the runway and many are escaping that way, people are desperate to get out.'

'Do you think NATO will ever intervene?' I asked.

'I doubt it. They haven't so far . . . The Serbs do as they please and they're getting away with it.'

'I feel sick when I see the Serb politicians on TV. They're behind all these atrocities and yet they have the gall to meet and smile and shake hands with foreign diplomats during so-called peace talks.' I was angry. 'But don't get me started on those idiots. Tell me, how are you?'

'I've just come back from the hospital again, I've had septicaemia.'

'What's that?' I was puzzled.

'Blood poisoning.' She sounded tired. 'It's because of my kidney.'

Two weeks previously, Atka had finally had an ultrasound for her kidney and the doctors discovered a two-centimetre stone. Usually, they would operate straight away but because Atka was pregnant they weren't able to. To help drain her very enlarged kidney, they had to insert a tube into it, which had to be left in there until the baby was born. The tube often became blocked, causing further infections and more pain, which meant that Atka had to go to hospital frequently to have the tube cleared or replaced. She was on painkillers, but because of her pregnancy could only take low doses.

'The pain's constant and tiring,' her voice was becoming quieter. 'Sometimes, I just want to give up. All I can do is stay in bed and sleep.' This was the first time that I'd ever heard Atka talking like that.

'You? You're such a fighter, Atka, you'll never give up . . .' I tried to encourage her and asked after Andrew and his parents.

'I don't think they could be more wonderful. His father's very sick but they spend a lot of time with me, driving me to the hospital, as though I were their own daughter. And Hana, hospitals in New Zealand are very well equipped. I wish I could send everything they have here to the hospitals in Sarajevo. All the nurses I've met are so capable and caring. They ask me about home whenever I'm in there. I feel so looked after, you know, I'm in good hands.'

'What's New Zealand like?' I was intrigued.

'It's like living in a fairy tale; everything's clean, organised and the people are so friendly and relaxed. Here, no one looks down on me because I'm from Bosnia. There are so many different nationalities, Indians, Chinese, Japanese, Italians, and Greeks . . . Everyone I've met has offered to help if ever I need anything.'

'It sounds like paradise.'

'It *is*.'

'So do you know when you're coming back?'

'Oh, Hana, I can't wait to come back but I have no idea how long everything will take. We'll have to stay here for the baby's surgery, then I'll have to have an operation to remove the kidney stone. We'll just have to wait and see how everything goes . . .'

Unsure of their immediate future, Andrew had relinquished his flat in Paris. He was coming to Europe next month to collect all his gear and Atka said that on his way there he would come to see us for a day.

That evening, I wrote a letter to Andrew's parents, Bill and Rose, to thank them for looking after Atka. I sent it to Atka and asked her to translate it to them.

The school library was crowded with noisy students. Our Croatian language teacher had organised a guest speaker for the evening and I was surprised when Professor Devide walked in. He sat down on a chair at the front of the library and talked to us for over an hour about his work on Japanese poetry. After his talk, slightly apprehensive, I walked to the front of the room to greet him briefly. He was very pleased to see me and asked if I'd had any news from my family. Our teacher, along with a small group of my classmates, joined us. Standing in a circle around Professor Devide, we listened as he was saying what a lovely city Sarajevo was and that he and my father were good friends. Someone of his standing complimenting my city filled me with pride and I chatted happily to him about my hometown. My classmates were listening to him carefully and I was pleased that they could hear how wonderful Sarajevo had been before the war. Although the distance between Sarajevo and Zagreb wasn't great, few of my friends had been there and it seemed that the only things they knew about Sarajevo related to the war. Some time later, our teacher thanked Professor Devide for coming and the gathering slowly dispersed.

The next day at school, some of my friends mentioned that their parents had been to the Olympic Games in Sarajevo and while talking to me they affectionately called it 'your dear Sarajevo'. After school, a group of us had agreed to meet at one of the sweet shops on the main road. I was rushing out of the school hallway on my way to the shop when two girls from another class stopped me.

'Hana, do you mind if we come along?' the blond-haired girl asked.

'Why are you asking me?' I was surprised.

'Your classmates told us to check with you.' It was strange that local girls had to come and ask me if they were allowed to do something but I was glad that no one thought of me as an outsider any more.

The wet autumn days slowly became colder and shorter and before we knew it winter had set in. Not a weekend passed without Nadia coming to see us with her baby. It was easier for her to move around since Atka had sent her money to buy a pram. She and Romana were due to leave the nuns' house at the end of February and I was looking forward to having them living next door again. Danica and Andrea's grandmother didn't mind the fact that the baby would be living there as well. I didn't see Lela much because she was either at work or at her boyfriend's. He seemed very friendly the few times I'd met him. Recently, Atka had sent Lela some money, making things a bit easier for her and for Nadia.

Two weeks before Christmas, Andrew came to Zagreb; he was on his way to Paris to pack up his belongings. He'd spent the whole day with the girls and after school I went to meet them at a café in town. I took my English textbook with me, hoping to make use of the vocabulary list at the back of it. It was strange to think that I was going to see my brother-in-law whom I'd only met once. But any apprehension or awkwardness about being with someone I hardly knew disappeared when Andrew greeted me with a hug and then gave me another one.

'This one's from Atka,' he said.

I asked him how Atka was but he spoke so fast that I couldn't understand everything he said.

'Sorry,' I apologised, opening my book. 'How's Atka's . . .' I glanced at Lela to check if she knew the word for *bubreg*, kidney, in English but when Andrew heard us, he said, partly in Bosnian, 'Bubreg, *ne dobro,* not good. But Atka will be OK, New Zealand has good doctors.'

From what we could understand, Andrew was still employed by his agency but with not much international news coming out of Australia and New Zealand he also started working for a local TV station as a cameraman.

'Do you miss working as a war photographer?' I asked.

'I'm not really thinking about it at the moment,' Andrew replied.

'Now that Atka and I are going to have a baby,' he continued, 'my priorities have changed. I've seen some of my colleagues ruin their marriages for the sake of their careers. My family comes first and I want my children to know me.'

'We know all about family . . .' Nadia said, looking at me.

We talked for a bit longer, then headed to one of the music stores in town. Lela couldn't come with us because she had to go to work, but Nadia and I helped Andrew buy some music cassettes for Atka who was missing our songs and language.

'Now,' he said, looking at my feet, 'you need some winter shoes. And you could do with a proper jacket,' he continued, looking at Nadia. We were embarrassed but he insisted, taking us to a shop nearby. He also bought each of us a pair of jeans.

'Thank you,' Nadia and I spoke in chorus.

'Hana, I'm very impressed at how much your English has improved since I first met you. Keep at it,' he said.

Over a hot chocolate afterwards, Andrew mentioned that his parents were going to try to bring us all to New Zealand.

'New Zealand?' I let out a nervous laugh. It sounded too good to be true so, thinking that I had misunderstood, I asked him to speak slower and repeat what he had said.

'Nothing's certain at this stage,' he said, 'but my parents are working on it.'

Speechless, Nadia and I looked at each other, then she started crying and giggling at the same time.

'It's all right, Nadia,' Andrew said. We chatted in the café for almost an hour, before he had to leave for the airport. We asked him to give Atka plenty of hugs and kisses from us and asked him especially to thank his family.

Later, at home, Danica was relaxing in front of the TV. When I walked in, she turned it off, wanting to hear everything about Andrew's visit. Excitedly, the first thing I told her was that Andrew and his family were going to try to help us go to New Zealand.

'You mean *all* of you? To the other side of the world?' She raised her arms in disbelief. 'The three of you here . . . well, now with Romana, the four of you, you can't travel on your refugee cards. And the rest of your family . . . they can't even get out of Sarajevo. How on earth do you think all of you will be able to go to New Zealand?'

I pulled my sleeves over my hands, 'I don't know . . . That's just what he said.'

Bill and Rose

Atka

Spring came and went but I hardly noticed. Sick with kidney infections and high fevers, I was in and out of hospital at least once a week. This time I was in Room 21 on the third floor of the Public Hospital in Christchurch. There were six beds in the room, mine was the first on the left, closest to the door. A couple of patients were talking quietly to their visitors while others were reading or sleeping.

'This might sting a bit, sweetie,' the nurse said as she slowly injected antibiotics into my arm.

'It's OK, I'm used to it by now,' I mumbled, holding the thermometer under my tongue and closing my eyes as I turned away. Once she'd finished the injection, she placed the needle and the syringe into a small container and then checked my temperature.

'Thirty-six point six degrees Celcius. That's good,' she said, writing it down on my chart. She placed a stethoscope on my stomach to check the baby's heartbeat. It was normal. 'I don't think your wife will have to stay here as long as she did the last time,' the nurse said to Andrew, who was sitting on a chair beside my bed. He smiled at me. The nurse put her pen back into her top pocket, then left the room carrying the container.

Andrew had just started telling me about my sisters and little

Romana who he'd seen in Zagreb a few days ago, when Bill walked in with a grin on his face. He was becoming thinner every day but always remained cheerful.

'Hi, little one, I brought you a couple of things.' He placed a box of chocolates on the bedside table and handed me a pile of neatly cut newspaper articles about Bosnia. Andrew offered his chair to Bill then moved to sit at the end of my bed. Bill told us about the endless calls he and Rose were making to the New Zealand Immigration Department in an effort to find a way of bringing my entire family here.

'We've spoken to someone in Wellington. It's not looking very promising at this stage, because you have such a large family and they're coming from a war zone.'

'I understand, Bill,' I replied. 'Nothing's easy for Bosnians. We are doomed to face barriers every step of the way, especially bureaucratic ones, even in our own country.'

'We'll keep on trying,' Bill assured me. 'For what it's worth, it might be a good idea for your family to start doing their paperwork. It might come in handy . . .'

'. . . Even if we never use it,' I joked, looking at him. 'Thank you, Bill, I'll tell them,' I said. 'I'm so grateful to you and Rose for everything you've done so far.'

'Something *will* come out of it, don't you worry,' Bill replied in his hoarse voice. When talking to my family I'd only mentioned in passing what Rose and Bill were trying to do. Mum was grateful that anyone was willing to help and assured me that they had no false expectations. She also knew that Dad was unlikely to leave because of Mayka.

Bill leaned back, resting his elbows on the arms of the chair. 'I'm glad you two have given up the idea of living with a baby in the middle of a war zone,' he smiled at us.

Sarajevo was constantly on my mind but I knew that for now it was impossible to return there. Sighing heavily, I looked through the newspaper articles. 'None of the aid is getting through to those besieged towns in eastern Bosnia,' I said bitterly. 'How miserable . . . those poor people . . .'

'Can I have a look?' Andrew asked. 'God knows how they're going to survive another winter. Things were pretty grim when I was in Gorazde in March.'

Bill looked at Andrew. 'I've always meant to ask you about Gorazde. How did you manage to get there?'

'Well, the place was completely surrounded,' Andrew began, 'and the Serbs weren't letting anyone or anything through, not even humanitarian aid. My friend John and I knew that a couple of journalists were trying to reach the town, so we drove in John's armoured car trying to get as close as we could to Gorazde. The roads were rough and covered in deep snow but we managed to get to the base that had been set up at the foot of one of the mountains near the town. This place was in the middle of nowhere. We'd call it the asshole of the world, but the Bosnians call places like that *vukojebina,* a place where wolves fuck,' Andrew said with an amused look.

'That's very apt,' Bill remarked.

'Local guys, smuggling food and weapons into town, were packing horses and mules for the journey. There were tents everywhere and smoke rose from the campfires into the freezing air. The scene was like something out of a black and white Second World War movie. We were told that from there on we'd have to walk over the mountains and down into the besieged town. It was so cold, it must've been twenty below,' Andrew said.

Bill listened with interest.

'A couple of photographers I knew were already at the

base. Sky TV was there and, unlike me, they were very well-equipped for the freezing weather. They carried plenty of food supplies, crampons and proper winter gear. Apart from the flak jacket and helmet that I was wearing, all I had was a small backpack, my cameras and a toothbrush. A local guy loaded my cameras on to one of his horses and I carried John's heavy suitcase, which was packed with his satellite phone gear.'

'Didn't you think to look out of the window to check the weather before you left?' Bill said, amused.

'There was no time to prepare, we had to leave in a rush,' Andrew said. 'We set out at four in the afternoon and walked for eighteen hours. We didn't reach Gorazde until the next morning.' Andrew shook his head. 'It started off as a nightmare and turned into a living hell. I could hear the trees cracking in the cold and wolves howling in the distance. We trekked up the mountain through the forest, with the terrain becoming steeper and more slippery as we climbed. I kept falling, I don't think I've ever sworn so much.'

'How did you find your way?' Bill asked.

'We just followed the locals. It wasn't easy. We weren't allowed to use torches or even smoke cigarettes, fearing that the Serbs would spot us. They didn't know exactly where we were but they just kept shooting blindly. Luckily, no one was hit.' Andrew paused. 'I've never been so cold and so tired in my life. I remember stopping for a rest in the forest for a moment. I closed my eyes and a delicious sense of warmth and comfort enveloped me. Someone kicked me and shouted at me to get up, "*Bijela smrt!*"'

'That means white death,' I translated to Bill.

'If the guy hadn't kicked me, I'm sure I would've frozen to death. I don't know how I managed to get up and keep walking. We staggered into Gorazde utterly exhausted at about ten o'clock the next day. People rushed out of their houses and ran towards the mules and horses, so happy to see that finally some foreign journalists had made it through. We took a couple of days to recover and heard that seven people had frozen to death on that trip. We were taken to the morgue to photograph their bodies so that the world could see, once again, the misery of these people. There was still ice in the nostrils of one of the men who'd died. They told me his name was Ramiz. I'll never forget that name.'

'Poor buggers,' Bill shook his head. Then he asked Andrew about the American airdrops.

'Apart from the small amount of food smuggled into the town on the pack horses, these parachute drops were the only way to get food to the starving people. Men, women and even small children ran frantically to the forest when the parachutes landed, scrambling to grab whatever food they could find. I remember thinking how surreal it looked as I took photos. I spent ten days in Gorazde, then I had to leave to take my films out and meet my deadline. My friend Gary was going to come with us but he became very sick and had to stay behind,' Andrew said, frowning. 'After another arduous journey we reached the base where we'd left the car and drove back to Sarajevo.'

'How did you get back in?' Bill looked at him quizzically.

'At times, the Serbs at checkpoints around Sarajevo were fairly lenient towards foreign journalists, letting us in and out,' Andrew explained. 'I took the first UN plane out, which was going to Ancona in Italy. There were no flights to Paris from there that day, so I rented a car and drove to Rome. There, I caught the first plane to Paris. I was still wearing my flak jacket and carrying my helmet. I was exhausted and I hadn't shaved or showered for two weeks. I was a real mess,' he laughed. 'When I boarded the plane the stewardess looked at me with suspicion, so I told her briefly where I'd been. She was fascinated by the story. When we landed in Paris she gave me a small bottle of champagne and said, "Welcome to France, sir."'

'Quite an effort,' Bill remarked.

'Absolutely,' Andrew replied. 'Gorazde was a big story. When I got back to Sarajevo, one of the journalists who'd been there with me invited me to a party. I was so tired and really not in the mood to go anywhere. All I wanted to do was sleep, but he insisted and I'm glad that he did because that's where I met Atka.'

Bill smiled at me and patted my hand.

The next day I was released from hospital. It was Christmas and with the January summer holidays, most government departments were operating with reduced staff. Despite their determination and concerted efforts, Bill and Rose were unable to get through to anyone who could help. Andrew was away for a few days in Australia, reporting for his agency on the bush fires that were raging there.

The pain in my kidney worsened and on the last day of January the doctors decided to induce our baby. We named our son William after Andrew's father. Andrew managed to convey the good news to all my family.

The heavy shelling continued through the freezing Sarajevo winter but to my relief everyone I knew was still alive.

Beep . . . beep . . . beep . . . The steady sound of the heart-monitoring machine was soporific. Five days after his surgery, William was still in his incubator. An oxygen tube was connected to his nose and another one had been inserted into his skinny little arm, feeding him precious fluids. Down the middle of his red, swollen tummy was a thin white tape, protecting the long, fresh scar.

'He looks so vulnerable,' I whispered to Andrew who was standing beside me.

'I think the worst's over now, he's a real fighter,' Andrew smiled.

'I can't wait to hold him . . .' I said, longingly.

'I know, neither can I.'

We spent our entire days in the neonatal unit, our eyes fixed on William.

One evening, when we arrived home I could tell that something was wrong the moment I saw the anxious look on Rose's face, 'Oh, darlings, there's been another terrible massacre in Sarajevo,' she said. We raced to the living room to watch the news that Bill had recorded for us. Petrified, I listened to the announcement before the report: *A large mortar shell has landed in the centre of the busy market in Sarajevo. More than sixty people are dead and over two hundred wounded. We advise our viewers that the following images are disturbing.* The shaky camera moved erratically, showing the chaotic scene at the market that was so familiar to me. Terrified people were running and screaming, lifeless bodies were lying in pools of blood on the ground.

Gasping for air, I stared at the horrific images. Suddenly, my mother's face appeared on the screen but then the camera moved quickly away from her. 'Oh my God, *that's my mother*!' I yelled. 'Pause, pause!' I felt dizzy.

Bill rewound the tape and we watched it again. And again and again. Mum was helping with the wounded and it was clear that she hadn't been hurt but in all the carnage and commotion we couldn't tell what was going on. We watched the tape in slow motion, studying every frame.

'What if someone else from my family was there with her?' I was hysterical.

'Oh, we'll have to get them out of there, Bill,' Rose said, with despair in her voice.

I wanted to scream loudly. Desperate to find out what had happened, I called Ariane's satellite phone. But there was no answer. I dialled over and over but to no avail, so I tried my friend Samra's number. I'd tried to call her many times in the past but had never managed to get through. This time though, I just kept on dialling and I was so surprised when her phone rang and she answered. Neither of us could believe that I'd got through; she told me that the phones worked sporadically. Straight away she assured me that everyone was alive then told me to stay on the line while she ran to get someone from my house.

'Everyone's alive,' I shouted to Andrew. He came over to me and hugged me.

'Thank God,' Rose said. We waited in silence for a couple of minutes.

'Atka . . .' I heard Mesha's voice, 'how did you get through?'

'I don't know, I just kept dialling. We saw Mum at the market on TV, what happened?'

'It was hell,' Mesha spoke fast, with a shaky voice. 'Mum and I were just a few hundred metres from the market when the mortar exploded. We ran to help. People were screaming, there were torn bodies and blood everywhere . . .'

'Oh my God, are you two OK?'

'Mum's totally freaked out, I'm still shaking . . . Mum spent all day at the hospital helping with the wounded. It was carnage . . .' Mesha's voice trembled. 'They're slaughtering us as though we're animals.'

'Oh, Mesha, I wish I were there with you.'

'Don't be stupid,' he replied angrily. 'There's no life here, I wish I'd never come back. You have to think of your child. Is he all right?'

'The doctors say that he's recovering extremely well. His heart stopped a couple of times during surgery but he's fine now.'

'And you?'

'Don't worry about me, I'm fine. How's everyone else? How are Grandma and Mayka?'

'They're all right but I'm not going to lie to you about Mayka,' Mesha said. 'She's in hospital with pneumonia—'

Then the line died. I called again and again but couldn't get through and eventually I gave up. I knew my sisters would be worried about the massacre, so I called them.

Nadia answered the phone, 'Atka, we saw Mum on TV,' she was panic-stricken.

'Don't worry, I just spoke to Mesha, everyone's OK,' I reassured her. 'But Mayka's ill in hospital . . .'

Before I went to bed, after talking to my sisters for a long time, Rose told me that she and Bill would do everything in their power to bring my family to safety.

That night I closed my eyes imagining that I was standing on the lookout on Mt Trebevic, where my friends and I used to go during our school trips. I could see my beloved Sarajevo sprawled out below me with its church towers and minarets scattered amongst the buildings. I wished I were there.

The doctors were amazed with William's speedy recovery; they were able to release him from hospital much earlier than they had expected. Finally, I was able to have my kidney stone removed and we were both home by mid-February. At last I was free of pain.

William's scar was large and, frightened that we might hurt him, Andrew and I handled him apprehensively. But with time and Rose's help we became more confident.

Bill grew tired more easily but he was determined to help my family, and he and Rose spent hours every day on the phone talking to various immigration officials.

'There's nothing I can do about this,' he said to me one day, pointing to his chest, 'but I can do something for your family.'

The garden in front of their house was in full bloom. I wished so much that I could send this warmth and sunshine to Sarajevo. I was devastated when at the end of February I found out that my dear Mayka had died. When I had left Sarajevo I was certain that I'd see her again but now she was gone and I hadn't even been able to go to her funeral. I respected and loved her so much. There was no one with whom I could grieve and I felt empty.

'I thought that we'd only be going away for three weeks,' I said to Andrew feeling guilty and full of regret. 'I didn't say a proper goodbye to Mayka, or to my friends.'

'But we didn't know that things would turn out the way that they have,' Andrew tried to console me. 'You can't blame yourself for that. Besides, if we'd known that we wouldn't be able to go back, you wouldn't have left in the first place. Maybe it's better it happened this way.'

But I was weighed down with guilt. For days I was sad thinking about Mayka. Then one afternoon as I was bathing William, the sweet scent of roses drifted in through the window, reminding me of Mayka's garden. I felt as though she were there beside me, telling me to look after and enjoy this little being in my arms.

Mayka's death changed Dad's mind and for the first time since the war had started he was willing to leave Sarajevo.

Bill rested frequently during the day but when he was up he and Rose pushed on with their immigration crusade.

'Atka, if you were a New Zealand resident,' Bill said to me one afternoon, as we all sat in the living room discussing the options, 'you'd be able to sponsor your parents and siblings under the family category.'

'How long is it going to take for me to become a resident?' I asked.

'A few months, darling. We're working on that as well,' Rose said.

'Anything could happen to my family in that time,' I said, troubled.

'What about me, as Atka's husband?' Andrew asked. 'Can't I sponsor them?'

'I'm afraid not,' Bill replied. 'You can't sponsor your in-laws.'

'So, what options do we have left?' Andrew said, rubbing his eyes.

'Well, Atka's family doesn't come under any other criteria . . . One of our immigration consultants thinks that soon New Zealand may allow fifty refugees from Bosnia to come here. Nothing is certain but if there's a way we'll find it.' Bill took off his glasses and stared thoughtfully at the pile of documents on the table.

I heard William crying and went upstairs to feed him. He was becoming stronger and more alert every day, and his scar was healing well. Every time he looked at me with his big eyes, I melted.

That night my sisters and I had a long conversation. Nadia was coping well on her own with the baby, and I admired her strength and devotion. Lela was still working full-time but the pressure on her had eased somewhat since Andrew and I had been sending money to them. It was no surprise that Hana remained completely focused on her schoolwork and, hoping that they would be able to come here soon, she'd started practising her English. Often when we talked she asked me to say a few words in English so that she could test herself.

The line to Sarajevo was always overloaded but on rare occasions I was able to get through. An eight hundred-metre phone line had been dragged through the tunnel under the runway allowing Sarajevans to have some contact with the outside world. Mum told me that they had started organising their passports and permits but for Mesha obtaining documents was particularly problematic since he was still in the army. Despite Mum's pleas to her contacts in the government, there was no certainty that Mesha would be discharged from duty or allowed to leave. Dad continued with his appeals for help. He had taught Janna and Selma the lyrics to 'Let the Doves of Peace Fly', a song which his father had written many years ago. The girls had learnt to sing the chorus of the song in twelve different languages, often performing it for foreign TV crews and hospitals. The year in the trenches had taken its toll on Mesha who sounded more and more defeated and resentful every time we spoke.

'While my friends and I are squatting in the mud with rifles, profiteers are becoming richer and richer by the day,' Mesha said angrily, when we talked one day in early March. 'They're just as bad as those who shoot at us from the hills. I was an idiot to come back, Hamo was right.'

'Hang in there, Mesha. You know that Andrew's parents are doing everything they can to get papers for you all,' I tried to encourage him. 'I'm sure something will come out of it.'

'I hope so. Mum's trying to get me a fake discharge from the army, but we still don't know what will happen,' he sighed. 'Atka, before I forget, we also need a statement from Andrew's family declaring that our destination is New Zealand, otherwise they won't let us go through Croatia.'

'OK, we'll arrange that straight away,' I assured him.

I asked Mesha to send us everyone's passport photos in case they were needed for the immigration papers in New Zealand.

'I'll find a journalist who's leaving soon. Consider it done,' he said, sounding more cheerful.

William was an easy baby, eating well and sleeping through the night. When he was awake during the day we put him on his blanket and watched him kicking. The sound of his contented cooing gave us all much joy.

Having exhausted all existing immigration options, all we could do now was wait. One day in March, Rose saw an article in the paper saying that the New Zealand government had indeed decided to allow fifty refugees from Bosnia into the country. She and Bill immediately rang their immigration consultant. The very next day we spent hours filling pages and pages of applications for each member of my family. When we had finished the last one I looked at Bill and Rose. 'Thank you, thank you so much,' I said, holding back the tears. 'Let's hope the applications are approved.'

'We'll wait and see . . .' Bill put his arm around me.

I couldn't wait to tell my family. That night I managed to get through to Mum. She was thrilled but expressed great concern for Mesha. She'd managed to get him a discharge from the army but government officials were still refusing to give him a passport.

It was uncanny that almost the same day that we'd sent the visa applications for approval, the UNHCR managed to negotiate with the Serbs to open a few roads out of Sarajevo, guaranteeing safe passage for the thousands of Sarajevans wanting to flee. These roads were named Blue Corridors. People who were entitled to leave, mostly women and children, were required to put their names on long waiting lists, then wait for approval from the Bosnian Government, the UNHCR and the Serbs. Although Mesha still had no passport my family put their names down on the waiting list anyway. Because so many people were clamouring to leave and my family was just another number, their names ended up on three separate waiting lists. If they were granted permission to leave, they'd have to travel in three different groups.

We spent most of April waiting anxiously to hear from the New Zealand immigration department. Towards the end of the month a courier bag was delivered to the house. I was very nervous as I watched Bill sign for it, knowing that the fate of my family depended on the contents of the envelope. We sat in the kitchen and Bill opened the bag. He looked at the letter and the smile on his face told us it was good news.

'They've been approved!' he said and we all shouted with excitement. Bill handed me thirteen grey documents from the bag. They were temporary identification papers with visas for my family. I looked through them to make sure that they were all there. Wildly we hugged each other.

'I never thought this would actually happen,' I said, looking at everyone.

'I never doubted it for a moment,' Bill had his arm around Rose.

'How are they going to get here, where are they going to live?' I asked. Thinking that it might bring bad luck, I hadn't dared to think that far ahead before.

'Don't worry,' Rose said, 'we'll all help. Andrew and his brothers have already discussed everything. They've got it all worked out and my sisters want to help too.'

I was so moved, I broke down in tears.

Later I called Sarajevo and Zagreb. Everyone was ecstatic. To make sure the documents would arrive safely, we decided to courier them to Andrew's editor in Paris, who offered to take them to my sisters in Zagreb.

By mid-May, my family's approval to leave had come through and the UNHCR allocated bus seats for them at the end of May and at the beginning of June. But Mesha still had no passport.

Although he'd won the immigration crusade, Bill was sadly losing the battle with his illness. He was confined to bed and the house became silent and still. Rose spent all her time next to him. Soon, he required an oxygen machine, which Andrew's older brother brought from the hospital, and a softly spoken nurse came to the house, making sure that Bill was comfortable. Just after midnight at the end of May, he died peacefully in his sleep. Although sadness and loss had become frequent visitors in my life, each visit was painful in a different way. Even though I'd known Bill for less than a year, I knew I'd just lost a good friend. I felt sad for Andrew and my heart went out to Rose who had lost the love of her life. Andrew's brothers and the whole family were there and we gathered in the living room, while Rose stayed upstairs with Bill. We waited for her for a few hours then she came downstairs. Later, I managed to get through to Sarajevo to tell them that Bill had died.

'I'm sorry for Rose and all her family,' Mesha said. 'Please give our condolences to them.' He paused for a moment when I told him what time Bill had died. 'How strange,' he said. 'Dad, Janna and Selma left on their bus at about the same time.' I shivered. Mesha continued talking, 'And just yesterday I was given my passport. Tarik and I are on the list tomorrow and Mum, Grandma and the twins are leaving in a few days.'

In a daze, I took the receiver away from my ear, and told everyone in the living room that some of my family members had just left Sarajevo. A roar of applause and cheers filled the room.

'Listen to that, Mesha,' I said holding the receiver for him to hear. He cried.

Later, when I hung up, Rose managed to say through her tears, 'Oh, Bill would be so happy for you . . . We'll have to open a bottle of champagne. That's what he would have done if he were here.'

The Arrival

Hana

The blossom on the apple tree in the front yard had fallen and the first fruits were starting to appear. Not daring to believe that we might be able to go to New Zealand, my sisters and I hardly ever mentioned the possibility. But when Atka rang early one morning to tell us that our documents for New Zealand had been approved, the three of us jumped for joy. With feelings of excitement and anxiety, we sat at the table in the living room along with Danica and Andrea's grandmother, talking for a long time after the call. Romana, who was now eight months old, was asleep on the sofa.

'I still can't believe that we'll be going there,' Nadia was smiling, her eyes wide.

'I have to admit, it all sounded like a bit of a fantasy to me,' Danica confessed. 'It's a real miracle. Let's hope that the rest of your family makes it safely out of Sarajevo . . .'

'Well,' I said, heaving a sigh, 'Mesha hasn't received his passport or his permit to leave yet.'

'We've been optimistic until now, let's keep believing that it'll happen,' Nadia said, adamant. Romana started crying but Nadia told us to leave her, she'd go back to sleep.

Danica stood up and, with the aid of her stick, went over to the windows. Although her hip was improving, she still needed support to walk. It was a hot day so she drew back the curtains and opened the windows. Birds were chirping outside.

'Someone up there must be looking after you,' she said, turning around. 'Spring's a good time for new beginnings . . .'

The next day at school, I shared my exciting news with my teachers and friends.

'So you really are going to go?' one of my classmates asked.

I nodded eagerly.

'There's only a month of school left. Will you be here for the end-of-year ceremony?'

'I don't know. As soon as our family arrives from Sarajevo we can leave but, that could take a few weeks or even months . . . who knows. And to be honest, the ceremony isn't going to be my priority.'

In the classroom that day I kept daydreaming about all of us in New Zealand, even though I had no idea what the country looked like. All I could imagine were beautiful green parks, lush trees and the ocean that Atka had described to me. Somewhere in all of this was a house in which my family would be together again. I was filled with hope.

With bated breath, we waited each day to find out if Mesha had received his papers, but a whole week passed without any change. A letter from Atka arrived at the end of the week, with a photo of her holding William and another one of Bill reading the paper on his bed, with William lying next to him. The photos cheered us up and I put them into the back of my textbook, often glancing at them during class.

I'd been looking forward to our May school trip all year but earlier in the week, my form teacher had told me that I wouldn't be able to join them. Pula, where we were going, was on the northern part of the coast and to get there we had to bypass parts of Croatia which were still unsafe. We'd have to make a detour through Slovenia instead, but because Slovenia was now an independent country, we needed passports to travel there. I didn't have one yet. It was another painful reminder that I was a refugee.

When my classmates heard that I wouldn't be able to go, they pleaded with our teacher to do something to help. She said she'd make some calls to the Slovenian Embassy. All evening I stayed by the phone, waiting to hear from her. It was almost ten o'clock when it finally rang. 'I've given them my guarantee that you'll be returning with us, so they've agreed to let you through,' the teacher said, triumphantly.

'Thank you, thank you,' I said, overjoyed.

The bus left early the next morning, often stopping for sightseeing and breaks. I sat at the back with my friends and we sang loudly all the way. We reached the town of Pula in the evening, driving past the amphitheatre which had been built by the Romans hundreds of years ago. When we'd first arrived in Croatia, Nadia and I'd spent three nights in Rijeka, which was near Pula. We were so scared and lost then. It had never crossed my mind that I'd be returning here one day with a group of my Croatian friends.

I shared a hotel room with three others and that night we stayed up until the early hours of the morning.

'You probably won't miss Croatia when you leave,' one of the girls said.

I looked across at her. 'I *will* miss it,' I insisted. 'I'm grateful to the people who looked after me here, for being able to go school and for meeting all of you. I'll always remember Croatia because of all the good people who've helped us. But, I'm *so happy* we're going, because my family will be together again and we can go back to living normal lives.'

'Do tell everyone how good we're at football,' one of the girls joked, 'and that our Adriatic Sea is the most beautiful in the world.' We kept on talking and I don't know how late it was when we finally fell asleep.

The trip was exciting and I became even closer to my friends. When we returned to Zagreb a few days later, Nadia showed me the documents that Andrew's editor had delivered from Paris. Each one had a passport photo in it. Until now, we'd had no photos of our family and it was a shock to see how grey and aged Mum and Dad had become. Nadia said that Atka had spoken to Mum again. There was no certainty that they would leave because Mesha was still waiting for his passport. We kept the New Zealand documents under the girls' mattress, thinking that was the safest place to hide them.

Now that there were only two weeks of the school year left, I kept my head buried in my books, preparing for my final exams. One evening, my Croatian teacher took me along to a literary competition in town. A selection of short stories from students across the city had been published and one of my stories was included. In a shaky voice, I read my story in front of a large audience, every now and then glancing at my teacher for support. There was a boy from Sarajevo who'd written a poem about the city and afterwards we talked for a few minutes about home and our families. On the bus back my teacher told me that I should show the story to my parents when they arrived in Zagreb.

Nadia was standing near the telephone, shaking her head, when I walked in through the door.

'Atka's just called. Bill has died and Dad, Janna and Selma have left on the bus from Sarajevo. I don't know whether to laugh or cry.' She leaned over to hug me and we both burst into tears.

'When did they leave? When did Bill die?' I asked, wiping away my tears.

'Just a few hours ago. On the one hand, I'm so happy they're managing to get out but, on the other, I'm so sorry we'll never meet Bill.'

'I know. Look how much he's done for us. What a generous man he was, to be so kind to people he'd never met.'

Nadia let out a deep sigh.

'Poor Rose. How are they all?'

'Atka said that all of Andrew's brothers are with Rose. I suppose they're all right, as much as anyone can be at times like this.'

'Did Atka say anything about Mesha?'

'Oh, yes! He has his passport and will be leaving with Tarik tomorrow,' she said with her fingers crossed. 'Mum, Grandma and the twins will leave next week. So now, we just have to wait.'

Four days had passed since Atka's phone call but Dad and the girls still hadn't arrived in Zagreb. Nadia spent all her time at Danica's waiting near the phone, not daring to leave the house. Every day at school I half expected Dad to walk through my classroom door.

The last few days the weather had been lovely, so my friends and I often took our time walking back from school, chatting along the way. Klaudia and another girl from my class were with me that day, they were going to stop at my place to look at my chemistry homework. When we turned the corner from the main road into my street Klaudia said, 'Isn't that Danica on the steps? She's waving her arms at us.' I looked up towards the house, Danica was shouting something.

'What?' I said, running towards her.

'Hurry,' I heard her say as we came closer. 'You have visitors! Go and see your sisters.'

'Is it . . .?' Before I could finish the sentence, I sprinted into the girls' house.

'We'll wait outside,' Klaudia yelled behind me.

As soon as I opened the door, I recognised the sweet voices of my little sisters and ran to the bedroom. Seated on the mattress were Janna and Selma, playing with Romana. The moment I stepped inside, they both jumped up. 'Haannaaaa!' they yelled as they hugged me.

'Ahhhhhh,' I screeched at the top of my voice and squeezed them tightly.

'You're crushing us,' Janna giggled.

'Hana, we wore our best dresses,' she said, stepping back to show me. Her red checked dress with its beautiful white collar had once belonged to Nadia. Selma was in a pink dress, her hair neatly parted to the side and held in place by a little bobby pin.

'You girls look so pretty,' I said. They both giggled, looking shy.

'Where's Dad?' I asked.

'He's upstairs talking to that woman with short hair . . .' Selma said, grabbing my hand. 'We'll come up with you.'

Klaudia and my friend were sitting outside on the small concrete wall in front of the house. Proudly, I took both Janna and Selma by the hand and introduced them.

'Hana's told us so much about you,' Klaudia said, smiling at the girls. 'She said you were cute, but not this cute.' The girls looked down in embarrassment.

'I don't think I'll be doing any chemistry today,' I said to Klaudia. 'I'll see you at school tomorrow, OK?' They waved to Janna and Selma as we raced up the steps into Danica's house.

Dad was sitting on a chair in the kitchen, in his brown suit. '*Hanico*, little Hana,' he called when I walked in, and stood up to give me a big hug. He looked even older than in his photograph. Deep lines were etched on his face, he looked worn out, thin and his eyes were sunken. Seeing him like this, I burst into tears. 'I know we don't look the best,' he said, patting my head with tears in his eyes, 'but we are alive.'

He pulled a chair out for me, and I sat down with Janna and Selma on my lap. Nadia sat closer to Dad, with Romana in her arms. Lela stood behind Dad, holding on to his shoulders.

'Your dad was just telling me about their trip out . . .' Danica wiped her eyes with a handkerchief, then poured more coffee into Dad's cup. He took a sip.

'Dad, *how* did you manage to get out?' I asked. 'When are the others coming?'

He slowly tapped his hand on the table. 'You see, this is how it was,' he spoke more slowly than he used to and his voice was flat. 'We came via Visoko,' Dad explained. Visoko was a small town some twenty-five kilometres north-west of Sarajevo. 'But, imagine,' he continued, 'it took us an entire day, *an entire day*, to get there. The Serbs stopped our bus at every checkpoint, holding us up for a few hours each time. We were never certain that they'd let us through. When we came to the first checkpoint, the Serbs asked if anyone wanted to stay behind, and one elderly Serb couple disembarked.'

'And, Hana,' Janna interrupted, 'at one checkpoint a young Chetnik with a rifle came on to the bus to look at everyone's documents.' Janna reached for Selma's hand. 'Selma was so scared, she was crying the whole time but he told her not to be scared because he wasn't like the others . . .'

Selma lowered her head, 'But I think he lied to us because when we started driving away, the Chetniks shot at our bus, and at the bus behind us.' It angered me to think of what my little sisters had had to go through and I hugged her close.

'We spent most of the trip lying on the floor,' Dad spoke with a mixture of sadness and anger.

Once they reached Visoko, they stayed the night with an acquaintance of Dad's who was still living there.

'Grandma had made pastries for our trip but Dad gave them all away to the people we stayed with,' Janna said.

'We were so hungry,' Selma added, staring at me with her big, brown eyes. 'But Dad told us they had nothing to eat and that soon we would have food.'

They left Visoko the next day and it took them two days to reach Zagreb.

'The entire bus was held up for hours at the Croatian border because there was one woman who was short of some documents. They threatened to turn us all back.'

'What about Mesha?' Nadia asked. 'How did he get his permit to leave?'

'Mum persuaded a doctor to write a note for her saying that Tarik needed urgent kidney treatment in Zagreb and Mesha was the only one who could accompany him.'

'Well done,' Danica laughed, 'anything to get them out.'

For the rest of the day, we stayed in Danica's house. One of her neighbours came to meet Dad, offering to have us all for lunch the next day. At dusk, Danica set a plate of *meze* on the table, bread, some dried meats and cheeses. Janna and Selma kept on asking if they were allowed to have some more and every time they ate a piece, they exclaimed that it was delicious.

I was reluctant to ask Dad about Nako, Zoran and Mayka and I decided not to say anything unless he mentioned something first. Listening to him talking about the war, I could only imagine what they'd been through, but all I cared about was that they were alive and safe. That night, Lela stayed at her boyfriend's place so that Janna and Selma could share the mattress with Nadia. Dad slept on the floor.

Early the next morning, Atka rang and talked to Dad and

the girls for a long time. She had some very good news: Mesha and Tarik had managed to leave the day before and we hoped that they would be here by the end of the week. Dad told me that I should keep going to school since there were only five days left till the end of the year. I sat my exams but was allowed to go home early. In the afternoon, I strolled through the neighbourhood with my sisters. Janna and Selma told us who had been killed, who was still trapped in Sarajevo and who had managed to leave. A sudden bang behind us sent Selma ducking and running to the side of the street.

'Is that a sniper?' she yelled, with a terrified look on her face.

'Selma, there aren't any snipers here,' Nadia replied. 'You won't have to worry about them ever again. No one's going to shoot at you any more.' She knelt down in front of Selma and hugged her.

'Now, let's see,' I said to distract the girls, 'who knows how to say "house" in English?'

Janna rolled her eyes, but Selma jumped to her feet. 'I don't know but can you teach me?' she asked, excitedly. We continued walking and Nadia smiled as she pushed Romana in her pram.

That evening, Dad told us that he had contacted some people at one of the radio stations in town, where he would be taking Janna and Selma to perform the song 'Let the Doves of Peace Fly'.

'It's a good song,' he said. 'They sing it well and we have to do something about Sarajevo. Most importantly, we can't let the world forget.'

The next three days passed in a blur. Dad and the girls were in town recording their song with the city children's choir and talking about Sarajevo on the radio. He took Janna and Selma to meet Professor Devide and Damir, but whenever they were home we played or went for walks. On the Friday of that week Dad came to my final parent-teacher interview. I was so glad that the teachers and some of my friends' parents were able to meet my father after all this time. But we didn't discuss the interview much because more important things were on our minds. Mesha and Tarik still hadn't arrived and we were becoming increasingly anxious.

'They're not here yet,' I told Atka when she called that evening.

'They'll come. Give them another day or two. I've just spoken to Samra. Mum, Grandma and the twins are on their way.'

'Oh, Atka, I'm so worried. What will we do if something happens to them?' I asked.

'I know, this waiting is torture,' she said, 'but don't lose hope now.'

'What if they stop Mesha?'

'Well, he has all his paperwork, they should let him go . . .'

I handed the receiver to Dad and he talked to Atka for a while.

Time had never passed so slowly and each hour seemed to drag on for an eternity. Every time a car drove past, we ran outside to see if Mesha had arrived. Finally, a week after he'd left Sarajevo, Mesha called us from the bus terminal in Zagreb and Lela raced to meet them.

While waiting for them, the girls, Andrea and I passed the time playing hopscotch in front of the house, glancing towards the street corner every few minutes. Suddenly, Janna let out a scream. 'There's Tarik!' she yelled, and started running towards him. Selma and I ran behind her.

'Go and get Nadia,' I shouted to Andrea, my heart racing.

Mesha let go of Tarik's hand and Tarik ran towards us, 'Janna, Selma!' he shouted. 'Whoohoo, Hana,' he exclaimed when he saw me.

I lifted him up into the air, staring at his skinny face. 'Give me ten kisses on each cheek,' I demanded.

He giggled, then kissed me, counting each one, 'One, two, three . . .' When he'd finished, I looked at him. He was scrawny, and his hair was so short that I could see his scalp. 'Look,' he said with a wide grin, 'my front teeth are missing.' He was clutching a short branch in his hand and when I told him to throw it away, he refused. 'I'm a soldier, this is my gun,' he said. Janna and Selma hugged him and took him by the hand. Nadia ran on to the street, carrying Romana. Mesha and Lela came over to us.

'Hello, little doll,' Mesha said, patting Romana's head. Nadia and I hugged him.

Nadia spoke through her tears, 'This is your Uncle Mesha and this is your Uncle Tarik.'

'Is that a real baby?' Tarik asked, making us all laugh.

Mesha pointed to the small rucksack on his back. It was the only luggage they had. 'I brought some old photos with me,' he said. 'We couldn't bring anything more.'

Mesha was exhausted. He slept for two days and it wasn't until a few days later that we learned how they had got out. To bypass the many Serb checkpoints, they had taken a less dangerous but much longer route out of town. They were able to cross the airport runway safely because it was now part of the Blue Corridors network. Afterwards, they hitchhiked and walked for three days, sleeping in abandoned army barracks, before reaching Visoko. From then on, they took the same route to Zagreb as Dad had taken, encountering the same hassles on the way.

'Mesha, tell them what I said to that man,' Tarik looked at him with a mischievous expression on his face.

Mesha chuckled. 'At the last Bosnian checkpoint out of Sarajevo, the soldier checking our papers asked Tarik what was wrong with his kidneys. Tarik looked at the soldier confused and said, "Nothing. I'm going to New Zealand to see my sister." I broke into a cold sweat, and thought that we'd be turned back but the solider smiled, wishing us all the best for "Tarik's treatment". We almost missed the UNHCR bus,' Mesha continued. 'A few hours before we were leaving, Tarik disappeared. We looked everywhere for him, but couldn't find him.'

'Well, I didn't want to leave,' Tarik exclaimed. 'I hid behind that yellow house at the top of the street and when you found me,' he said, looking at Mesha. 'I cried a lot, didn't I?' Mesha nodded.

Mesha was restless. He was only twenty-one but seemed so much older now. He smoked cigarette after cigarette, finishing an entire packet in one afternoon.

'Are you all right?' Nadia asked him, as he was going to lie down.

'I'm pretty fucked at the moment,' he said, rubbing his head. 'But I'll be fine once we leave.'

Lela raced home every day after work. With six people staying in the girls' house it was very crowded, so at night she took Tarik to sleep at her boyfriend's family's house. Dad and Mesha slept on the floor.

I was glowing with pride when on the last day of school, my form teacher handed us our certificates. I had finished with straight As in all of my fourteen subjects, coming top of the class. For a long time after the form meeting, my teacher and the rest of us remained behind, talking. My friends wanted to know what high school I'd be going to in New Zealand. 'Whichever one will take me,' I joked. 'I have to learn to speak English first.'

Before we parted, we walked around the school, saying goodbye to all our teachers. I found it difficult to say farewell to my Croatian language teacher, thanking her for her support. 'When you've settled in, write to me,' she said.

I promised my friends that I'd remember them for the rest of my life.

Two days later, Mum and Grandma arrived with the twins. When I walked into Danica's house, Grandma's back was turned. She was in the hallway, taking off her shoes.

'Grandma!' I yelled, and ran to hug her.

Her bright blue eyes widened when she saw me. 'Hana,' she said, pulling me closer to her. I was taller than her now. 'Grandma's good girl,' she said. Seeing tears in her eyes made me cry too. 'Come,' she said, and holding tightly on to my hand she led me into the living room. Mum stood up from her chair and the twins ran up to me. Emir couldn't stop kissing my cheeks.

'Asko, Emir, do you remember me?' I asked. The boys looked so tiny and I was overwhelmed by a mixture of joy and sadness.

'A little bit,' Asko said. 'Have you seen Nadia's baby?' he asked in his quiet little voice, then put his thumb back into his mouth.

'I have, Asko. I've lived here with them.'

Mum came over to me with open arms. Just like Dad, she had aged. Her hair was completely grey, her frame so slim and bony that it looked like that of a young girl. Her cheekbones were prominent and her eyes seemed bigger than before. If I hadn't known that she was only forty-four years old, I would have sworn she was sixty.

'This is the only thing that I could take with me,' Grandma said, pulling the coffee grinder from her bag. The only belongings that they had been allowed to take were packed in two small bags.

'We brought as many photos as we could,' Mum said. 'Nothing else matters.'

It didn't seem real to be with my family after all this time.

With Danica's house, the girls' flat and Lela's boyfriend's place, we managed to find somewhere for everyone to sleep. We had a few days to wait before our flight to New Zealand. Excited, all of us were up early every morning and stayed up late every night.

The day we flew out was sunny and warm. Andrea's Dad, together with Danica's neighbours and Lela's boyfriend, had arranged to take us to the airport. Klaudia and a few of my friends came to Danica's house. They would also accompany us.

Danica, Andrea and her grandmother decided to stay behind.

'Thank you for looking after our daughters so well,' Dad said to Danica, shaking her hand.

Mum hugged her, crying, then left the house. Everyone had gone outside to get into the cars, but Danica, Andrea and I stayed behind in the kitchen.

'I don't want to see any tears from you,' Danica said, smiling at me.

'I don't know how to thank you . . .' I said as we hugged.

'I wrote something in your diary,' Andrea whispered in a shaky voice. 'Read it when you get to New Zealand.'

I kissed them both and ran outside before they could see my tears.

We drove to the airport. Because we had little luggage, we were checked in quickly. I said goodbye to Klaudia and my friends for the last time, then walked backwards to the departure gate, waving to them. They blew kisses to me.

On the plane, I sat next to Grandma. Several hours into the flight, there was some turbulence. Frightened, I looked at her and asked, 'Are you scared?'

She thought I was talking about our destination because she waved her hand and replied, 'Is there war where we're going?' I shook my head. 'Then there's nothing to be scared of,' she shrugged her shoulders and smiled.

We talked all the way. At one point, I mentioned how sad it was that we couldn't thank Bill for what he'd done for us.

'You can,' she said, adamantly. 'Just work hard and do your best when we get there. He'll know.'

We stopped in Tokyo for several hours. Intrigued, I looked around, thinking of Professor Devide and his wife. I'd never dreamt that I'd see Japan one day! Dad took Janna and Selma to the duty-free store and the girls sang the chorus of 'Let the Doves of Peace Fly' in Japanese to everyone there. People clapped and gave the girls some sweets.

On the flight from Tokyo to New Zealand, we were served a rice dish for dinner. Grandma looked at her tray, then said to me apologetically, 'Hana, can you ask that woman if there's anything else but rice. It's all I've eaten for the last two years.'

I tried to explain this to the stewardess, but she didn't understand me, so in the end Grandma just ate the pudding.

After almost thirty hours of travel we were exhausted but nothing could dampen the excitement we felt when we arrived in Auckland early the next morning. It was two hours before our next and final flight to Christchurch. As we walked from the international terminal to the domestic one, Mesha looked at the sky in awe and said, 'It's so blue and bright . . . I've never seen a sky like this before.'

None of us could sit still during our eighty-minute flight to Christchurch. As soon as we landed, we all rushed through the gate. Amongst a small group, I saw Atka and Andrew. Atka was holding William, waving his little arm towards us.

'Atka, Atka,' Tarik screamed, racing ahead of everyone. 'I've been good, where's my chocolate?'

We took a long time kissing and hugging each other, before Andrew finally managed to introduce us to his family and friends who had come to greet us.

He turned to me and said, 'This is my mother Rose.'

Rose looked younger than I had imagined and hugged me as though we'd known each other for ever. 'Oh, at last we've met,' she said and smiled at me through her tears.

Mesha walked towards her and gave her a hug. 'Don't cry, Rose,' he said.

Happy to see my whole family together at last, I couldn't stop laughing. Andrew and his family drove us to our new home, which was a beautiful, two-storey house just across the road from a river.

I ran around with my brothers and sisters, looking through the rooms and soon we joined everyone in the large, bright living room. It was the first time in three years that my entire family was under one roof, this time with the addition of Romana and William who kept Tarik and the girls amused. The fire was crackling in the fireplace, everyone was chatting. It seemed surreal and I felt as though my prayers had been answered. Grandma appeared from the kitchen holding her coffee grinder. 'Shall I make us some coffee?' she asked, her eyes lighting up.

'Yes please, Grandma,' we yelled from all corners of the room.

Atka was sitting on a large bench next to the fireplace.

'Hana, come over here,' she said, tapping the space next to her. Smiling, I sat down. Atka put her arm around my shoulder.

'We're very fortunate to be here, but we must never forget what happened to our family, to Sarajevo and Bosnia . . .'

'I know, how could I ever forget?' I replied. 'Besides, I've been writing everything down every since that day I left Sarajevo.'

'I'm glad you have,' she said. 'Who knows, maybe our children will want to be told all about it one day.'

Epilogue

The war in Bosnia and Herzegovina lasted from March 1992 until November 1995. The siege of Sarajevo lasted for forty-six months. It is estimated that over 10,000 Sarajevans were killed during the siege and more than 60,000 injured. By the end of the war, upwards of 100,000 Bosnian people had been killed and over 1.8 million displaced by the conflict.

Acknowledgements

T here are many people to whom we owe our heartfelt gratitude. We'd especially like to thank the following:

Rosie Reid for being an integral part of this project. Without her dedication, passion and hitherto unknown editing skills, this book would not be what it is.

William and Sam, for their support, understanding and enthusiasm.

Our parents, brothers and sisters; we greatly appreciate their courage in revisiting 'memory lane', as well as their valuable individual insights and contributions.

For their encouragement and individual input Selma and Janna, Merima, Mirza and Haris, Charlotte Curtis, Gill Clark, Anna Rogers, Jim Espie, Janine di Giovanni, Andrea Louisson, Linda and James Schofield, Kate Owens, John Burns, Dubravka Rovicanac, David Hall, Nevena Sijercic, Amela Vukotic, Ash Hill, Fiona McLeod and the Staff at Christchurch Public Library.

Our many friends and wider family, whose continued interest in the book and its progress gave us the motivation and confidence to tell the story. We feel privileged and fortunate to have such an incredible group of people in our lives.

David Godwin, our agent and his very capable assistant Charlotte Knight.

Alexandra Pringle, Alexa von Hirschberg, Anna Simpson

and the wonderful team at Bloomsbury, it's been a pleasure and a privilege to work with them.

All the people whose random acts of kindness helped us during the war in Bosnia and the refugee life in Croatia. We'd like to express our thanks to Samra and Ako Bitevija, Sabrina Hajdarpasic, Aida Kelic, Hamo Zubcevic, Mira and Elvir Hadziselimovic, Christopher Long, Mladena Mihanovic, Cvitar Family, Nada Levi, Ciro Blazevic, Kenan Mazlami, Lovorka and Milan from Rijeka, Imre i Vera from Belgrade, Damir Medvesek, Philip and Sandi Morgaman, Ariane Quentier, Gary Knight, Susan Sontag, David Rieff, Emanuele Scorcelletti, David Crary, Xavier Gautier, Aida Cerkez-Robinson, Filip Horvat, Maglic Family, Sahinovic Family, Klaudija Ancic, the staff at the Marina Lucica Hotel in Primosten and the staff and friends from Ante Starcevic School in Zagreb.

For their kindness and generosity, and for enabling us to start a new life in New Zealand, we'd like to express special thanks to Rosie and Bill Reid and their sons; such kindness and generosity is seldom found, we'll forever be thankful to them. Our gratitude also goes to Charles and Carolyn Reid, Richard Reid, Andrea and Doig Smith, Audrey and Karl Burtscher, Joanna and Noel Todd, Helena Malfroy-Todd, Pedro Carazo and D'Arcy Waldegrave.

And lastly, our profound thanks to Andrew and James for their unconditional love and unshakeable belief in us.

A NOTE ON THE AUTHORS

Atka Reid was born in Sarajevo in 1970. At the outbreak of the Bosnian war, she was a political science student. During the war, she worked as a reporter for a local radio station and as an interpreter for the foreign press. Upon her arrival in New Zealand in 1993 she worded as a journalist in Christchurch. She later gained a diploma in graphic design and worked as a graphic designer. She and Andrew, the New Zealand photo journalist she met in Sarajevo, live in New Zealand with their two sons.

Hana Schofield was born in Sarajevo in 1979. She spent two years living as a refugee in Croatia during the siege of Sarajevo. In 1994 she arrived in New Zealand with her family, speaking no English. In 2002 she graduated from the University of Canterbury with first class honours in law and a bachelor's degree in Russian. Since then she has worked as a lawyer for a leading New Zealand law firm, and more recently for a city law firm in London. Hana is also a qualifed performance consultant. She lives in New Zealand with her husband James.

A NOTE ON THE TYPE

The text of this book is set in Bembo. This type was first used in 1495 by the Venetian printer Aldus Manutius for Cardinal Bembo's *De Aetna*, and was cut for Manutius by Francesco Griffo. It was one of the types used by Claude Garamond (1480–1561) as a model for his Romain de l'Université, and so it was the forerunner of what became standard European type for the following two centuries. Its modern form follows the original types and was designed for Monotype in 1929.